these images of the city share the qualities of a matrix. In *The Four-Gated City* and *The Diaries of Jane Somers,* Doris Lessing portrays the city as a palimpsest, a fragment of layered text. Margaret Drabble uses the image of the city as a network in *The Middle Ground* and *The Radiant Way,* novels that celebrate the connections between people. Iris Murdoch selects the more problematic image of the labyrinth to describe the city and her complex morality in *A World Child* and *Nuns and Soldiers.* P. D. James employs the image of the mosaic to convey the city and the method of the detective novel in *A Taste for Death* and *Innocent Blood.* And in her brilliant lyrical novels, *Londoners* and *Capital,* Maureen Duffy uses the image of the archeological dig to convey the passage of time in the city.

As she examines the novels, Sizemore finds that women characters tend to notice the elements of the city that architect Kevin Lynch describes as "edges" and "districts." Male characters, on the other hand, often remain fixated on only the landmarks. In looking for reasons for these differences, Sizemore draws on the work of feminist psychologists Nancy Chodorow, Carol Gilligan, and Jessica Benjamin and their writings on flexible ego boundaries and intersubjective space.

The Author: Christine Wick Sizemore is associate professor of English at Spelman College.

A Female Vision of the City

A Female Vision of the City

London in the Novels of Five British Women

Christine Wick Sizemore

Photographs by Susan Cavanaugh

The University of Tennessee Press / *Knoxville*

PR 888 .L65 S59 1989

Sizemore, Christine Wick.

A female vision of the city

Frontispiece: Statue of the Celtic warrior queen Boadicea who led a
revolt against the Romans. She died in 61 A.D. The statue is located
near Westminster Bridge. Doris Lessing refers to her in *The Four-
Gated City.* (see p. 37)

Library of Congress Cataloging in Publication Data
Sizemore, Christine Wick.
      A female vision of the city: London in the novels of five
   British women / Christine Wick Sizemore; photographs by
   Susan Cavanaugh.—1st ed.
        p. cm.
      Bibliography: p.
      Includes index.
      ISBN 0-87049-599-2 (cloth: alk. paper)
      1. English fiction—20th century—History and criticism.
   2. English fiction—Women authors—History and criticism.
   3. London (England) in literature. 4. City and town life in literature. 5. Women and literature—Great Britain—History—20th century.
      I. Title.
   PR888.L65S59 1989
   823'.914'0932.42—dc19   88-31609 CIP

For Mike, Christi, and Jamey

Contents

List of Illustrations

Acknowledgments

I have found imagery of networks not only in novels by contemporary women and in the works of feminist psychologists but also in my own life. It is because of the supportive network of family, friends, and colleagues that I have been able to write this book.

I would like to thank both my chairpersons at Spelman College, Richard Carroll and June Aldridge. Richard Carroll spent many afternoons discussing my ideas with me and encouraging me to continue. Later, June Aldridge gave me equally valuable help in telling me about available grants and in advising me how to apply. Thanks to her advice and to Spelman College's generosity and support, I received a half-year sabbatical, a half-year United Negro College Fund "Strengthening the Humanities" grant, and a Bush Foundation grant for one course released time. Without these this book would have taken infinitely longer to write.

I am grateful to all the friends and colleagues who read portions of this manuscript and responded to it. Ideas also grow in networks, and I am happy to have had so many people to share ideas with. My thanks to Linda Bell, Richard Carroll, Judy Gebre-Hiwet, John Hannay, Anne Harper, Rhoda Hendrickson, Lyssa Higgins, Nancy Kearns, Debra Sitter, Anne Warner, and Susan Ward.

I feel fortunate to live in a time when there is a real community of scholars who share interests in urban literature and feminism. I appreciate Susan Squier's publishing my first article on Doris Lessing in her anthology, *Women Writers and the City;* Susan Squier's work continues to be an inspiration for all those working in urban literature. I would also like to thank those who sent me their articles and unpublished manuscripts: Patrick Byrne and Richard Carroll Keeley, Helen Druxes, Gayle Greene, Amy Kaplan, Richard Lehan, and Dale Salwak. Carol Orr, Director of The University of Tennessee Press, has been very encouraging in her continuing interest in this subject.

I am grateful to the librarians at Atlanta University and Emory University for helping me get materials on interlibrary loan and track down obscure references. I thank the library of King's College, London, for letting me see their Maureen Duffy collection.

I especially thank Mike, Christi, and Jamey Sizemore. I have spent many hours walking through cities with Mike, discussing architecture and urban design. He was the one who first interested me in cities. I thank him for his intellectual interest in my project and his unfailing support and encouragement. I thank Christi and Jamey for both their enthusiasm and their patience.

The following publishers have generously given permission to use extended quotations from copyrighted works: From *The Middle Ground,* by Margaret Drabble. Copyright © 1980 by Margaret Drabble. Reprinted by permission of Alfred A. Knopf, Inc., and Weidenfeld & Nicolson Ltd. From *The Radiant Way,* by Margaret Drabble. Copyright © 1987 by Margaret Drabble. Reprinted by permission of Alfred A. Knopf, Inc., and Weidenfeld & Nicolson Ltd. From *Capital,* by Maureen Duffy. Copyright © 1976 by Maureen Duffy. Reprinted by permission of George Braziller, Inc., and Methuen London Ltd. From *Londoners,* by Maureen Duffy. Reprinted by permission of Methuen London Ltd. Excerpts from *The Cocktail Party,* copyright © 1950 by T. S. Eliot, renewed 1978 by Esme Valerie Eliot. Reprinted by permission of Harcourt Brace Jovanovich, Inc., and Faber & Faber Ltd. Excerpt from "Burnt Norton" in *Four Quartets,* copyright © 1943 by T. S. Eliot, renewed 1971 by Esme Valerie Eliot. Reprinted by permission of Harcourt Brace Jovanovich, Inc., and Faber & Faber Ltd. From *A Taste for Death,* by P. D. James. Copyright © 1986 by P. D. James. Reprinted by permission of Alfred A. Knopf, Inc., and Faber & Faber Ltd. P. D. James, excerpted from *Innocent Blood.* Copyright © 1980, P. D. James. Reprinted with the permission of Charles Scribner's Sons, an imprint of Macmillan Publishing Company, and Faber & Faber Ltd. From *The Diaries of Jane Somers: The Diary of a Good Neighbor and If the Old Could,* by Doris Lessing. Copyright © 1983 by Doris Lessing. Reprinted by permission of Alfred A. Knopf, Inc., and Michael Joseph Ltd. From *The Four-Gated City,* by Doris Lessing. Copyright © 1969 by Doris Lessing Productions Ltd. Reprinted by permission of Alfred A. Knopf, Inc., and Collins Publishing Group. From *Nuns and Soldiers,* by Iris Murdoch. Copyright © 1980 by Iris Murdoch. All rights reserved. Reprinted by permission of Viking Penguin Inc., and Chatto & Windus. From *A Word Child,* by Iris Murdoch. Copyright © 1975 by Iris Murdoch. All rights reserved. Reprinted by permission of Viking Penguin Inc., and Chatto & Windus.

A Female Vision of the City

CHAPTER 1

Introduction

We get the cities we imagine. But first, in order to imagine new or better cities, we must learn to see the cities that we have. Imagination is rooted in past experience and perception. We see the city we have been taught to see, and literature teaches us to see cities. Novels in particular portray cities well because they have the potential for detailed descriptions of varied settings and they can communicate values and attitudes towards those settings. Furthermore, the novel is an urban art form. The contemporary novelist Maureen Duffy ties the origins of the novel to cities: "Writing itself grew up with cities. . . . Printed prose fiction is essentially an urban art, even when the urbs was a court or castle, cities in miniature which provided the readership for Marie de France and Malory."[1] The city and the novel thus create each other. Historically the novel was born from the city, as Duffy points out, but the urban novel can also teach readers to imagine cities and to observe existing cities in new ways. Architects and city planners also recognize this connection. For instance, the architect Kevin Lynch writes, "Dickens helped to create the London we experience as surely as its actual builders did."[2]

If Dickens created Victorian London, London now exists, in Doris Lessing's words, in "women's brains":

Iris, Joe's mother, had lived in this street since she was born. Put her brain together with the other million brains, women's brains, that recorded in such tiny loving anxious detail the histories of window sills, skins of paint, replaced curtains and salvaged baulks of timber, there would be a recording instrument, a sort of six-dimensional map which included the histories and lives and loves of people, London—a section map in depth. This is where London exists.[3]

It is in "women's brains," as revealed in the novels of Doris Lessing, Margaret Drabble, Iris Murdoch, P. D. James, and Maureen Duffy, that the London of the 1960s, 1970s and 1980s exists. *The New York Times Book Review* called Margaret Drabble "the person who will have done for late 20th-century London what Dickens did for Victorian London."[4] Louis Martz called Iris Murdoch "the living writer who is . . . the most important heir to the Dickens tradition."[5] Actually, all five of these novelists belong in the Dickens tradition because the characters in their novels do not observe the city from behind curtained windows; they literally walk the streets of the city at all hours of the day and night. These novelists portray the actual city of London with all its varied districts and buildings and alleyways. The city is not just a backdrop or setting in such novels as Lessing's *The Four-Gated City* and *The Diaries of Jane Somers*, Drabble's *The Middle Ground* and *The Radiant Way*, Murdoch's *A Word Child* and *Nuns and Soldiers*, P. D. James' *Innocent Blood* and *A Taste for Death*, and Maureen Duffy's *Londoners* and *Capital*. It is an active component of the novels that reveals the nature of the protagonists in their observation of the city.

The Tradition of Urban Novelists

Up until the twentieth century, it was the male imagination and the male experience that shaped the view of the city.[6] The great women authors of the nineteenth century like the Brontës and George Eliot[7] did not portray London much at all. As Elizabeth Abel notes, "[W]omen in nineteenth-century fiction are generally unable to leave home for . . . the city. When they do, they are not free to explore."[8] In the nineteenth century, women were confined to the domestic sphere, and even those middle-class women who did write were not free to wander around the city at any hour of the night or day as Dickens did. Not until the twentieth century did women begin to write about the city. Now in the late twentieth century a whole group of British women novelists are writing about the city. As contemporary British male writers like Graham Greene, William Golding, Angus Wilson, and John Fowles turn increasingly to exotic or historical settings, Doris Lessing, Margaret Drabble, Iris Murdoch, P.D. James, and Maureen Duffy are picking up the tradition of writing about the city.

On the periphery of this tradition are some contemporary women novelists who focus on a particular district or neighborhood of the city. Blanche Gelfant borrowed the sociological term "ecological" to classify this kind of novel. She defines the "ecological novel" as one that "focuses upon one small spatial unit [of the city] such as a neighborhood or city block and explores [it] in detail."[9] Ecological novels thus do not portray the breadth and variety of the city. They scrutinize a small social group usually within a particular class or ethnic group. Muriel Spark's early novels, such as *Memento Mori, The Bachelors, The Ballad of Peckham Rye,* and *Girls of Slender Means,* focus on what one critic has called the small "semi-closed community."[10] Even her more recent London novel, *Loitering with Intent,* focuses on a small group, the members of an autobiographical society. Barbara Pym's city novels, such as *Excellent Women* and *A Glass of Blessings,* portray upper-middle-class Anglican neighborhoods. Anita Brookner's *Look at Me* describes the neighborhood of a young single librarian. Beryl Bainbridge describes working-class or lower-class groups in novels like *The Dressmaker* and *The Bottle Factory Outing* in which the tightly focused atmosphere borders on claustrophobic. Nell Dunn's *Up the Junction* is a vivid collection of portraits of the working-class inhabitants of Battersea. Although some of Fay Weldon's novels, like *Down Among the Women* or the frame story in *The President's Child,* are set in London or its outskirts, she does not analyze neighborhoods or the city in as much depth as the other novelists just mentioned. All these writers are interested in the city, but they do not teach us to see an entire city differently because they do not portray its breadth as Dickens did for Victorian London or Doris Lessing, Margaret Drabble, Iris Murdoch, P. D. James, and Maureen Duffy do for contemporary London. Olivia Manning is a contemporary urban novelist who portrays the breadth of cities, but after an early London novel, *Doves of Venus* (1955), she turned to other cities, Bucharest and Athens in her Balkan trilogy and Alexandria and Cairo in her Levant trilogy.

Women's portrayal of London actually began earlier in the twentieth century in the modernist period with writers like Dorothy Richardson, Jean Rhys, Katherine Mansfield, and Virginia Woolf. The awareness that the city is not just a male domain and that it can reflect female experience is an important legacy of the modernist women writers to contemporary women writing about the city. Nevertheless, there are some important differences between the modernist women writers and the contemporary ones in their portrayal of the city. Partly some of the modernist women writers focus on only one particular urban character, such as Richardson's "shabby genteel teacher" or Rhys's "female victim." The contemporary women's urban novels, in contrast, achieve variety not only in setting but also in the kinds of urban characters they create. Even more importantly, there is a crucial difference between modernist and contemporary urban writers in their basic vision of the city: contemporary British women novelists celebrate the city. The "modernist legacy" as Irving Howe describes it is one of "established hostility to the idea of the city." For Howe the modernist view is the "vision of the city we inherit from Eliot and Baudelaire, Céline and Brecht— with its ready nausea, packaged revulsion, fixed estrangement."[11] Shari Benstock finds the same negative image of the city in modernist novels by expatriate women living in Paris, particularly in novels like Djuna Barnes' *Nightwood*, Anaïs Nin's *House of Incest*, and Jean Rhys's *Good Morning, Midnight*. Rhys's urban vision is particularly grim. Benstock explains why: "Rhys represents an extreme example of woman's marginality in the modern urban environment. . . . although she continued to prefer Paris to London, Rhys herself was never comfortable in the city setting. The city's margins, its peripheral limits, drew Rhys like a magnet: disgusted by the sordid, she was nonetheless incapable of resisting it."[12] Katherine Mansfield's vision was not quite so bleak. Sydney Janet Kaplan feels that London continued to attract and inspire Mansfield even after she had left it, but Kaplan quotes one of Mansfield's last letters in which she rejects London and urban life: "[I]t's the people who live remote from cities who inherit the earth. London, for instance, is an awful place to live in. Not only is the climate abominable but it's a continual chase after distraction. There's no peace of mind."[13] In contrast, Doris Lessing's "expatriate" character in *The Four-Gated City* comes from a colonial setting to find tremendous freedom and exhilaration in the city.

The influence of Virginia Woolf's vision of the city is more complex than that of other female modernists because Woolf is not as negative about the city. Susan Squier explains in *Virginia Woolf and London: The Sexual Politics of the City* that Woolf's vision of the city evolved over the years: "In her earliest years Woolf saw the city as a competitive environment that excluded her and that stressed hierarchy, property and patriarchy. Yet her mature work portrays the city as an environment holding out the possibility of a feminist, egalitarian society."[14] Even at its most celebratory, the tradition of contemporary women urban novelists does not view London as having achieved a feminist or an egalitarian society, but it does portray London as being open to women's experience and to women's perception of it. Contemporary women urban writers inherit Woolf's fascination with the city and her love of London, and like her they portray the city as having a place for women.

Iris Murdoch is the most influenced by Woolf. Murdoch evokes Woolf's London when she uses Ebury Street, where Martin Pargiter lives after the war in Woolf's *The Years,* as the central London setting in *Nuns and Soldiers.* Deborah Johnson finds Woolf a stronger influence on Murdoch than Sartre, on whom Murdoch wrote a book. Johnson notes that Murdoch "shares something of Woolf's striving after an aesthetically rendered *plurality* of vision and her stress on human sympathy and interconnection. She also shares Woolf's playfulness, her subverting of set assumptions about gender roles and gender identity."[15] Peter Conradi, however, thinks that Woolf's influence on Murdoch is limited; Murdoch "has a firmer grasp of human difference than Woolf, as well as a much fiercer sense of the dangers and urgencies of the moral life."[16]

An appreciation of human difference is precisely what Lessing, Drabble, and Duffy find lacking in Woolf. In a 1962 interview Lessing says: "I've always felt this thing about Virginia Woolf—I find her too much of a lady. There's always a point in her books when I think, my God, she lives in such a different world from anything I've ever lived in, I don't understand it. I think it's charming in a way but I feel that her experience must have been too limited."[17] Claire Sprague emphatically denies any Woolf influence on Lessing. She thinks that Lessing's work is "determinedly antimodernist" because "modernism was not exactly in the fifties and rarely in England a viable choice. . . . Nor did the example of Virginia Woolf affect her fictional forms."[18] Although Margaret Drabble uses Woolf when she ends *The Middle Ground* with what she tells Diana Cooper-Clark is a "literary joke, a Mrs. Dalloway-type party," Drabble continues to be bothered by Woolf's lack of knowledge about "ordinary people." Drabble explains that she identifies strongly with Arnold Bennett, whom she contrasts with Woolf: "He came from a very poor background himself, as did my family, and he never forgot it. And because of this grounding in knowledge of ordinary people, which Virginia Woolf, for example, did not have, Arnold Bennett tells you things that Virginia Woolf simply didn't know."[19] In her biography of Bennett, Drabble is even more direct in her criticism of Woolf: "But there was something in her, some really fundamental recoil from grocers and shops, that blinded her appreciation both of his subject matter and of his meaning. Her recoil was an involuntary movement of class."[20] Maureen Duffy, a writer with strong working-class roots, shares Drabble's concern about Woolf's class limitations. Duffy in fact says that her stream-of-consciousness style was influenced by Joyce, not by Woolf.[21] Nevertheless, Duffy did write a play on Woolf, *A Nightingale in Bloomsbury Square,* in which Woolf has a fictional encounter with Freud. Woolf's love of London and the positive aspects of her vision of London were thus a strong influence on later female urban writers, but many contemporary women urban writers are also committed to portraying a breadth of characters, the "ordinary" people of the city, and for that they look back to writers like Arnold Bennett and Dickens.

Urban Images

Doris Lessing, Margaret Drabble, Iris Murdoch, P. D. James and Maureen Duffy analyze London in their novels by celebrating its variety and its many parts, but they also provide a unifying image of the city as a whole. Each of these five novelists uses a spatial image that is nonorganic and nonhierarchical: the palimpsest, the network, the labyrinth, the mosaic, and the archeological dig. Lessing portrays the city as a palimpsest, a layered text, that shows the passage of time through its layers. This palimpsest is also a fragment of a text and reveals the fragmentary nature of any one observer's perception of the city. Margaret Drabble describes the city as a network that includes the streets on the surface of the city and the sewers below it as well as the many interrelationships of the female protagonists. Iris Murdoch's image of the city as a labyrinth is related to Drabble's imagery of network, but it lacks the sense of connectedness. The qualities of this image reflect not only Murdoch's inheritance of the image from Dickens but also the morally limited character and perception of her male protagonists. P. D. James' detective novels and particularly her more traditional novel, *Innocent Blood,* depict the city as a mosaic, a collection of villages that connect together to make a coherent image. Maureen Duffy brings history and the passage of time in the city to the foreground in her image of the city as an archeological site, each layer of which has riches worth treasuring.

These five images, the palimpsest, the network, the labyrinth, the mosaic, and the archeological dig, are female images in that they all share the spatial configuration of a net, a web, or a multidimensional matrix. The term *matrix* is a particularly appropriate description of all these urban images because of its several layers of connotations. The association of matrix with the female lies in its anatomical definition, *womb*. (This definition is not in common use today, but as recently as 1923 Arnold Bennett used it in *Riceyman Steps:* a doctor, explaining a woman's medical problem to her husband, uses the term "matrix" to refer to the uterus.) In its mathematical and spatial definitions the matrix retains the idea of expandability that is associated with the uterus. A mathematical matrix, which is adaptable in having potentially any number of dimensions, contrasts sharply with a "grid," which is limited to two dimensions. In addition, a mathematical matrix, like a net or a web, is nonhierarchical; all intersections of points are equally important. A matrix is also associated with texts when it is defined as the mould in which type is cast. These implications are all contained in the five images used by the novelists. These implications might also be the reason why a group of British women architects have chosen the name "Matrix" for their architecture group; they have written a brief, nontheoretical book on housing entitled *Making Space: Women and the Man Made Environment.*

The five different urban images used by Lessing, Drabble, Murdoch, P. D. James and Duffy stress different aspects of the overarching matrix image. Lessing's palimpsest combines the idea of text with the dimension of time. The layers of text, one on top of the other, form a matrix. Drabble's network is a matrix that emphasizes the connection between points. The labyrinth, which Murdoch uses, is similar to a network but twisting and irregular. A labyrinth can be unicursal like the labyrinths in church floors which represent the faithful's pilgrimage to Jerusalem. In these labyrinths there is only one path, and it leads to the easily visible center. A labyrinth can also be multicursal. Multicursal labyrinths, in which there are many branchings and dead ends, are more complex,[22] and they can add the dimension of time if one cannot see them from above but only move through them. In both kinds of labyrinths the emphasis is on the intricacy and irregularity of the pattern, unlike the pattern of a net, which is often regular. P. D. James' image of the mosaic shares with that of the labyrinth an emphasis on intricacy of pattern, but its pattern is always intelligible to those who can see the whole picture. In the mosaic, small colored tiles are fitted into a matrix to form a glittering whole. The emphasis again is on connection. Duffy's image of the archeological dig involves three or even four dimensions in its emphasis on layers of time. A matrix is laid out over a site, and the dig proceeds down through layers of time. The matrix as a mass in which fossils or gems are embedded is also related to this image.

Not only do these five images share in the female and spatial configurations of a matrix, but each one also carries its own rich history of use in psychology, literature, and contemporary feminist criticism and planning theory. The image of the palimpsest occurs in Freud's *Interpretation of Dreams* to explicate the nature of the dream beneath whose surface lie "traces of an old and precious communication."[23] Sandra Gilbert and Susan Gubar use it to describe women's writing.[24] The image of the city as a palimpsest is also a popular one in contemporary urban theory, where the emphasis is on decoding previous strata of culture.[25] The network, an image applied to the city by some urban planners, has also been applied to female thinking and morality by the feminist psychologist Carol Gilligan. The city as labyrinth has a long literary history and is also used by architect Kevin Lynch.[26] The image of the mosaic comes from art, but Lynch also applies it to the city.[27] The archeological site, another image popular among contemporary urban theorists,[28] is also, according to Judith Kegan Gardiner, implied in Freud's reference to the preoedipal stage in girls as the Minoan-Mycenaean civilization in his 1931 essay, "Female Sexuality."[29] Such associations with psychology and urban theory reveal further female and spatial dimensions of the five urban images.

These nonhierarchical, spatially-focused images contrast sharply with some traditional male urban images. One of the oldest images of the city is that of an organism, in particular, a body or a part of a body. This image, especially strong in the eighteenth and nineteenth centuries, often took on negative overtones. Defoe describes the city as a plague-ridden body.[30] Another eighteenth-century writer describes London as a "monster, with a head . . . out of all proportion to its body," and William Cobbett in the nineteenth century referred to London as "the great wen."[31] Twentieth-century architectural and planning theory, adopting this earlier image of the city as an organism, repressed some of its negative aspects until, as Lynch explains, it became "the view that is most prevalent among planning professionals today."[32] Lynch feels that the image of the city as organism is destructive to planners: "The fundamental ineptness of the metaphor . . . leads us unthinkingly to cut out slums to prevent their 'infectious' spread." Lynch also criticizes the concept of hierarchy implicit in the organic image: "It is difficult to maintain hierarchy in very complex organizations such as cities. It is harmful to the easy flow of human interactions. . . . There are no 'higher' and 'lower' functions in cities."[33]

Two more recent male images, the city as a machine and the city as an atom, have equally negative connotations. Lynch explains that the image of the city as a machine, which dominates the thought of Le Corbusier, Paolo Soleri, and those who would apply systems analysis to cities, produces cities that would be "alien places. The separations, the oversimplification, the pure esthetics of the working machine, seem cold and repellent."[34] The city as atom, an image that William Sharpe finds in the United States government's 1983 publication *Metropolitan Statistical Areas,* involves "a nuclear city and 'orbiting' electron-suburbs . . . combining connotations of both space and energy."[35] This seems at first an appropriate image to describe the "nonplace urban realm," or the contemporary cities of poststructuralist novelists like Alain Robbe-Grillet and Thomas Pynchon, but Lynch notes its limitations as a theory for planning cities: "[T]here are values implied in this view. Persons are static, unthinking units which must respond in prescribed ways to the whirl of dynamic forces which surround them. The model is dynamic, but the rules are immutable."[36] These male images of the city as organism, machine, and atom are rigid and leave little room for people. In contrast to these, the female images of the matrix are especially appropriate to the city because they can incorporate elements of time as well as space and because they focus on connections. Furthermore, these images leave room for people and are flexible enough to allow people to define the urban spaces around them.

Because the images of the palimpsest, the network, the labyrinth, the mosaic, and the archeological dig are spatial images of the city, it is useful to have a way of classifying the spatial elements of the city. Lynch provides this classification in one of his earliest works, *The Image of the City,* identifying five elements of a city that an observer usually notices: the *landmarks* are well-known buildings or reference points; the *nodes* are "strategic spots," places of junction and concentration, or a "convergence of paths"; the *districts* are "recognizable" sections of the city; the *paths* are "streets," "walkways," and "transit lines"; and the *edges* are "linear elements not . . . considered as paths," "boundaries . . . barriers . . . [and] seams, lines along which two regions are . . . joined together."[37] An interesting pattern of observation concerning these spatial elements occurs in the urban novels of contemporary British women. It is the male characters who idealize the landmarks; the egocentric males in Murdoch's novels are especially fixated on them, but males in Drabble's and Duffy's novels also comment on them. Lessing's female characters laugh at landmarks and instead notice the edges of the city and the changes in districts. Both male and female characters in P. D. James' novels focus on districts as urban villages and note specificity of detail in them, as detectives usually do, but it is her female characters who notice the connections be-

The Albert Embankment is an example of an edge and a path.

tween districts. And although both male and female characters comment on the paths, the streets, and subway lines in
works by all five novelists, the female characters notice the
subtle changes of street life more than the male characters.
Some of these women writers also deal with time and the
changes in the city over time much more than male writers,
even Dickens. For Lynch the perception of the spatial elements of the city allows the formation of an "image" of the
city. The five contemporary women authors considered here
use these spatial elements of the city to form their own distinctive urban images.

Female Psychology: Chodorow, Gilligan, and Benjamin

Doris Lessing, Margaret Drabble, and P. D. James portray the
city through female protagonists who exhibit qualities of nurturance and flexible ego boundaries that psychological theorists Nancy Chodorow, Carol Gilligan, and Jessica Benjamin
think are typical of twentieth-century, middle-class western
women. In contrast, many of Iris Murdoch's male narrators
are egocentric characters who are afraid of connection to others. Nancy Chodorow argues that in families where child-
rearing is done primarily by the mother, girls resolve the oedipal stage differently than boys; girls "grow up with a sense of
continuity and similarity to their mother, a relational connection to the world."[38] Boys raised in a similar family must sever
the primary bond with the mother in order to resolve the oedipal phase and identify with the father. Boys, according to
Chodorow, thus "come to define themselves as more separate
and distinct, with a greater sense of rigid ego boundaries and
differentiation." Girls, because they do not have to break the
preoedipal bond with the mother as they identify with her to
resolve the oedipal phase, "come to define and experience
themselves as continuous with others; their experience of self
contains more flexible or permeable ego boundaries."[39] Carol
Gilligan, in investigating women's moral development, finds
that women solve moral dilemmas differently than men be-

cause they see "a world comprised of relationships rather than of people standing alone, a world that coheres through human connection rather than through systems of rules."[40] Gilligan finds this same concern with connection in the imagery that girls and women use. Where men use images of hierarchy, women use imagery of networks and webs.[41]

Chodorow, and particularly Gilligan, have been criticized on several points. Although Chodorow explicitly rejects arguments from nature and the concept of maternal instinct, Gilligan sometimes sounds like an essentialist, arguing that women's difference is innate.[42] She is not an essentialist, however; at the beginning of her book, she says that the different voice she describes is "characterized not by gender but theme. Its association with women is an empirical observation, and it is primarily through women's voices that I trace its development. But this association is not absolute."[43] Gilligan thus believes that gender difference is a result of social and cultural conditioning and that men can achieve these qualities, but she would have avoided misunderstanding if she had restated this throughout her book.

Even when gender difference is acknowledged as social and cultural, a discussion of it is sometimes seen as dangerous by some critics because of the dangers of dualism.[44] Difference, say these critics, can easily lead to oppression or neglect. Jonathan Culler answers this criticism in terms of urban imagery: "when discussing women writers of the past and present should one seek to identify a distinctly feminine achievement, at the risk of contributing to the isolation of a ghetto of 'women's writing' within the city of literature, or should one insist on the undesirability of categorizing authors by sex and describe the magnificent *general* achievements of particular women authors?" For an answer he turns to Jacques Derrida: "Analytical writings that attempt to neutralize the male/female opposition are extremely important, but, as Derrida says, 'the hierarchy of the binary opposition always reconstitutes itself,' and therefore a movement that asserts the primacy of the oppressed term is strategically indispensable."[45] Thus in spite of the valid dangers of discussing difference, studies that analyze female psychology, female morality, and women's literature, the oppressed terms, are especially important.

Gilligan has also been criticized as a social psychologist because, unlike neo-Freudian theorists Chodorow and Benjamin, she bases her conclusions on data from interviews. Gilligan is criticized primarily for using a very small and privileged sample of people in the abortion studies that led to her formulating an ethic of care. Joan Tronto argues that moral difference and the possession of an ethic of care might be "a function of social position rather than gender,"[46] that it is subordinate social position that gives one an opportunity to develop an ethic of care. Tronto does not deny that the ethic of care is possessed by women, only that the cause is a result of caretaking roles and responsibilities and is thus possessed by minority men and women as well as white women. Working-class men in Maureen Duffy's novels, particularly in *Capital,* exhibit a humility and an ethic of care that parallel Tronto's theories. Gilligan has also been criticized for not taking women's anger into account in the interpretation of her interviews,[47] although that is less a concern for the novels of these five women because they do not focus primarily on women's anger. Although one needs to use both Chodorow and Gilligan with care, they are helpful in a discussion of twentieth-century white western novelists because these female novelists and many of the female characters they create are similar to the women on whom Chodorow and Gilligan base their studies. Although there is much debate as to the cause of gender difference, there is considerable agreement as to what the different qualities associated with gender are in twentieth-century, middle-class, western groups.

Jessica Benjamin, a psychoanalyst, builds on Chodorow's and Gilligan's work in "A Desire of One's Own: Psychoanalytic Feminism and Intersubjective Space" and proposes that "intersubjective space" can be a psychic structure for girls just as the phallus is for boys. The concept of "intersubjective space" is influenced by the object relations theorist D. W. Winncott's concept of transitional space, the space between the mother and the child at play. Benjamin uses this image of space to represent females' concerns with others and their relational connection with the world. Benjamin defines the intersubjective mode as "aspects of the self that each individual brings with her from infancy—agency and receptivity toward the world," a "capacity for connection," and an acknowledgment of the other person that each individual develops from infancy onwards.[48] It is these qualities rather than envy of the phallus that can become a way of explaining female desire. Benjamin specifically links this psychic mode to spatial imagery:

> the intersubjective mode of desire has its counterpart in spatial rather than symbolic representation, and . . . this mode does have something to do with female experience. I would have to say that Erik Erikson was not all wrong in his intuitions about inner space, though he was wrong in some of the conclusions he drew from them. . . . Rather, inner space should be understood as part of a continuum that includes the space between the I and the you, as well as the space within me; and, further, the space within should be understood as a receptacle only insofar as it refers to the receptivity of the subject.[49]

Benjamin emphasizes that feminine desire is a positive force. Her theories stand in sharp contrast to those who see feminine desire as "penis envy" or "lack" or "passivity." Benjamin theorizes that this psychic mode would develop more strongly in a family in which girls saw their mothers as "subjects" as well as "objects" of desire and in which "girls should get what boys get from their father [during the crucial separation phase that takes place at about age two] recognition of agency, curiosity, movement toward the outside—and . . . they should get it from their mothers as well as their fathers."[50] Even though Benjamin's ideas are theoretical and still tentative, the images she associates with male and female interestingly parallel the spatial pattern of observations used by contemporary women urban novelists. Male characters in Drabble's and Murdoch's novels are fixated on phallic structures of landmarks; female characters notice boundaries of spaces and relationships between spaces. Once inner space is redefined as a capacity for relationships and an ability to see relationships between inside and outside, female characters can leave the domestic inner space and move outside to see the exterior urban spaces in new ways.

Doris Lessing, Margaret Drabble, Iris Murdoch, P. D. James, and Maureen Duffy all describe characters who are not only sensitive to the quality of spaces but who also value qualities of nurturance, connection, and responsibility for others. These characters differ from typical nineteenth-century characters of feminine virtue, however, by having a strong sense of their own autonomy. These contemporary female characters can maintain their autonomy because these authors mostly do not use a marriage plot. Moreover, the female characters' qualities of nurturance and connection are outwardly directed toward many others, not just toward a spouse. In *The Four-Gated City* and *The Diaries of Jane Somers,* for example, Doris Lessing concentrates on her protagonists' relationship with the mother or mother figure. As the protagonist in *The Four-Gated City* focuses on boundary issues with her mother, she notices the boundary areas of the city. When the main character in *The Diaries of Jane Somers* overcomes her fear of engulfment by a mother figure, she views the city with increasing euphoria. Although Lessing's Canopean novels do not focus on urban issues, "the substance-of-we-feeling" (SOWF) that Canopus sends to its colonized planets to support them illustrates how Lessing values an emphasis on relationship and connection. Margaret Drabble's two female protagonists in *The Middle Ground* are mothers themselves and spend time thinking about their own mothers. As they contemplate their many connections with family and friends, they see a strong connectedness throughout the city. (In *In A Different Voice,* Gilligan uses Drabble's novel *The Waterfall,* which focuses on childbirth and a woman's love affair, to illustrate women's relationship-centered morality.) Iris Murdoch first gives a negative example: in *A Word Child* an egotistical male character who lacks connectedness and concern for others focuses on landmarks, and the city he perceives is dank and dismal. Then in *Nuns and Soldiers* light continually radiates through the snow and fog as Murdoch portrays some "good" characters who develop a concern for others.[51] Connectedness is also a concern for P. D. James, who shows a clear difference between her male and her female detectives in their willingness to get involved. In *Innocent Blood* the female protagonist, who has been adopted, must get to know her real mother before she can learn to observe the city and connect the villages that make up London. Maureen Duffy too believes in an "ethic of compassion," and her characters either already possess this quality or must learn to develop it in order to explore fully the history of the city.

In the nineteenth century the city was associated with individuality and rationality, not empathy and otherness. Sharpe explains that for the turn-of-the-century classic urban theorists, Max Weber, Georg Simmel, and Oswald Spengler,[52] the city bred a "rational, impersonal, alienated, unemotional and autonomous" character.[53] Richard Sennett, schooled in the works of Weber and Simmel, decries "men's" neglect of others in cities and thinks it is the cause of urban violence. In *The Uses of Disorder: Personal Identity and City Life,* he writes:

> people feel most uneasy and most challenged by perceiving the "otherness" of people around them. . . . The fear of "otherness," of that which one does not know, is exactly of a piece with what men fear about *themselves* and their own powers when those powers ripen in adolescence. From adolescence people take a power for mythmaking into their adult community lives to blunt the conscious perception of "otherness."[54]

Although Sennett probably did not intend to refer only to a male fear of "otherness" when he used the plural "men," Chodorow's, Gilligan's, and Benjamin's theories of women's relational connection to the world and concern with others reveal such a fear as more applicable to the average man than to the average woman. Drabble, paralleling philosopher Sara Ruddick's concept of "maternal thinking,"[55] ties female concern for otherness to motherhood: "Having children gives you an access to an enormous common store of otherness about other people."[56] Gilligan would at least applaud Sennett's calling this "fear of otherness" adolescent. Too many psychologists, according to Gilligan, describe adulthood as a time when "relationships are subordinated to the ongoing process of individuation and achievement. . . . among those men whose lives have served as the model for adult development, the capacity for relationships is in some sense diminished."[57]

Sennett not only finds this lack of feeling for others adolescent, he also sees it as leading to an intolerance of disorder and a cause of violence:

> this inability to deal with disorder without raising it to the scale of mortal combat, is inevitable when men shape their common lives so that their only sense of relatedness is the sense in which they feel themselves to be the same. It is because men are uneasy and intolerant with ambiguity and discord in their own lives that they do not know how to deal with painful disorder in a social setting.[58]

Again, the plural "men," for readers of feminist psychologists, implies that this tendency toward violence is more typical of men, with their higher levels of aggression, than it is of women. Chodorow's theories also suggest a psychoanalytic reason for men's greater tendency toward aggression when they are faced with ambiguity and discord. Women, according to Chodorow, have more flexible ego boundaries,[59] and thus they are perhaps better able to tolerate ambiguity in their own lives. It is men, with their more rigid ego boundaries and their stronger sense of differentiation, who are made uneasy and intolerant of ambiguity and discord and thus react aggressively. Sennett calls for a greater tolerance of disorder, for he believes that only life "in the diverse disorganization of a dense city"[60] can lead to the full complexity of life and adulthood. To find the concern for "otherness" for which he is searching, he needs to look to the qualities of women in dense cities as they are portrayed by women novelists.

American Urban Literature

A major difference between the portrayals of the city by these five British women novelists and those in other recent traditions in urban literature is that these authors celebrate the city. A celebration of the city is rare not only in British and European modernism (see pp. 4–7, above) but also in twentieth-century American literature. Certainly the urban novels of contemporary British women writers show the crime and the sordidness of the contemporary city but these negative aspects are balanced by the women's sense of freedom in the city and their delight and fascination with the variety of the city. As Blanche Gelfant points out, the city liberates women from the traditional and limiting associations of the female with nature and from the prescribed roles for women in farm and small-town life. Gelfant finds some of this sense of freedom in twentieth-century American city novels in the intellectually "hungry woman" character who can find libraries and education in the city, but in American novels the price this hungry heroine must pay for her freedom is solitude. There are very few close relationships among women to balance the city's isolation in the novels Gelfant discusses (for instance, *Sister Carrie, A Tree Grows in Brooklyn, Daddy Was a Numbers Runner, The Crying of Lot 49*) compared to Lessing's *Diaries of Jane Somers,* Drabble's *The Middle Ground,* and P. D. James' *Innocent Blood.* Gelfant's American heroine is also in conflict with the city; she must resist "the forces of urban anonymity and indifference, turning them into a test of her own will."[61] Although the city in the American novel provides some freedom for women, it does not nurture them as it does in some of the British novels.

American literature has a greater history of antiurbanism than British literature. Sharpe points out that "American culture . . . has never developed a positive image of the city. . . . antiurbanism [is] . . . a preeminent motif in American literature."[62] This American antiurbanism appears not only in literature but sometimes in the very structure of American cities. Jean-Paul Sartre, tying American antiurbanism to the lack of a sense of time and history in American cities, says that American cities "are not constructed in order to grow old . . . the past does not manifest itself in them as it does in Europe, through public monuments." Furthermore, according to Sartre, streets function differently in American cities: "In Europe, a street is half-way between the path of communication and the sheltered 'public place.' . . . The American street is a piece of highway. . . . It does not stimulate one to walk."[63] These aspects of the American city and the tradition of American literature make it hard to find a celebration of the city in American novels. There is a chance, as Gelfant's essay intimates, that more positive images of the city will begin to appear in American women's novels, but pessimism is still dominant in such works as Joyce Carol Oates' *Them* (1969) and Gloria Naylor's *Women of Brewster Place* (1982). In Marge Piercy's *Going Down Fast* (1969) and *Fly Away Home* (1984), the heroine is locked in a bitter fight with the male forces that control the development of the city. In *Fly Away Home* the heroine moves back to the city from the suburbs and wins some battles, but this novel still does not celebrate the city or portray it in as much detail as the British women's novels.

Ancient Urban Literature

This celebration of the city in contemporary British women writers actually reestablishes the balanced attitude toward the city that was typical of premodern times. The image of the city in ancient literature is often of the city as woman, an image infrequently employed in contemporary literature, and in ancient literature the city as harlot alternates with the city as goddess or bride. Vincent Scully, an architectural critic, points out that the "archaic Athena Polias was . . . the embodiment of what the city state might be—the polis which helped to liberate men from their terror of the natural world."[64] The goddess Athena Polias, a deity separated from the earth, represented the city's protection of its inhabitants from the wilds of nature. "As such," Scully explains, "she crowned the acropolises of archaic Mycene, Athens, Megara and many other places."[65] In ancient literature as well as in buildings and sculpture the city was the protection from the wilderness. The Homeric and Virgilian epic tradition, that which glorified cities, balanced out the tradition of Juvenalian satire that criticized the ills of the city. The Biblical city of Babylon was counterbalanced by the New Jerusalem. Gail Paster describes how the dual images of the "city as a visionary embodiment of ideal community . . . or the city as a predatory trap"[66] dominated the drama of the Renaissance. In the eighteenth century, as the historian Carl Schorske explains, the city of virtue characterized by industry and pleasure balances the Blakean vision of the city of vice.[67] In the nineteenth and twentieth centuries, however, this balance was beginning to be lost. The city became the wilderness and the jungle only or as Howe describes it "the pesthole."[68] In their celebration of the city of London, the novels of Doris Lessing, Margaret Drabble, Iris Murdoch, P. D. James, and Maureen Duffy restore the positive image of the city and thereby redress the late nineteenth- and early twentieth-century traditions of modernism and naturalism.

City Planning Theory

City planners as well as literary critics need to read these novels that celebrate varied, mixed-use cities and value "otherness" and a sense of time in cities. Although there are some planners like Kevin Lynch and Jane Jacobs whose values match those of these five British women authors, the more dominant tradition in architecture and planning has been the rationalist and patriarchal tradition that stretches from Ebenezer Howard, the turn-of-the-century theorist who advocated the Garden City, and the early modernist architect Le Corbusier to contemporary American planners and architects like James Rouse and Philip Johnson. Patrick Byrne and Richard Keeley describe these architects and planners as belonging to a tradition "cast within the rigorous bounds of a Cartesian rational consciousness" and characterized by "rectilinear simplicity, functional foreclosure, and domination over nature."[69] Byrne and Keeley connect this rational and geometric concept of space and design to elitism, a contempt for "otherness" and for the actual people of cities. This tradition, they conclude, views

> the city as a disastrous mess, capable of being tidied up only by dint of massive reorganization along rational-geometric-artistic lines. This tradition also carries an implicit political judgment, a distrust of the people who inhabit cities: who, but they, could be responsible for the lack of grand vision, for unplanned and unadministered growth that disfigures the city?[70]

In contrast to this tradition, Byrne and Keeley place the thought of Jane Jacobs and Kevin Lynch, which they define as characterized by subjectivity, plurality, and a street level perspective. One of the most significant values in the work of Jacobs and Lynch is the emphasis on other people, on community. Byrne and Keeley contrast the hierarchical and deterministic values of the first tradition with the communal and relational values of the second:

> The tradition of LeCorbusier suffers under the weight of environmental determinism: alter the streets and buildings, and the good life will result. The Jacobean tradition locates the source of the possibility of the good life within the community of subjects who, by their virtues, loyalties, friendships, sacrifices, and commitments, create the meanings of the city.[71]

In the emphasis on connection and community, Jacobs' tradition shares the values that Chodorow, Gilligan and Benjamin describe as female values. Thus it is not surprising that in their analysis of cities Jacobs and Lynch value some of the same qualities that contemporary British women novelists portray, such as the mixed-use city that connects parks and streets, backyards and alleyways.

Jacobs in *The Death and Life of Great American Cities* (1961) praises diversity, vitality, plurality, and responsiveness to human need in her discussion of city sidewalks, parks, neighborhoods and districts. She particularly criticizes a quality "meaner than outright ugliness or disorder . . . the dishonest mask of pretended order,"[72] which she sees as the legacy of Ebenezer Howard's Garden City theories and of Le Corbusier's Radiant City. Lynch also rejects these planners and with them Howard's image of the city as an organism and Le Corbusier's image of the city as machine. Jacobs calls Howard's planning concepts "paternalistic, if not authoritarian"[73] and sees as especially dangerous the trend still used by planners of segregating and containing urban uses. Jacobs feels that successful districts and neighborhoods have a variety of primary and secondary uses; for instance, they mix commercial and residential uses although maintaining compatible scale. This mixed-use city is more typical of London than American cities, and it is precisely London's mixture of shops and residences that is so vividly portrayed in the novels of Lessing, Drabble, and P. D. James. Like these novelists, Jacobs and Lynch eschew what Chodorow, Gilligan, and Benjamin would call the typically male values of separation, distinction, and hierarchy. Instead they value continuity, connection, flexibility, and, above all, other people.

Jacobs in fact writes much like a novelist when she uses an extended image to convey her values of connection and interrelationship. She describes city sidewalk life as a ballet:

> Under the seeming disorder of the old city, wherever the old city is working successfully, is a marvelous order for maintaining the safety of the streets and the freedom of the city. . . . This order is all composed of movement and change, and . . . we may . . . liken it to the dance—not a simple-minded precision dance with everyone kicking up at the same time, twirling in unison and bowing off en masse, but to an intricate ballet in which the individual dancers and ensembles all have distinctive parts which miraculously reinforce each other and compose an orderly whole. The ballet of the good city sidewalk never repeats itself from place to place, and in any one place is always replete with new improvisations.[74]

This ballet is not the image of the cosmic dance that echoes through the works of modernists like Yeats and Eliot. Nor are there any prima ballerinas. It is rather the image of an ordinary corps de ballet with lots of dancers each playing a small role and improvising within the pattern. All are connected together in the overall network of the dance, but they are not forced to dance in precision sameness. The order of the city sidewalk, and the city itself, is that of intricate, connected, and mutually reinforcing choreography which has not been designed from above but rather improvised from below. The success of city life according to this image depends upon human interrelationship.

Nature and the City

Contemporary British women's urban novels also differ from the dominant tradition of rationalism in planning and from many nineteenth- and twentieth-century urban writers in refusing to contrast the city with nature. As Raymond Williams points out, this idealization of pastoral settings and small towns is primarily nostalgia, an idealization of a past set of values seen as a Golden Age.[75] Childhood memories of rural innocence may have brought nostalgia for male authors, but for women the roles available in rural life were limited. Furthermore, the city/country dichotomy also implies the older culture/nature dichotomy which associated men with culture and cities and women with nature and enclosed space. As Susan Squier points out, this led to women's being judged as "less fit" for the "urban marketplace" and caused "women's experience of the city . . . [to have] generally been mediated by men."[76] If the city is no longer contrasted with nature, as is the case in many contemporary British urban novels by women, then the female observer is as "at home" in the city as the male and feels no need to separate nature and city. The protagonists in the novels of Lessing, Drabble, P. D. James, and Duffy constantly notice urban trees and birds in the backyards, squares, and small parks of London. This inclusion of nature Sidney Bremer finds to be typical of women's late nineteenth- and early twentieth-century novels about Chicago: "Chicago novels by women usually embrace nature as a powerful, complex presence within the city, whereas the men's novels tend to idealize nature and to present it as apart from the city."[77]

Jane Jacobs and Kevin Lynch also refuse to separate city and nature. Jacobs writes:

> Human beings are, of course, a part of nature, as much so as grizzly bears or bees or whales or sorghum cane. The cities of human beings are as natural, being a product of one form of nature, as are the colonies of prairie dogs or the beds of oysters.[78]

In this view, shared by female novelists and some progressive city planners, cities are a part of nature, not a separate order from nature. This is not the same as seeing the city as organic. In the nineteenth-century view of the city as organism, the city was seen as subject to "Nature's Laws." In Jacobs' and Lynch's theories the city is not itself organic, but since it is created by human beings, it is a "product" of nature and other natural beings and other products of nature can be found within it. Nor is there the direct opposition between the city and Nature that is implied by the image of the city as machine. According to Jacobs, a belief in a false dichotomy between nature and city is one of the reasons why earlier planners ran into problems. They thought the green belt of a Garden City or grass around public housing would automatically guarantee the health of the city. Jacobs, however, shows that if parks or even small grassy areas function as seamless boundaries that cut out diverse pathways, they can actually harm city life. Her focus is on people; parks, for her, are dependent for their health on the patterns of use rather than the presence of what is traditionally and, according to Jacobs, falsely called "nature." Lynch too rejects the false contrast between nature and the city:

> The mental sense of connection with nature . . . is a basic human satisfaction . . . but the urban landscape can also convey [it]. . . . The movements of sun and tides, the cycles of weeds and insects and men, can also be celebrated along the city pavements. Once we can accept that the city is as natural as the farm . . . we work free of those false dichotomies of city and country, artificial and natural, man versus other living things.[79]

The acceptance of the city as natural, with cycles of light and seasons and vegetation, also introduces a new awareness of time within the city and an appreciation for the passing of time. Just as these women novelists value fluidity and relationships, so do they also notice the cycles of natural time within the city. Iris Murdoch's novels, for instance, portray the quality of light at different times of the day and describe the variation in seasons by noting the changing color of leaves on the trees in the city. In Duffy's *Londoners* the protagonist notices city daffodils poking up through a spring snow and comments on "how the city drains of colour in summer."[80] Lynch, in *What Time Is This Place,* emphasizes the value of using natural elements in the city to convey the rhythms of the seasons and the day. Deciduous trees, for example, help to provide the "episodic contrast," the awareness of "rhythmic recurrence" in nature that contributes to a city's livability.[81]

Not only do feminist observers and novelists perceive that nature has all along been part of the city, but they also perceive the "manmade" structures of the city and the complex relationships of people within the city in new ways. Thus readers of the novels of Doris Lessing, Margaret Drabble, Iris Murdoch, P. D. James, and Maureen Duffy learn to see the city of London in new ways, and by extension, other cities as well. If planners and architects and designers want to produce livable cities, ones that reject elitism, segregation of use and people, and contempt for time and history, they need to read not only theorists like Jacobs and Lynch but also the urban novels of contemporary British women novelists who love the city and dramatize the values of Jacobs and Lynch. All those who create cities and all those who live in cities need to learn what it means to imagine the city as a matrix, whether it be palimpsest, network, labyrinth, mosaic, or archeological dig.

CHAPTER 2

The City as Palimpsest:
Doris Lessing

The architect Kevin Lynch was one of the first to envision the city as a text. In *The Image of the City* (1960) he wrote that a city has "legibility." Like the "printed page . . . [which] can be visually grasped as a related pattern of recognizable symbols . . . a legible city [has] . . . districts or landmarks or pathways [that] are easily identifiable and are easily grouped into an over-all pattern."[1] Lynch's terms are useful for an analysis of the city's linear elements, but the city has other dimensions as well, and in that sense it is not just any text; it is a specific kind of text. Another urban planner suggests that a city is a palimpsest, a text that is built up layer after layer, each layer preserved partially or wholly underneath the other:

> A city . . . is the pulsating product of the human hand and mind, reflecting man's history, his struggle for freedom, his creativity, his genius—and his selfishness and errors. It is the palimpsest on which man's story is written, the record of those who built a skyscraper or a picture window, fought a pitched battle for a play street, created a bookshop or a bakeshop that mattered. It is a composite of trials and defeats, of settlement houses, churches, and schoolhouses, of aspirations, images, and memories.[2]

Whether one thinks of the seven layers of Troy or of a contemporary new town like Cumbernauld outside of Glasgow with its separate layers of traffic and pedestrian circulation, the image of the palimpsest fits the city well. The city is not just any text; it is a layered text.

To those familiar with women's studies, the image of the palimpsest recalls another application. Women's novels have been called palimpsests because the real story about women is hidden beneath the surface text.[3] Women have a long heritage of writing and reading beneath the surface and of being aware of the layers of meaning. If both the tradition of the city itself and of women novelists is "palimpsestic," then women ought to be particularly capable "urban novelists." Novelists who themselves can decipher and portray the multiplicity of layers in their own lives and histories ought to be those who can portray the experience of the city.

Doris Lessing is such a novelist. Several critics have noted how important the image of the city is in Lessing's work. In one of the earliest works on Lessing, Mary Anne Singleton contrasted the image of the veld with the archetypal image of the city.[4] Ellen Cronan Rose, has found the image of Lessing's ideal four-gated city to be based on the utopian Italian Renaissance city, the *città felice*.[5] More recently, Claire Sprague describes the city as central to Lessing's work:

> Unlike so many other writers, Lessing refuses to damn the city and extol nature. She is stubborn in her insistence on the city as the center of human interaction. The city must be confronted, accepted, altered. It is the quintessential locus of human history.[6]

Like the planner Jane Jacobs and like Margaret Drabble, Iris Murdoch, P. D. James, and Maureen Duffy, Lessing values the city and sees no inherent contrast between it and nature. Nature, even if only in the form of a tiny flower growing out of an old timber, is part of the palimpsest that is the city.

The Four-Gated City

Although mythological cities occur in Lessing's work from the vision of the ideal white foursquare city in *Martha Quest* to the grim disintegrating city of *Memoirs of a Survivor* to the "mathematical" cities of the Canopean novels, it is in her vivid evocation of the real city of London in *The Four-Gated City* that she portrays most vividly the city as a palimpsest, a layered text built up over time, perceived by women. In *The Four-Gated City*, Martha Hesse arrives in London just after World War II. She walks around London, noticing its districts and boundaries and its bombed-out buildings. As she walks, she notices the details of the city herself and also thinks of how her landlady, Iris, who runs "Joe's Fish and Chips," would view these sights:

> Iris, Joe's mother, had lived in this street since she was born. Put her brain together with the other million brains, women's brains, that recorded in such tiny loving anxious detail the histories of window sills, skins of paint, replaced curtains and salvaged baulks of timber, there would be a recording instrument, a sort of six-dimensional map which included the histories and lives and loves of people, London—a section map in depth. This is where London exists.[7]

The city here is portrayed as multilayered. It exists not only in three dimensions of space, but in three additional dimensions, perhaps of time: the *histories, lives,* and *loves* of people. This concept of the city is symbolized by a fragment of thirteen layers of wallpaper all fused together, a miniature palimpsest, that Martha scrapes off the wall of a bombed-out house and puts in her pocket as she starts thinking about the nature of the city. Furthermore, this miniature palimpsest of wallpaper fits into a pattern of actual palimpsestic texts that occur throughout the novel: Thomas Stern's ant-eaten testament with his own "additions and riders, in red pencil" and Mark's insertions layered over those in red pen (176), Dorothy's diary (413–14), Mark's layers of clippings on his walls (282–83), and even the "appendix" itself, in which the accounts and letters of several characters overlap (560–614). The piece of wallpaper, however, is a particularly significant "text" here because it is an image of the city and a statement of how to read the city.

The piece of wallpaper is an appropriate image of the city and a method of perceiving the city because it is both layered and a fragment. As Lynch emphasizes, "Most often, our per-

ception of the city is not sustained, but rather partial, fragmentary, mixed with other concerns."[8] This kind of perception, partial, fragmentary, and mixed with other concerns, is
precisely the kind of perception that women are good at, as
Nancy Chodorow implies in *The Reproduction of Mothering.*
She argues that because women go through a less clear-cut
oedipal stage than men, women "define and experience themselves as continuous with others; their experience of self contains more flexible or permeable ego boundaries."[9] This re-
sults partly because mothers "tend to experience their
daughters as more like, and continuous with themselves. Cor-
respondingly, girls tend to remain part of the dyadic primary
mother-child relationship itself. This means that a girl continues to experience herself as involved in issues of merging and
separation."[10] Later, Chodorow says, "Throughout their development women have been building layers of identification
with their mothers upon the primary internalized mother-
child relationship."[11] Because women do not separate out the
sense of self as rigidly as men do, they are more comfortable
with seeing the city as mixed, partial, and layered, as districts
overlapping with one another in space and in time, rather
than definite precise areas. Perhaps it is also because of this
fluid ego boundary that they do not feel so threatened by fragmentation, and because they are comfortable with layers of
identification that they can perceive the layers of time in the
city.

Martha herself becomes an astute observer of the city not
only because she is a woman, but also because for her this
issue of merging with and separation from her mother and
acceptance of a fragmentary identity is what she must work
out in *The Four-Gated City.* Martha has been struggling with
psychic separation from her mother throughout the *Children
of Violence* series. In *The Four-Gated City* she doesn't even
read her mother's letters because they seem to threaten her
so much. Her mother seems to be able to invade Martha's ego
boundaries not only in person but even in letters. Martha had
sought to escape her mother earlier in *A Proper Marriage,* but
the sensuous, soporific Zambesian town (Zambesia is Les-

sing's fictional country that she based on her own experiences growing up in Rhodesia) and her marriage threaten to engulf her just as her mother does. When Martha looks out of her window shortly after her marriage to Douglas Knowell, she sees that the

> small, ramshackle Colonial town had become absorbed in a luminous dark. A looming pile of flats was like a cliff rising from the sea. . . . Whiffs of petrol-laden dust, staled scent from the flowers in the park . . . drifted past . . . towards the back of the building, where it would mingle with . . . that smell which comes rich and heavy out of the undertown. . . . The fun-fair had come to town; and over the straggling dusty grass . . . rose swings and roundabouts and the great glittering wheel. . . .
> The great wheel was revolving slowly, a chain of lights that mingled with the lamps of Orion and the Cross.[12]

Martha fears that her life will be like the ferris wheel,[13] merely an endless repetition of her mother's life. In *A Proper Marriage* Martha feels caught "in the grip of the great bourgeois monster, the nightmare, repetition" (102).

Paradoxically, the boundaries of the Zambesian town in *A Proper Marriage* seem at the same time both potentially engulfing and too rigid. On the one hand, Martha fears that the sensuous town will swallow her up and that the people she meets, all of whom know her life history, will force her into a role just like that of her mother. On the other hand, the boundaries seem too rigid. Martha seems to be caught in a grid just like the grid design of the town:

> The town-planners, when faced with a need for more houses, always solved the problem by laying a ruler neatly over the map which represented a patch of unused veld, causing a pattern of streets to come into existence which crossed each other regularly at right-angles. Everything was straight, orderly, unproblematical; grey strips of tarmac stretched endlessly, the naked earth at either side sprouted grass and wild flowers. (315)

Martha knows these grids and the boundaries within the town that carefully divide areas for whites, coloreds and Africans. Those boundaries are especially tightly drawn for women. Her Jewish male friend, Solly Cohen, can start a commune in the colored area, but Martha, as a white woman, is not welcome. In the small colonial town, Martha continually has to fight the forces that threaten to engulf her and lock her into a narrow way of life.

Not until *The Four-Gated City,* when Martha comes to London alone, does she experience freedom and begin to accept herself:

> For a few weeks she had been anonymous, unnoticed—free. Never before in her life had she known this freedom. Living in a small town anywhere means preserving one's self behind a mask. Coming to a big city for those who have never known one means first of all, before anything else, . . . that freedom: all the pressures are off, no one cares, no need for the mask. (4)

In the freedom and anonymity of the city Martha recognizes the various personas and masks she has worn in the past and realizes that she can control them. She is no longer forced to be "Matty," the clowning persona she adopted to fight her mother. She accepts herself as having many personas and as being multilayered.[14] This recognition of herself as multilayered allows Martha to read the city, and finally after she has come to understand the city which gives her freedom, she comes to terms with her own mother. Then she reads all the letters and allows her mother to come to visit. Martha finally develops an ability to feel comfortable with fluid ego boundaries. Later in the novel Martha goes down to the basement apartment of Lynda, Mark's "mad" wife. Martha is able to cross Lynda's ego boundaries and "understand" the nature of madness. Her development of this ability, however, starts with her reading of the city of London.

It is precisely Martha's focus on boundaries and her growing acceptance of fluidity and fragmentation that allow her to read that fragment of wallpaper and the city. When she learns about the people of the city, she does not restrict herself to a single class or layer of society any more than she restricts herself to a single persona. Nor does she feel that she must stay with any one person long enough to learn his or her entire life story. She accepts knowing people as fragments. Likewise, when Martha observes the spatial qualities of the city, she does not focus on the "landmarks" or "nodes . . . the strategic spots" that are the two broadest elements of a cityscape, according to Lynch. Rather she focuses on boundary areas, more fragmentary areas that Lynch calls "districts," "paths," and "edges."[15] It is in the variety of overlapping districts connected by paths and edges that Martha constructs her section map of the height, width, and depth of the city.

The final dimension in which Martha has to learn to read the piece of wallpaper and the city is that of time. After she has scraped her piece of wallpaper off the wall and observed it spatially, noting the "thick sog of papers: layers of it . . . fused together, like a kind of felt" (73), recognizing the overlapping pieces, and identifying the boundaries and layers, she reads it in terms of time:

> Picking at the layers, she counted thirteen. Thirteen times had a man stood on trestles, . . . and stretched new clean paper over the stains and dirts of the layer beneath. Thirteen times had a wife or children said, Yes, that's very nice, I like that, Dad; or had said, No, we chose wrong. The two papers at the very bottom were rather beautiful, . . . they got progressively uglier as the decades slid by. The one at the top was hideous, must have been an acid green, with a bad jangling pattern. In the middle was a rather pretty sprigged pattern, like a Victorian young lady's morning dress. (74)

This incorporation of the aspect of time is perhaps another important reason why Lessing said that cities are recorded in "women's brains."

This sense of historical time is not strongly present in Dickens, for instance, in spite of his intense visual imagination and his tremendous scope and breadth as an urban novelist. Although Dickens captured the movement of the city[16] and "the city dweller's experience of architectural change," Alexander Welsh says that Dickens had "little historical imagination."[17] John Raleigh puts it even more strongly:

> I think . . . that London or any of the new large cities must have been equally disturbing, at almost a subconscious level, for two other reasons (not that the squalor was to be disregarded): one,

it was so large that no one could grasp it; and second, it was always changing and growing, so that it constituted a new paradox in man's history: a huge "thing" that was "alive." And in some ways it is these aspects that were finally to defeat the imagination even of a Dickens or a Balzac.[18]

What stands out strongly in Raleigh's comment is that something "changing and growing . . . constituted a paradox in *man's* history." For any parent who has watched a child grow, it is not a paradox at all. In fact, as Sara Ruddick argues in an essay on "Maternal Thinking," a mother's "realistic appreciation of a person's continuous mental life allows a mother to expect change, to change with change." Furthermore, she continues, "if we attend to maternal practices, we can develop new ways of studying . . . the changing natures of all peoples and communities, for it is not only children, who change, grow."[19]

Although Doris Lessing rejects the idea that there is a particular style that is feminine,[20] she does imply that women have a distinct perception when she says of *The Golden Notebook* that it was written with "that filter which is a woman's way of looking at life."[21] She links that filter with maternal thinking when Anna in *The Golden Notebook* explains to Tommy that women see their children in phases:

> But I think that's how women see—people. Certainly their own children. In the first place, there's always been nine months of not knowing whether the baby would be a girl or a boy. Sometimes I wonder what Janet [Anna's child] would have been like if she'd been born a boy. Don't you *see*? And then babies go through one stage after another, and then they are children. When a woman looks at a child she sees all the things he's been at the same time. When I look at Janet sometimes I see her as a small baby and I *feel* her inside my belly and I see her as various sizes of small girl, all at the same time.[22]

Because of motherhood, women are trained in seeing many different ages or layers[23] all at the same time. Although Martha did not raise her own child in the earlier volumes of the *Children of Violence* series, in *The Four-Gated City* she not only comes to terms with her own mother, but she also takes over the responsibility of raising Lynda's child and also Mark's nephew, Paul, since his mother committed suicide.

In a later novel in the *Canopus in Argos* series, Lessing implies that this way of perceiving experience and accepting change is open to men as well as women. In the matriarchal zone three of *The Marriages between Zones Three, Four and Five* the queen Al.Ith explains that all children have "Mind-Fathers" as well as "Gene-Fathers" and that these Mind-Fathers "considered themselves joint-parents, forever available to [the child] . . . any time they were needed."[24] Thus adults involved in parenting, but particularly the women in *The Four-Gated City,* expect change over time and cherish the memories of earlier stages. The image of the city as a huge "thing" that is alive is not profoundly disturbing nor a paradox if one associates it with a growing child. Instead, that perception allows one to notice aspects of the city, both in space and in time, that others have missed. It is why women can record "in such tiny loving anxious detail the histories of window sills, skins of paint, replaced curtains . . . the histories lives and loves of people—London a section map in depth" (10), why women can read palimpsests.

Martha starts her reading of the city by learning about and experiencing fragments of the lives of urban characters. In fact, when Phoebe, the earnest Labour party worker and sister of Martha's friend in the colonies, questions her, this is what she says London means to her.

> And now, because it was Phoebe who sat there, opposite, the past weeks changed their aspect and presented "London" to Martha as a series, containing dockland Stella, the café and Iris; Jack; Henry; and the people in the streets and pubs. Fragments. (79)

Stella and Iris are particularly important characters not only because they take Martha in, but also because they are lower-class women who represent the variety of social classes she gets to know. Stella, who first befriends Martha, is "the matriarchal boss of her knot of streets, among the body-proud, work-proud men who earned their wages by physical strength and who judged everyone by strength and their capacity for work—was Stella the only Boadicea [the Celtic warrior queen who rebelled against the Romans] among the masculine communities of the river's edges?" (15). Iris, "a small fatish smeared woman . . . [who] wore an overall washed so often it had gone a greyish yellow" (4) runs a small café and rents a room to Martha after Martha leaves Stella. Like Stella, Iris takes care of Martha and values her:

> Iris felt for Martha, or rather Martha's experience that enabled her to drop into the life of Joe's café like a migrating bird, exactly the same emotion as she felt for a baulk of timber hauled up out of the tides of the river. . . . Martha had been something extra, something given, something unearned. . . . Treasure. (18)

Martha has to leave Iris, and she feels guilty about that, but she feels that Iris's very kindness might threaten her new-found freedom. Martha can't afford to take on a new mother in Iris just at the moment when she most needs her experience of separation, of anonymity and freedom. Nonetheless, Iris has given Martha a treasure she can take with her. It is Iris who has taught Martha how to read the "histories and lives and loves" of people in the details of the London street. Martha can now walk "in a double vision as if she were two people: herself and Iris" (10).

Iris and Stella do not reappear in the later three parts of the novel. Even Henry Matheson, who is upper-class and might know the Coldridge family with whom Martha goes to live, does not reappear after Martha has lunch with him at Baxter's and turns down his offer of a secretarial job. These characters do not reappear because their lives have intersected with Martha's only in fragments. Their stories are soon to be papered over by lives of other characters Martha will meet, but Martha has learned from them all. She knows London in a way that the London journalists editorializing about socialism do not: "Had the editors and journalists never met Iris . . . and Stella, did they know nothing of what they could find out by getting onto a bus, crossing the river, and living for a week or so with Stella or with Iris? It seemed not" (15). For Martha a very significant dimension of the city is made up of its urban characters, "that current of people, that tide, which always flows in and out of London" (6).

For most urban novelists, however, the city is not just a group of urban characters. The spaces of the city, its physical presence, are an equally significant aspect. Martha brings the same concern for variety, interest in boundaries, and tolerance of fragmentation which allowed her to learn about the people of the city to the reading of the spatial qualities of the city. Here the variety and fragmentation are like a collage: sometimes a new structure is superimposed on an old district; sometimes boundaries are clearly observable as one area barely overlaps or is merely contiguous to the next. Kevin Lynch's five categories of cityscape (see Ch. 1, p. 11) are useful here in defining the nature of Martha's spatial perception. Lessing particularly contrasts Martha's reactions to landmarks, which are those well-known buildings or reference points that give a city imageability,[25] and nodes, the central places of juncture and meeting of streets, with the more subtle elements of the city, its paths or streets and its edges, those "linear elements not . . . considered as paths," "boundaries . . . barriers . . . [or] seams, lines along which two regions are . . . joined together."[26]

Martha is aware of the landmarks and nodes of London. She listens to Big Ben chime (72), she looks at the bomb damage to St. Paul's (17), and she rides the bus up to Piccadilly Circus, but because her mother spent so much time trying inauthentically[27] to instill the values of British culture into her colonial child by repeatedly mentioning these landmarks, they evoke only alienation and pain for Martha now. As the bus goes past Trafalgar Square, Martha thinks of "the haphazard insignificance of it, and the babyish statue," and begins to laugh. She tries to explain her feelings to her upper-class companion, Henry: "This . . . is the hub of the Empire" (22), she says laughing, but he doesn't understand. Her laughter subsides into pain. She recognizes the significance and power of the landmarks and nodes; for her, however, they evoke not identification and pride but only pain: "all kinds of half-buried, half-childish, myth-bred emotions were being dragged to the surface: words having such power! Piccadilly Circus, Eros, Hub, Centre, London, England . . . each tapped underground rivers where the Lord only knew what fabulous creatures swam! She tried to hide pain, Henry not being a person who knew how to share it" (22). As both a woman and a colonial, Martha is unable to identify with the battle of Trafalgar, and she does not glory in Britain's colonial past. She considers herself an "alien," and, despite Henry's offer of a job, she realizes she will never fit into his society. "She had discovered, swapping notes with other aliens in pubs, that it was not only she who had to fight paranoia, so many invisible rules there were to break, rules invisible to those who lived by them, that was the point" (22). As an alien, however, Martha is able to see other elements of the city that remain invisible to men like Henry, men who are too blinded by the landmarks and the power they represent to see the districts and paths and edges that thread through a city as invisible rules thread through a society.[28]

Because Martha rejects the vision of the city as a single towering landmark, she is able to notice the variety of districts within London. When she first gets to London, she wanders around both the district of the dockyards, "a world of black greasy hulls" (13), and the district of fashionable Oxford Street with its "lit glass" and "dark weights of masonry" (32). She often walks the districts of the many small shops "passing shop fronts, each one the face of a low oblong room like Joe's café: haberdasher, grocer, chemist, greengrocer, hardware, fishmonger, then all over again, chemist, grocer, hardware, grocer, laundry, a pub. All over London: millions of little shops, each one the ground floor of an old house. On either side of her the terraces: damp. Stained with damp. Under her feet, a damp concrete" (8). As Martha moves from one district to another, she notes the boundaries of the districts, both the paths she walks on, the "damp concrete" under her feet, and the edges, the terraces on either side of her.

The paths and edges of the city are those elements that are

Piccadilly Circus is an example of a node, a place where paths meet, a place of juncture. It is mentioned not only in Lessing's *The Four-Gated City* but also in Drabble's *The Middle Ground*, P. D. James' *Unnatural Causes*, and Duffy's *Londoners*.

most often completely invisible to those like Henry who see a
city in terms of landmarks and who restrict themselves to certain fashionable districts. Martha, however, is sensitive to
boundary areas both in human relationships like that with
her mother and in spatial perception. As Martha works to define for herself what Jessica Benjamin calls "intersubjective
space," the "space between the I and the you,"[29] in her relationship with her mother, she also notices the subtle spatial
transitions in areas around the city. These transitions between areas and the nonstructural boundaries between them
are often missed by many observers, but just as Martha noticed that the fragment of wallpaper which seemed like a solid
piece of felt was actually thirteen overlapping pieces of wallpaper, so also she notices edges and subtle boundaries between districts, whether they are specific streets or merely
linear seams. Martha thus sees much greater variety in London than those who only see landmarks and certain districts.
One particularly vivid portrayal of city edges occurs as Martha
walks one night from Baxter's, the fancy upper-class restaurant, to Jack's house by the canal. First she walks down Oxford Street. When the shops that form the edge of Oxford
Street end, Hyde Park becomes the new edge on one side:

> She walked down the pavements at the Bayswater Road, with the
> park on one side, balances and patterns of leaf dramatically
> green where the street lights held them, retreating into mysteri-
> ous shadow beyond. . . . On her right hand, the great ponderous
> houses that stood so assertively on damp soil. Great ugly grey
> houses. They were boarded up or empty or in makeshift use. . . .
> (32)

One edge is the park; she sticks close to it, walking "under
the trees that edged the pavement." The other edge is "the
grey cliff of buildings on her right" (32). Martha walks close to
the edge that is the park. She finds in this edge both the excitement of the street lights reflecting on the green leaves and
a comfort from the overarching trees. Martha is not afraid of
edges.

Bayswater Road, along Hyde Park, is an example of what Lynch calls an edge, a linear element that functions as a boundary or a seam.

As Martha observes the edges, the linear forms stretching between districts, she also observes the subtle boundaries between districts:

> There had begun, from the moment she left Oxford Street and the shops, that heightened wary atmosphere which meant she must walk careful of her eyes, because in this stretch of the Bayswater Road, men prowled after women. Invisible boundaries, invisibly marked territories—just as, across the river a boundary could be marked by an old hulk of timber with river salt in its seams . . . here the corner of a street or the hour of a day could say: Here a certain kind of order ends. (32–33)

She walks fast until she passes "another invisible boundary. From here until past Queensway, the pavements were lined with prostitutes. . . . But Martha was freer here than she had been in the other territory she had only just left, whose boundary was simply a bisecting street. She was protected precisely by the line of girls for sale, who knew she wasn't one of their trade union" (33). The boundaries are subtle. Sometimes they are just a bisecting street; at other times they are invisible because they are signaled not by a change in structure but by a change in the groups of people in the street. A sensitive observer, which a woman walking alone in a city at night automatically becomes, can perceive these subtle changes in district.

After Martha leaves the prostitutes, she reaches Notting Hill and braces herself "before turning off . . . into an area which was worse than anything" (34). Even in the squalor of the area and the stench rising from the refuse thrown into the canal, Martha acknowledges the value of the city to herself: "Far from being an enemy . . . [London] was her friend. This was the best thing she had known, to walk down streets interminably, to walk through mornings and afternoons and evenings, alone" (35). Although Martha has to be wary as she walks around the city, she experiences a heightened level of consciousness as she walks because of the freedom in the city and the intense powers of observation that being in the city requires and evokes. During this walk Martha is able to think back to her childhood and accept some of her personas. She gets a glimpse of the fluidity and boundlessness of consciousness that she will later explore more systematically.

Before Martha descends into the depths of consciousness, however, she must explore the depth of the city. Her attitude toward the depths of the city reveals that she is not afraid of this dimension. She does not see in the lower layers of the city the sewers of Margaret Drabble's *The Middle Ground* or the subway tunnels of Iris Murdoch's *A Word Child*. Rather, Martha sees riches and treasure:

> The great market that was London had opened . . . where it seemed as if wealth had swum together just here, to offer congealed money, furs, carpets, silver, gold, robes, but like icebergs, only a fraction of them visible. . . . above all, it was a sense of hidden wealth: and walking over the damp grey pavements it was to feel that under one's feet stretched invisible warehouses of luxury and richness and beauty—miles of them, caverns of them. . . . A secret city. A hidden city. And, if instead of walking past . . . one pushed open a door . . . suddenly, hey presto! a great descending stairway to the underground city beneath London where were stored for miles and miles the most fabulous carpets and tapestries and silks in the world. (77)

It is perhaps this conviction of the richness rather than the terror of the depths that later allows Martha to descend to the basement of the Coldridge house and enter into Lynda's madness.

Martha also keeps with her a sense of the passage of time in the city. When she first scraped the piece of wallpaper off the bombed-out house, she projected back into time, thinking of the stories that could accompany each layer. Ten years later, after Martha sees the rebuilding of London, she still remembers that earlier bombed-out city, maintaining the simultaneity and layering of different points of time:

> The city had lost its grey shoddiness; that dirty, ruinous, war-soaked city . . . it was gone. A fresh soft air moved through it. . . . She walked through this [rebuilt] city and kept that other one in her mind, so that a long street of fashionably bright buildings had behind it, or in it, an avenue of nightmare squalor, a darkness and a lightness together. . . . London heaved up and down,

houses changed shape, collapsed, whole streets were vanishing into rubble, and arrow shapes in cement reached up into the clouds. . . . it seemed as if the idea of a city or a town as something slow-changing, almost permanent, belonged to the past. (287–88)

The city is in constant flux literally as well as in the eyes of a single perceiver walking through it, but the past of the city is not lost. It is preserved, even if covered over with a layer of paint like a palimpsest, by one who can read it carefully.

By the end of Part I, Martha must leave the multitude of people and the spaces of the city to continue her education by exploring one family in depth and learning about the spaces within a single house and within herself.[30] She takes with her, however, the knowledge of people, and of districts, boundaries, and edges, that she has gained from walking through London and the acceptance of fragmentation and layering that both comes with and is necessary for the experience of perceiving the city. As Dagmar Barnouw points out, "Martha's 'education' in [the rest of the novel] is toward the conscious recovery of that space with its pictures and voices that she received here by chance, made sensitive, receptive by her 'aimless' walking"[31] through the city of London and her observation of it.

The ability to read even the most challenging of texts, however, is no guarantee that one can preserve them. By the end of the novel, London has been bombed again, this time in some kind of nuclear holocaust from which only a few characters have escaped. Mark went to Africa, but he never was able to build his ideal city; he was too busy administering a refugee camp. His last notes before his death say pessimistically: "Ninevah and Tyre, and Sodom and Gomorrah, and Rome, Carthage, Balkh, and Cordova—but that never meant anything. A desert which was a graveyard becomes a place where cities are not built" (611). Mark's word is not the last one, however. His comment is only one in the palimpsestic appendix that closes the novel. On top of the stack of documents that comprise the appendix is an official note saying that Joseph Batts, a young boy whom Martha recognizes as having superior sensitivities, has come to Nairobi to Francis, Mark's son, to work as a gardener.

The focus on the young gardener recalls a symbol from Part I of the novel, that baulk of timber which not only survived the bombing of London but also produced new growth:

> This door to this bomb site was . . . held shut by a bolt or a baulk of timber. . . . It was splintered, eaten, beaten, battered. Touching it was not touching wood, but nearer to water-eaten stone. . . . "they" had pulled this great beam out of the river at some point. . . . It had . . . been used as a base for a stair . . . before the bomb had destroyed [the] house . . . though not the timber itself. . . .
>
> In the hulk of timber was a cleft, more like a crack in rock than a split in wood. Moss grew in it. Salt lay seamed in finer cracks, salt from the salty, tide-washed river. Iris said the timber was probably part of a ship once. (9)

That hulk of timber which has been reused again and again and has survived both water and fire is referred to several times throughout Part I. It is one of the details of the city recorded in "women's brains" (10); it is a treasure to Iris, like Martha's own arrival (18); it marks boundaries between districts (33) like the other visible and invisible edges. It is an urban artifact that has survived many uses, but at first it seems barren. When Martha returns to it after her night with Jack, however, she "greet[s] . . . the slab or hulk of timber. In the less than two days since she had seen it, a minute yellow flower had emerged from a crevice. That great salty, sour, more-stone-than-wood monument had put out a coronet of green leaves and a flower. A small wind tugged at it, but the flower held firm, its roots being well dug in" (73). The old baulk of timber "with river salt in its seams" that has marked "invisible boundaries" (33) is another palimpsest. Seasoned wood is made up of layers and seams itself, and the baulk was used to mark boundaries that were invisible to those who were blinded by landmarks and could not read palimpsests. This wood, however, is not just a fragment; it has also served as soil for a flower, a new order. In spite of the seeming destruction of the novel's ending, there is hope that people with a new kind of consciousness, people who can read palimpsests, can survive. If that old splintered, battered, seamed timber can put out a flower, perhaps a city too can be rebuilt, maybe not an ideal city but perhaps an ordinary, many-layered city with many districts, edges, and pathways, and multitudes of urban characters. And perhaps it can be recorded again in the minds of women who "passing a baulk of timber remember, smiling, how it came rolling up out of the Thames on that Thursday afternoon it was raining, to lie on a pavement until it became the spine of a stairway" (10).

"Inner space" and Outer Space Fiction

In the early 1970s Lessing wrote three novels that have been called "inner space fiction" or "apologues,"[32] *Briefing for a Descent into Hell* (1971), *The Summer Before the Dark* (1973) and *Memoirs of a Survivor* (1974). All three focus on an individual's spiritual quest, and the cities are not as realistically portrayed as in *The Four-Gated City*. In *Briefing for a Descent into Hell* there are only the ruins of mythological cities. In *Memoirs of a Survivor,* the ills of contemporary cities are projected into the future to portray a city in its death-throes. There are some vivid scenes of blocks of apartments and hotels being taken over by gangs once all the city services and utilities have been cut off, but the city functions primarily mythologically by contrasting the life of the failed rational ego with the intuitive life behind the wall. In *The Summer Before the Dark,* Kate Brown returns to London after her trips to Istanbul and Spain. In walking the city streets, Kate learns how dependent the image of the attractive, efficient Mrs. Brown is on carefully dyed hair and well-fitting, expensive clothes. When she wears a baggy dress and grey frizzy hair as she walks past construction workers, she is invisible. When she borrows a tight shift of Maureen's and does up her hair, she receives the whistles she expected. Kate Brown's primary self-revelations, however, come in her dreams, not in the city.

In this novel, like the other three, the city plays only a minor role.

In 1979 and the early 1980s, Lessing turned to the space fiction of the *Canopus in Argos* series, where the focus is on the collective. These novels employ large spans of time and space and do not emphasize an individual's perception of the city, although, as Mona Knapp notes, the ideal "geometrical" cities perceived by Kassim at the end of *Shikasta* recall Martha Quest's vision of the four-gated city.[33] However, just as Lessing interrupted her *Children of Violence* series in the 1950s and 1960s to write *The Golden Notebook* (1962), so she interrupted the *Canopus in Argos* series to write *The Diaries of Jane Somers* in 1983 and 1984. These differ from all her other novels in that Lessing did not publish them under her own name, but rather published first *The Diary of a Good Neighbour* in 1983 and then *If the Old Could . . .* in 1984 under the name of Jane Somers. It is in these novels that Lessing returns to the realistic mode and to a detailed portrayal of London.

The Diaries of Jane Somers

In the Preface to the 1984 edition of *The Diaries of Jane Somers,* Lessing explains that she took on the pseudonym for several reasons: partly so she would be reviewed on merit and not on reputation, partly to encourage younger writers, partly to see if she would be recognized, and, finally, partly to achieve a new kind of freedom. "As Jane Somers," she explains, "I wrote in ways that Doris Lessing cannot. . . . Jane Somers knew nothing about a kind of dryness, like a conscience, that monitors Doris Lessing."[34] Gayle Greene offers yet another reason for the anonymity. In the Preface, Lessing remarks that "thoughts of women like my mother did feed Jane Somers." Greene comments: "In the Jane Somers novels . . . Lessing returns to the subject of the mother, distanced and deflected this time by a surrogate relationship [like that of *Memoirs of a Survivor* where the narrator is a surrogate mother for Emily] and by a pseudonym, and again attempts to confront this relationship."[35] Greene suggests that the relationship with a mother figure is still so intimidating in its threat to cross ego boundaries that it takes the double layering of a surrogate relationship and a pseudonym to approach the subject. This time the palimpsest occurs not just as a symbol like the wallpaper or a fictional method like the appendix at the end of *The Four-Gated City*, but in the production of the text itself.

In *The Diaries of Jane Somers,* the character Janna and her perception of London share several characteristics with Martha Quest and her earlier perception of London in *The Four-Gated City.* There is the same focus on the fear of losing and the effort of maintaining ego boundaries, first in Janna's interaction with the old mother-figure, Maudie Fowler, in *Diary of a Good Neighbour* and then in her romantic involvement with Richard Curtis and concern for her niece Kate in *If the Old Could. . . .* Janna, must, like Martha, accept knowing fragments of lives, whether those of another generation like Maudie and Annie Reeves, or even that of Richard, who has a thirty-five-year-old marriage and three children Janna cannot share. Janna, like Martha, enjoys the anonymity and freedom of the city, and it is within the city that she develops new ways of seeing people and relating to them. Like Martha, she sees the city as multilayered, with rich depths that encompass time as well as space. And like Martha, she notices the women of the city and focuses on women's perception of the city. Once Janna has opened her eyes and allowed herself to be involved in relationships, she finds a joyousness in the city that even goes beyond that of Martha Quest. For Janna, especially in *If the Old Could . . . ,* the city is a theater;[36] each encounter or overheard conversation is a scene, a fragment of city life that enchants her: "I have spent hundreds of enjoyable hours by myself in and around London, my great bazaar, my lucky dip, my private theatre."[37] Janna's image of the city as a theater is another kind of palimpsest, less spatial, but still multilayered. There are numerous layers of reality to the theater just as there are in the city, and each scene, each episode of city-life, is a many-layered fragment to be read and enjoyed.

Although Janna describes herself as having always had an "urban, street-loving life" (421), as the novel opens she in fact has not noticed many things about the city nor has she let herself become really involved in her relationship with her mother, her sister, or her husband: "for thirty-odd years Janna James, then Janna Somers, has presented herself polished, finished, arranged, and this is what people see and know. But it is an artefact!" (273).[38] As an editor of the fashion magazine *Lilith*, Janna Somers is always impeccably groomed and efficient, but she has never let herself be involved deeply with others. She is an "urban artefact," a typical London career woman like the one Kate Brown learned to become when she worked for Global Foods in *Summer Before the Dark*.

Unlike Kate Brown, however, Janna's discovery of self occurs not on an inward journey but on the streets of London. Salman Rushdie, a British-Pakistani novelist whom Lessing cites as evidence that we are "living in a Golden Age of the novel,"[39] describes the "city eyes" that such successful middle-class women wear. The narrator's mother in Rushdie's novel, *Midnight's Children*, goes into the oldest part of Delhi:

> as she enters these causeways where poverty eats away at the tarmac like a drought . . . something new begins to assail her. Under the pressure of these streets . . . she has lost her "city eyes." When you have city eyes you cannot see the invisible people, the men with elephantiasis of the balls and the beggars in boxcars don't impinge on you. . . . My mother lost her city eyes and the newness of what she was seeing made her flush.[40]

Janna loses her "city eyes" when she meets Maudie Fowler:

> I thought how I rushed along the pavements every day and had never seen Mrs. Fowler, but she lived near me, and suddenly I looked up and down the streets and saw—old women. . . . They stood in pairs or groups, talking. Or sat on the bench at the corner under the plane tree. I had not seen them. That was because I was afraid of being like them. I was afraid, walking along there beside her. It was the smell of her, a sweet, sour, dusty sort of smell. (21)

Janna, who had emotionally absented herself during both her mother's and her husband's deaths from cancer because she hated "physical awfulness" (15), now becomes involved with Maudie Fowler, an over-ninety, working-class woman who is dying of stomach cancer.

Janna is mistaken for a "good neighbor," one of the women paid by the Council to check on the elderly, but Janna is not a good neighbor. She becomes Maudie's friend, even though "one did not have *friends* with the working classes" (46). She shops for Maudie, listens to her stories, cleans out her filthy basement rooms, and even washes Maudie herself when the old woman becomes incontinent. With Maudie, Janna experiences the "physical awfulness" she had earlier avoided, but she also learns to love and to commit herself in a way that she never had before either with her mother or her husband. Later Janna thinks to herself: "I know what it is to become committed to an old woman whose needs are so great that your own needs become secondary, your whole life gets swallowed up. . . . I am not sorry I did it—far from it, for I loved Maudie" (368). When she becomes involved with Richard, Janna tries to explain her relationship with Maudie to him:

> I said that I had met this old woman, she was in need of help, I offered it, got in deeper than I had meant, and had ended by being something not far off a daughter to her, for a long time— years. (415)

Janna avoided a close relationship with her own mother, but she achieves a mother-daughter relationship with Maudie and is not afraid of being "swallowed up" by that relationship. As Gayle Greene points out, Janna " 'delivers' herself—Learning to risk the intimacy that enables subsequent relationships with Richard and Kate, Jane is released from her bounded, guarded self."[41] Janna is also released from her "city eyes" and sees new aspects of London that she had not noticed before she befriended Maudie.

Janna had always loved the city's "anonymity, the freedom of being alone in a crowd" (70), but once she has gotten to know Maudie and the other old women, Eliza Bates and Annie

Reeves, she notices different elements and different people in the city than she would have previously. Janna stops defining herself only in terms of her job, and she takes time off, which she spends wandering around the city of London: "By nine I was down in the streets, sauntering along, enjoying myself in the way I do. Oh, the good humour of this city, the pleasantness, the friendliness!" (206). She notices

> the old ladies I once did not see at all but, since Maudie, have watched creeping about the streets with their bags and their baskets—and I could never have guessed the companionableness, the interest of their lives, the gaiety. They love shopping, it is clear; and what shop they will patronize and what not on a given day is the result of the most intricate and ever-shifting tides of feeling. That Indian doesn't keep a clean shop, but he was observed sweeping out yesterday, so they'll give him a second chance. (156–157)

It is women who take over the city, once the office workers have gone to their jobs. Janna notices that

> the bus is full of women. The freemasonry of women, who sit at their ease, shopping baskets and bags all over them, enjoying a nice sit-down and the pleasant day. A bus at half past ten in the morning is a different world: nothing in common with the rush-hour buses.
>
> These women who keep things together, who underpin our important engagements with big events by multifarious activities so humble that, asked at the end of the day what they did, they might, and often do, reply, Oh, nothing much.
>
> They are off to a shop three stages away to buy knitting wool for a jersey for a grandchild . . . or to pay the electricity bill, or to get their pensions. The Home Helps are on their way to get prescriptions made up for Eliza Bates, Annie Reeves. . . . A parcel is being sent to Cape Town to an emigrated niece. . . . Some are off down to Oxford Street, on a weekly or monthly jaunt, regarded as a holiday. . . . They will later go to visit housebound relatives. . . . They are at it all day, these women, and the good nature that is the result of their competence at what they do overflows and splashes about the inside of the bus. (207–208)

Janna sees the life of the city in a new perspective during "women's time" (208). For the first time, now that she is involved in nurturing someone else, she notices how women's seemingly small and humble acts of nurturing actually sustain life in a big city. Furthermore, the good nature these women create sets the tone for the city. In *The Four-Gated City* Lessing focuses on the boundaries between the self and others and the boundary areas of the city; in the Jane Somers novels, the focus is on the connection between the "I" and the "you." The spaces of the city are filled with women who hold relationships together. Janna identifies with these women and feels for the first time the joy of connectedness with others.

When Janna starts to view London during "women's time," not even a worsening of Maudie's illness can take away Janna's enjoyment of the city. She goes to the Victoria and Albert Museum, eats at a café in High Street, visits Maudie, and then walks through Golders Park to drink coffee on the terrace. Janna writes in her diary: "A day in London, the great theatre, lovely London whose quality is sardonic good humour, and kindness, a day to myself, in solitude. Perfect enjoyment" (209). The day was spent in solitude, but Janna can now see the women who populate the city and make it work. Before she met Maudie, Janna didn't notice the old people, but now she sees not only the old women, but the Home Helps like Bridget, the poor housewives who live in Council flats and who work keeping house and shopping for the elderly of the city, and the social workers like Vera Rogers who decide when the elderly must be taken to the hospital and who accept the resulting fury as part of their job, and the ward maids in the hospital, "the Spanish or the Portuguese or Jamaican or Vietnamese girls who work for such long hours, and who earn so very little, and who keep families, bring up children, and send money home" (248). Janna notices all these women of the city and collects the fragments of their lives, like scenes from a play, that compose the city of London.

Listening to Maudie's stories has also allowed Janna to see London in terms of time. Maudie describes pre–World War I London as she tells stories of her childhood: "Her father had had a corner shop in Bell Street, and sold hardware and kept free coal and bread for the poor people, and in the cold weather there was a cauldron of soup for the poor" (37). Then he sold that house for a lot of money because the Paddington railway line was coming through, and they moved to St. John's Wood, but there her father took up with a "fancy-woman" who "poisoned" her mother. Janna is not quite sure how much of the stories to believe or even whether they are historically accurate: "None of it adds up. There couldn't, surely, have been a deep grassy garden behind the hardware in Bell Street? And in St John's Wood she would have been too old for swings" (37). Nevertheless, Janna receives from Maudie those "bright pictures . . . that she has painted for herself" (37) of London in the past. Janna also gets a sense of the growth of the city as Maudie describes going out to her Aunt Mary's village, but then Maudie comments, "It's part of London now, you'd not know it was a village so recently, it was beyond Neasden" (81). It is Maudie's story that Janna turns into an historical novel, *The Milliners of Marylebone*. She recognizes that it too isn't purely historical: "Oh, I know only too well why we need our history prettied up. It would be intolerable to have the long heavy *weight* of the truth there, all grim and painful. No, my story about the milliners of London will be romantic" (149), as Maudie would want it to be.

From Annie Reeves, another old woman, Janna learns about growing up in a poor family in Holborn, but also about what fun Annie and her sister had as young women buying "clothes on the never-never from the shops in Soho" (178). In Annie's stories she and her sister made "the West End . . . their oyster, using it, knowing how to evade dangers. They would allow themselves to be picked up . . . had a real slap-up dinner, . . . but they knew ways out and about and around, and remained in debt to their salesmen" (179). Annie may now refuse to move from her chair in the third floor flat, but her stories of "Annie, the pretty raider of the West End streets" (180) add to Janna's image of London's past.

Janna's new awareness of the pleasure of "women's time" in the city and of the passage of time in the city is carried over to the next novel *If the Old Could . . . .* In this novel Janna looks up at the old house which serves as the offices of *Lilith* and sees the history behind it:

I stood as I sometimes do, looking at the old houses, externally unchanged, and wondering what the people who lived in them— let's say, up to the First World War—would make of us, of *Lilith,* who spreads herself over two houses, who has knocked down walls and removed barriers and boundaries where once separate families might have heard the odd sound through thick brick and plaster. I was thinking of how these houses were layered once, the family on the ground floor, first floor, second floor; the servants in the basement and at the very top; and, as I thought of those servants, going in and out down the steps where now the typists and secretaries go, it was as if there was a time-blur, for there was a skivvy, a kitchen maid, someone like that, standing on the pavement. (406)

The kitchen maid turns out to be Janna's bedraggled punk niece, Kate, who evokes the same pity and concern Janna would have felt for the pre–World War I scullery maid. Janna sees the city's past both in Kate and in the old many-layered house. Janna's rigid boundaries have come down just like the partitions of the house, and she can see not only the vertical layers of the house and the activities of each story but also the layers back through time when scullery maids once worked where now the secretaries do. Like Martha Quest, Janna preserves the past beneath the layer of the present. She too can read the city as a palimpsest.

Because Janna has once let herself be "swallowed up" in a relationship, she no longer fears the engulfment in *If the Old Could . . .* that she was so cautious about approaching in *The Diary of a Good Neighbour.* In the latter novel Janna was unsure of whether she wanted even her competent, attractive niece Jill to come live with her. She thought to herself: "having admitted Jill into my life . . . my gates are down, the defences breached, my territory invaded." (244). When the pathetic Kate comes, uninvited, to live with Janna in *If the Old Could . . . ,* Janna responds with a very different emotion: "I was in the grip of such pity for the wretch. . . . there was something about Kate that went, smash, to my heart" (406). Kate's desperation reminds Janna of Maudie. Janna thinks to herself, "I felt like that when Maudie made me her prisoner, not by what she said but by her need" (407). In commenting on the novel, Lessing says that Janna "is rather better off after her experience, firstly, with the old, and secondly, with this very unfortunate niece of hers who is a disaster area. I feel that Jane Somers has changed a great deal by . . . the end of volume two."[42] Janna has changed in that she has developed qualities of sympathy and openness, and these qualities influence her perception of the city in *If the Old Could.* . . . In *The Four-Gated City,* as Martha Quest walks alone at night, she notices the boundaries of the city, partly because she is concerned with issues of ego boundaries. In *If the Old Could . . .* Janna has established the ability to connect to others. Rejoicing in her newfound ability to connect, Janna walks ebulliently through numerous districts and parks with her lover, Richard Curtis, and she perceives the variety of the city with joy and fascination. Together she and Richard savor a city filled with richness and plenitude. London for Janna is a "wonderhouse" (299), a "bazaar" (322), a "feast of people" (445), "a theatre . . . a pageant" (336), a "stage set" (510). Janna rests her head on Richard's shoulder and listens to him hum: "London, London, London, I love you, how I love you, London, my love" (334). Even the quality of light in the city that Janna observes is always bright and dazzling, as it would be in a theater. At night Janna looks out her window and ponders: "I am looking into the sky, which has light in it even though there are no clouds and nothing to reflect back London's brilliances. Is London ever dark? Is our sky ever without light? I don't think it is" (338). This image of London's brilliance and richness is the opposite of the dank, dark city portrayed in Iris Murdoch's *A Word Child.* Janna's love for Richard and concern for Kate bring her to reach out and embrace the entire city.

There is a hint of the darker side of London, one Lessing will develop further in *The Good Terrorist,* where Kate's friends from a "squat," the urban homesteaders and revolutionaries, come to Janna's flat and eat all her food, leaving stains all over her linen chair covers. Janna, who once lived solely for the elegance of her "artefacts," now ignores the lingering smell of marijuana and the grubby chairs. In a burst of pity, Janna says, "Never mind, Kate" (383). Likewise Janna is aware of the class and racial differences in the city. As Janna waits to buy an apple at a vegetable stand, she admires how the stall man jokes with a young black girl and gives a banana to an old "crone." She is aware, however, that he will treat her differently: "I have stopped there in my good clothes, the very picture of expensive well-being, and all that quick joky good humour has suddenly, savagely, been switched off, and I have stood there, exposed, the enemy" (388). Yet even this potential hostility, Janna relates to the theater: "A stall-holder playing at being a stall-holder, with all the tricks: entertainment, people queuing for that as much as for a lettace or a toffee apple. I have been the entertainment" (388). Janna is willing to play the role of the rich woman, to be the entertainment, because the dazzling experience of London as theater outshines the potentially darker side of the city; and usually Janna does not have to be the participant in street theater but can just enjoy the scenes as audience: "My days are full of pleasure, delights, little treats, listening to the amazing exchanges between people on London's pavements, so surreal and suggestive of hidden continents of experience, looking at people in restaurants, buses, shops" (371). For Janna, in love, each overheard conversation, each fragment of life observed, is another scene in the great pageant that is London.

The city is the meeting place for Janna and Richard. Their excursions through the city cover numerous parks, districts, and streets and illustrate the variety and details of city life. Nature is clearly seen as part of the city in Janna's and Richard's wanderings through the parks of the city: St. James's Park, Regent's Park, Green Park, Hyde Park, and Hampstead Heath. They throw freesias and daffodils in the fountain at Trafalgar Square. They explore various districts and streets of the city. They eat take-away meals in Soho Square. They walk down Bayswater Road, enjoying the details of city life: "a building being done up, with scaffolding up its side for four storeys, and on a platform on the fourth-floor scaffolding a little house, in scarlet, . . . and in the doorway sat a workman with a bucket in front of him in which must be a wisp of fire, for he held a sausage on a fork over the heat . . . so comical and pleasant" (288). They walk down Old Brompton Road and Cromwell Road until they find themselves "between Shepherd's Bush and Hammersmith, in a maze of streets, the dense crammed London people live in . . . and push prams and shop for everything from Rice Crispies to yams and flying fish and Mars Bars, and stand talking on pavements" (306). They take a boat up to Richmond; they walk around the streets of Holborn in the rain. One day as Janna sits having tea with Annie, she envisions herself and Richard as a "handsome pair of adventurers." She thinks "of how we range around London, from Greenwich to Richmond, from Highgate to the docks, of how on a whim we go to the theatre or decide to walk ten miles; the glitter and colour of our being together" (370). London in *If the Old Could . . .* is a lover's city, full of variety, richness, and glitter.

The pubs where they stop to eat are like the city in miniature, both in the image of the theater that is used to describe them and the fragmentary views they offer into others' lives. Janna muses "how pleasant they are, London pubs. Every public place is like a theatre, but pubs most of all, because people coming in are so often regulars. . . . What companionable and good-natured places they are, these pubs; how people do come and go . . . each caught tight into his or her little pattern, their trip into the pub a fragment of the pattern which is invisible to us" (303). Richard and Janna see only the fragments of others' lives, but they treasure these views because they can share with one another only fragments of their own lives. Richard must tend to his mother in a nursing home and his anxious daughter, Kathleen, who attempts to follow Janna and Richard. Janna can't give up her trips for *Lilith* or her visits to Annie Reeves' deathbed or her concern for Kate, who halfheartedly stages a suicide attempt. Janna and Richard realize they can only have fragments of each other's lives, just as they can only perceive fragments of the city life around them, but it is enough to give them the joy and ebullience of theater.

Like Martha Quest, Janna also finds richness in the depths

of the city. It is as she is coming out of the underground at
Tottenham Court Road that she catches her heel and falls,
literally, into Richard's arms. Together she and Richard ride
the underground, getting off at Charing Cross, Baker Street,
King's Cross. The emphasis is not on these stations as nodes
or even as transportation. Instead, they represent yet one
more of the varied districts, this time an underground one in
the rich bazaar that is London. When Janna thinks of her life
and Richard's coming together, she thinks of them as each
having rich cargo, like rivers of great depths. She even mentions the baulks of timber, the image that figures so promi-
nently in *The Four-Gated City:*

> as if our two lives, running for so long invisibly to the other and
> coming together so improbably in that comic little accident on
> Tottenham Court Road underground, carried along with them a
> rich cargo that had been invisible, too, to ourselves, like rivers
> whose depths know nothing about the baulks of good timber . . .
> packing cases that have who knows what things in them. (370)

By the end of the novel, Richard and Janna must part, like
rivers branching out again—he to go to Canada with his wife
and family to start a new clinic, and Janna to remain in London, working for *Lilith* and perhaps befriending his daughter
Kathleen now that Janna recognizes that her niece Kate will
be better off in a woman's commune.

Even when Richard and Janna say good-by, the city still
glitters with light:

> Night fell at King's Cross station, and we walked slowly along Eus-
> ton Road. . . . The great buildings dazzled with lights. . . . We
> stood on the pavement at the bottom of Hampstead Road, and
> looked at the new building, all of mirrors, that reflects . . . lights
> and stars and people. Tonight it reflected part of the towering
> building behind our backs: black that had regular stars of light
> up and down it . . . and at one side of it a transparent glass lift
> outlined in smaller starry yellow lights. (509)

Janna weeps at Richard's departing, but her perception of the
city is not dependent on him. She loved their time together,
but even as she says good-by, the city buildings still remain

solid and brightly lit. When she returns to her flat, she still keeps the image of London as theater and thinks of the pleasures of solitude in which she earlier enjoyed the city:

> And I look around at this quiet, white, cool, orderly room where soon, I know, into the emptiness will steal one by one, at first lacklustre and inconsiderable, but then familiar and loved, all the little innumerable pleasures and consolations of my solitude. . . . Beyond are the windows where in black panes blur and blend the lights from the street.
>
> A stage set! House lights down . . . the sudden hush . . . the curtain goes up . . . (510, Lessing's ellipses in last paragraph)

London is the brilliantly lit theater still. The hints of the problems of the city, the urban homesteaders, the desperate teenagers, the potential racial and class conflict are there, but this particular "play" has been a love story and Janna's newfound emotions color her vision of the city. It is significant, however, that the novel does not end in the typical romance plot of marriage. Both Janna and Richard have complex public lives which they cannot give up. Janna's elation and her vision of London as dazzling theater continue even after Richard's departure because her joy is not just in a single love relationship but in her discovery of a capacity for relationship within herself.

The Good Terrorist

The achievement of a good surrogate mother-daughter relationship in *The Diaries of Jane Somers* and its resulting enhancement of other relationships and of the ability to read the city does not last in Lessing's novels. In 1985, Doris Lessing returned to her own name to publish *The Good Terrorist* and returned to that "kind of dryness, like a conscience, that monitors Doris Lessing."[43] This time the focus of the novel is on the darker side of London, the "squat," barely hinted at in *The Diaries of Jane Somers*. The squat is inhabited not by benign urban homesteaders like Nicholas Manning and Ilse Nemorova in Drabble's *The Radiant Way*, but by a group of would-be terrorists. The novel is realistic, like *The Diaries of Jane Somers,* but the tone shifts dramatically. Irony pervades the novel, and almost all of the characters are unsympathetic. The irony directed toward the naive but fervent politics of the unattractive young terrorists and the senseless bomb explosion that kills one of them at the end of the novel recalls Joseph Conrad's *The Secret Agent,*[44] but *The Good Terrorist* differs from *The Secret Agent* and from Lessing's earlier urban novels in its narrow focus on this one slice of city life, the political squat. Because of this focus, *The Good Terrorist* can be classified with ecological novels (see Ch. 1, pp. 3–4). Alice Mellings, the heroine, travels about the city, but unlike Martha Quest or Jane Somers, she fails to notice the details of the city itself or of city life. Some of the same qualities of the city portrayed in the other novels are hinted at, but Alice does not notice them. The narrator refers to London as "that great lucky dip"[45] when some of the inhabitants of the squat come back with furniture that they have collected from rubbish piles, but Alice thinks only of the waste that people create in throwing things out. Nature is still in the city; forsythia blooms next door to the squat, but Alice is only interested in nature if it can work for her to get rid of waste. She is attentive only to the needs of the house and its inhabitants.

The Good Terrorist is a negative example of the pattern set by Lessing's urban novels in that the heroine of this narrowly focused, negative ecological novel is incapable of in-depth relationships. Martha Quest's willingness to explore the boundaries of her relationship with her mother and to investigate the fragments of others' lives enables her to read London. Janna Somers' establishment of a nurturing relationship with Maudie opens her up to "women's time" in the city and the joy in urban life. In contrast, Alice Mellings, the thirty-six-year-old "hippie" who is the "good" terrorist, is able neither to resolve her relationship with her parents nor to establish a meaningful commitment to her peers.

Alice's relationship with her parents is defined by her resentment at their unwillingness to take care of her any longer. Alice is furious at her father, who has since remarried and has a new young family, for not continuing to give her money. She steals money from him and throws a rock through his window, narrowly missing one of the children. Alice and her homosexual friend Jasper have lived at her mother's flat for four years until her mother is bankrupted by their sponging on her. Alice is angry that her mother moves to a small cramped flat and no longer seems willing to feed and house her. Claire Sprague notes that the relationship between Alice Mellings and her mother, Dorothy, "both reverses and sustains Lessing's earliest interpretation of the mother-daughter configuration. The rebellious, dependent daughter and the powerful mother are still there, but their psychic organization has undergone an ironic revolution. The daughter cannot escape her dependence, but the mother can. Dorothy abandons Alice instead of vice-versa. Furthermore, the mother figure is wholly sympathetic and the daughter figure wholly unsympathetic."[46]

Alice's relationships with her peers are just as unsatisfactory as those with her parents. Her closest relationship, at least on her side, is with Jasper, an anarchistic young homosexual. Jasper allows her to cook for him and to give him money, but he will not allow her to touch or embrace him. His one gesture, repeated throughout the novel, is to grab her hard by the wrist to restrain her: "His hand shot out, and her wrist was encircled by hard bone. It hurt" (5). This motif of painful encirclement by hard bone illustrates Alice's constriction. Alice allows herself to be dominated by Jasper, and she restricts her life to the small group of terrorists. She is asexual. Alice tolerates Jasper's homosexual weekends, but she herself is repulsed by both the heterosexual and the lesbian couples in the squat: "Anything to do with sex! It simply made people unbalanced. Not themselves. One simply had to learn to keep quiet and let them all get on with it! Provided they left her out of it . . ." (233, Lessing's ellipses). Alice likes some of the other residents of the squat, like Pat and Philip, but she never learns much about them. She uses whoever is willing to work on the house or contribute, but she does not learn to see as they do or to read the fragments of their lives the way Martha Quest does those of the people she meets.

Alice at first seems a nurturing figure for the terrorists, who finally begin to call themselves a commune, but it turns out that she is merely a good housekeeper, not unlike Martha Quest's mother. When Alice and Jasper first come to the squat, Alice is horrified by the cemented-up toilets, the dangling electric wires, and the buckets of human waste. She uses the money she steals from her father and begs from her mother's friends to make the house habitable. She cajoles Philip, a frail young workman, to fix the plumbing, the electricity, the roof, and the waterheater. She uses all her middle-class skills with the bureaucracies to keep the house from being demolished. She cooks cheap and nourishing meals for the commune. Finally, however, she cannot protect any of the members of the commune or keep them from leaving her. She helps Philip on a job, but she cannot help him get paid for it nor can she protect him from the construction accident that kills him. She likes Pat, but she cannot help Pat resolve her relationship with Bert nor keep her from leaving. Alice nurses the psychotic Faye through a suicide attempt, but she cannot persuade the group to abandon an ill-conceived bombing attempt that kills Faye and others. Alice personally harms Jim, the young black man who first found the house and let the others in. Alice gets her father to give Jim a job that he very much wants, but then he is fired because he is blamed for stealing the money that actually Alice has taken. Alice cannot even keep Jasper, who leaves with Bert after the bombing since they had agreed to disperse. At the end of the novel, Alice is left alone in a restored but empty house. She has alienated her father, argued with her mother, and been unable to establish any lasting peer relationships. She knows neither others, nor the city, nor herself.

Doris Lessing describes *The Good Terrorist* as being "about a girl—rather loosely based on something I've seen—who drifts into becoming a terrorist out of sheer stupidity or lack of imagination."[47] Alice is the "good" terrorist because she always has "good intentions," but she does not imagine the consequences of her actions. She spends no time analyzing either her own motives or those of others. She does not intend to have Jim fired when she steals from her father; she does not intend to ruin her mother's chances to sell the flat when she takes the curtains. Alice certainly does not intend for the bombing, which she herself does not like, to end in violence, but she never tries to persuade the others to change their plans. Alice does not like waste and does not intend to waste her life, but that is what she seems to be doing.

An undertone of irony in the novel focuses on the waste of all the young lives. The politics of the commune are strongly satirized as Bert and Jasper attempt to attach their commitment to violence first to the I.R.A. and then to the Russian communists, only to be rejected by both. Their independent bombing is senseless and destructive: it is connected to no real political aim, only the desire for attention. The novel's surface motif of human excrement parallels the young lives wasted in self-indulgent anger. Alice can dig a pit and bury the human excrement or wash down the walls when a bag of excrement is thrown into the house, but neither she nor any of the others are interested in preventing the waste of their own lives. They cannot even help others like the young mother living in a welfare hotel who wants a better place to live.

At the end of *The Good Terrorist,* the empty restored house[48] is useless without human beings to inhabit it. The lack of a full portrayal of the city in *The Good Terrorist* is a reflection of the characters' inability to relate to one another. Their "commune" has no community, and Alice's seeming nurturance is only unimaginative good housekeeping. In this negative example Lessing again illustrates what it takes to read the city as palimpsest. One needs intelligence, imagination, knowledge of self, attentiveness, openness to others and a willingness to observe carefully. These are qualities that allow Martha Quest and Janna Somers to celebrate the city and read well its many layers. These are qualities that women often make an effort to develop, but not all women, as Alice Mellings demonstrates, take the time to cultivate them. Lessing's negative example in *The Good Terrorist* makes the need to read cities properly all the more urgent. Alice Mellings illustrates that those who cannot read the city, destroy it.

CHAPTER 3

The City as Network:
Margaret Drabble

Margaret Drabble is the contemporary urban novelist who most celebrates the city. In her middle novels, London is alluded to as a new Jerusalem or a realm of gold. In her most recent novels, *The Middle Ground* and *The Radiant Way,* London is portrayed in all its complexity and fascination. While Drabble does not ignore the crime and other problems of the modern city, her London is a place of freedom and interconnection, particularly in her 1980 novel, *The Middle Ground.* It is in this novel that her image of the city as an interconnected network emerges most clearly.

The image of the network blends female ways of thinking with a way of visualizing the city. For the psychologist Carol Gilligan, the image of the network, often found in women's writings, reveals women's emphasis on relationships. In studying children's moral development, Gilligan discovered that the "contrasting images of hierarchy [male] and network [female] in children's thinking about moral conflict and choice illuminate two views of morality," which Gilligan defines as based on the contrast between a "self defined through separation [male] and a self delineated through connection [female]."[1] Gilligan found the same characteristics and images in her work with adults in Thematic Apperception Tests. Gilligan notes that women describe "life as a web rather than a succession of relationships, . . . stressing continuity and change in configuration, rather than replacement and separation."[2] The network image is thus characteristically female in its emphasis on connection and continuity.

The network is also an urban image. It refers not only to the physical networks of city streets or support systems like sewer pipes or gas lines[3] but also to relationships within cities. The city planner Jane Jacobs, describing the social networks needed to make cities livable, points out

> the self-government functions of city streets: to weave webs of public surveillance and thus to protect strangers as well as themselves; to grow networks of small-scale, everyday public life and thus of trust and social control; and to help assimilate children into reasonably responsible and tolerant city life.[4]

City networks are social as well as physical. As social networks they link together different classes and kinds of people. As physical networks they exist in several dimensions, not only on the linear plane of the streets, but below the streets in several layers of service networks.

The Middle Ground

The emphasis on connection and on layers are the aspects of the network image that resonate through the female protagonists' description of the city in Margaret Drabble's most celebratory urban novel, *The Middle Ground* (1980). Kate Armstrong and Evelyn Stennett are two middle-aged working mothers. When they contemplate the city of London, they both celebrate the connections they see as the essence of the city. The two male protagonists,[5] Hugo Mainwaring (Kate's friend and Evelyn's cousin) and Ted Stennett (Evelyn's husband and Kate's former lover), ruminate about politics and middle age, but they do not notice the city around them. It is the two women who perceive and describe the city. What Kate sees as she looks out of Evelyn's hospital window epitomizes her view of London:

> the sky had been washed clear, and a clear pale luminous band of duck-egg blue-green light lay low over the city, . . . a gold evening radiance fell on the glittering distance. From the twelfth-

floor window, London stretched away, St. Paul's in the distance, and the towers of the City, and beneath them, nearby, the little network of streets, back yards, cul-de-sacs, canals, warehouses, curves and chimneys, railways, little factories tucked into odd corners; unplanned, higgledy-piggledy, hardly a corner wasted, intricate, enmeshed, patched and pieced together, the old and the new side by side, overlapping, jumbled, always decaying, yet always renewed; London, how could one ever be tired of it? . . . When there it lay, its old intensity restored, shining with invitation, all its shabby grime lost in perspective, imperceptible from this dizzy height, its connections clear, its pathways revealed. The city, the kingdom. The aerial view. . . . The aerial view of human love, where all connections are made known, where all roads connect?[6]

The city may be "higgledy-piggledy," but as Kate looks down from the twelfth floor,[7] she perceives the city's "network" of streets and railways and backyards, and they parallel for her the connection of human love and relationship. The view not only links the elements of the city together, but it is antihierarchical. St. Paul's and the city towers are no more significant than the little factories in odd corners and the backyards. The new does not replace the old, nor is it separated from it. It forms a collage, the old and new are "side by side, overlapping, jumbled, always decaying, yet always renewed." This view, which stresses continuity and accommodates change without separation, corresponds to Gilligan's findings about female imagery. Kate and Evelyn affirm the multiplicity of the city and see the connections among the collage of the city's urban districts and multiethnic urban characters.

The collage image, like the network image, connects things, old and new, found objects and created objects. Also a collage often avoids separation. Elements of it "overlap" each other, and the sense of connection and continuity in spite of contrast is maintained. It is this image of the city that Margaret Drabble especially praises in the poet Adrian Henri's description of Liverpool:

Henri's city is a good-hearted, swarming, jostling jumble, with Chinese Duck, bottles of brown ale, take-away curry, pie and chips, Beatles records, double-decker buses, butcher's shops, electric clocks, nylon panties, cream-painted bedsteads, PVC shopping baskets and cats waiting for their Kit-e-Kat all thrown together in an ideal (and idealized) cosmopolitan harmony—the kind of city that ought to be possible, but which people have to assemble for themselves, from unpromising materials—a collage city, for those who can love what is there, rather than yearn for what is gone.[8]

Although it is the word "network" rather than "collage" that echoes throughout *The Middle Ground*, *The Middle Ground* achieves the same celebration of the city in all its multiplicity and "jumble" of old and new, foreign and familiar. Buildings are described in terms of their uses through time, and the multiethnic mixture of contemporary London is evoked. Kate's "small terraced house" in Dacre Road NW 6 "used to be a fish-and-chip shop" (88). Kate hands out ten-pound notes for take-away curry from the Taj Mahal around the corner when she arrives home late and finds too many people to cook for. When Hugo arrives at Kate's house for a drink, he finds a pile of miscellaneous objects reminiscent of Drabble's catalogue of Henri's. Hugo has to stumble "along the narrow hall, over a collection of plastic carriers, broken furniture, piles of books, Adidas bags, and bicycle spare parts, into the sitting room, which used to be the chip shop" (88–89).

Kate's collection of urban characters is just as eclectic. A rock group is represented; this time not the Beatles like in Henri, but Joker James of the Black Ice, who grew up in the same lower-middle-class East London suburb, Romley, that Kate did so she invites him in. Mujid, the French-speaking Iraqi, is the fiancé of the daughter of Beatrice, a half-French, half-Lebanese woman with whom Kate shared a hospital room when their sons were born. Kate is saddened to learn that Beatrice's son has died in the street fighting in Beirut, so she takes in Mujid: *"he seemed to expect it"* . . . she says "and anyway, I expected it of myself" (83). And Kate always makes room for Hunt, an aging homosexual, alcoholic scavenger and "antique" dealer, for whom she saves a blanket and a place on her sofa because he first taught her the limitations of Romley "good taste." There are numerous teenagers, her own, the

Stennetts', and their various friends. Evelyn, as a social worker, collects an equally eclectic group of day-care workers, Pakistani children, a South African widow, and a Jamaican Rastafarian. Although she does not invite them to her home as Kate does (they sometimes come uninvited, like her client Irene, who is an unwed mother), she sympathizes with them and admires many of them, maintaining her faith in human nature. Out of these similar "unpromising materials" and a variety of people, Kate and Evelyn construct the network that comprises their lives and their city.

Kate's and Evelyn's perception of networks is particularly acute at this stage in their lives not only because of what the psychologist Nancy Chodorow calls their "relational connection to the world"[9] as females (see Ch. 1, pp. 13–14), but also because of their active involvement in mothering. Drabble herself says that "once you've had a baby, it's terribly hard to pretend that reality doesn't exist. Somehow life becomes so basic, and you know other people are there. Having children gives you an access to an enormous common store of otherness about other people."[10] Sara Ruddick adds that maternal thinking not only gives one a sense of realism and connectedness with others, but that it also allows one to perceive the consciousness and connectedness of a child who "is itself an 'open structure' [and] whose acts are irregular, unpredictable, often mysterious."[11] Drabble does not sentimentalize motherhood, as her portraits of Emma Evans in *The Garrick Year* (1964), Janet Bird in *Realms of Gold* (1975), or Clara Maugham's mother in *Jerusalem the Golden* (1967) illustrate, but in *The Middle Ground* it is clear that she believes that motherhood connects one to others and makes one pay attention to the openness and potential of children. To their perception of the city, Kate and Evelyn bring the tolerance for open structure and the "attentiveness"[12] developed by their years of mothering and their respective careers as journalist and social worker.

In addition, both women are in their middle years and are going through a "bad patch" that forces their attention on the networks of their own lives, not only the present social network of their jobs and families but also the networks of their past. One of the authorial insertions describes the predicament of the middle years:

> The middle years, caught between children and parents, free of neither: the past stretches back too densely, it is too thickly populated, the future has not yet thinned out. No wonder a pattern is slow to emerge from such a thick clutter of cross-references, from such trivia, from such serious but hidden connections. (185)

Both Kate and Evelyn are caught up in the networks of the past, their parents and their jobs, and in the networks of the future, their children. Evelyn has managed to reconcile herself to her husband's infidelity, but she worries intensely about her truant, antisocial teenage son, Sebastian, and she "was going through a bad patch of her own. Her work had once seemed worthwhile. . . . But it too was becoming repetitive; she spent too much of her time . . . filling in forms. She saw more of failure than of success. The welfare state itself, and all the caring professions, seemed to be plunging into a dark swamp of uncertainty" (59). Kate is also finding limitations in her job as a writer on women's issues: "She found herself trapped in stale repetition, and depressed by the fact that as everyone else got more interested in Women she became less and less so" (58). Then an event in her personal life sends her "into the nastiest patch of her hitherto charmed life" (65). She discovers she is pregnant by Ted, Evelyn's husband, and after she decides to keep the baby because she could afford it, her three teenagers would enjoy it, she liked babies, and it would give her "fifteen years of purpose and selflessness" (66), she discovers it has spina bifida and has to be aborted. The loss of the baby agonizes her: "She had murdered it. For every good reason, she had murdered it. Maternity had been her passion, her primary passion in life, and she had been forced to deny it. Fate had forced her to undo her own nature" (235).[13]

Cut off from additional future mothering, Kate turns to the past, that other area of dense and "thickly populated . . . connections," to analyze the depths of her relationship with her parents. Her relationship with her parents and her past is strongly associated with another aspect of the city that she sees as a network: the sewage system. As she analyzes her own psychological depths, she sees parallels between them and the sewers.[14] Kate grew up in a lower-middle-class area called Romley. Her father was an intellectual sewage worker, and her mother an overweight, agoraphobic, class-conscious housewife. "All seemed set, says Kate, looking back, for a life of truly gruesome neurosis" (19), but early in life Kate learned to turn "shit into gold." In the childhood game Confessions, "her Mum, her Dad, Peter . . . Arblay Street, the secrets of her body . . . the sewage works, out they all came, translated into art. It was like a kind of magic, turning shit into gold" (22–23). It is not just that Kate is able to turn the sewage into art that makes the image significant. Drabble's use of the image reverses the typical negative associations with sewers.[15] Later in the novel Hugo recommends that Kate read a book by the anthropologist Mary Douglas, *Purity and Danger*. Kate never reads the book, but, as Michael Harper points out, Drabble clearly did.[16] Douglas' thesis is that "dirt is essentially disorder. There is no such thing as absolute dirt." She thinks that "ideas about separating, purifying, demarcating . . . have as their main function to impose system on an inherently untidy experience."[17] Kate tolerates disorder and in fact enjoys the multiplicity and variety in "jumble."

It is not surprising, given Drabble's use of Douglas, that Kate finds the sewers a positive memory.[18] As Kate heads back to Romley to interview some of her former classmates for a TV documentary on women's lives, she walks along the old sewage bank, remembering it as her favorite place to play as a child:

> The smell, powerful and secret, of drains and rainwater rose towards her. A vegetable, organic smell. Well, she had to admit it, a pleasant smell. She actually like it. . . . When small, she used to climb up this very bank . . . and when no one was looking she would lie on her belly and press her face against the grating and inhale. She knew it was both wicked and silly . . . and possibly dangerous, but it was also irresistible. There had been some-

thing magical about the dark race of water and the powerful odour of London. She had lain there and thought of the mysterious network of drains and pipes and tubes and gulleys and sewers linking the underground city, her small flat child's belly pressed to the warm summer grass. (116)

Even as a child Kate sensed the network below the city's surface; far from seeing it as unpleasant, she thought of it as "magical," "mysterious," "powerful," and interconnecting. The sewage bank was for her "a secret thoroughfare, a walk through . . . the surrounding brick industrial wilderness, a link with scrubby open space which counted, to the children of the district, as countryside" (17–18). Unlike the arbitrarily planned and artificial park of the new town, Romley Riverside, the "pleasure gardens of concrete . . . civic landscape-gardening . . . with a funny serpentine river, and a little Chinese bridge, and . . . thin young planted trees . . . [that] quaked in lonely gatherings" (112–113), the sewage bank provides meaningful connections. It is rooted in natural functions and provides a link to nature, to open space. It serves as natural connector of the many districts of the city and contrasts with the arbitrary and antiseptic landscaped pleasure gardens of Romley Riverside, that "grey monolith of expensive planning for cheap people . . . [which] in the midst of construction . . . looked derelict, abandoned: raw, ugly, gigantic in scale" (111–112). Nora Stovel identifies the sewage bank as "the middle ground itself . . . symbol of contemporary society,"[19] but she is wrong to imply that it is a negative image. Instead, it is the antiseptic new town, falsely ordered by concrete, that points to the ills of contemporary society. The new town, in Douglas' terms, is imposing a "system on an inherently untidy" existence, and Drabble makes clear in *The Middle Ground* as well as in her earlier novel, *The Ice Age*, that it is the superimposed system that is negative. The sewage bank as the middle ground is a positive image, one which furthermore echoes Gilligan's findings about safe places in female network and web imagery. For women, the safe place is the center of the network or web; it reflects "the wish to be at the center of connection."[20]

As an adult, Kate maintains the same positive associations and the same image of the sewer as a network when she goes down into the sewers to write a piece on them. As an adult she sees the detailed reality of the sewers and yet still retains the sense of mystery and network and vital connectedness:

> She had persuaded the Thames Water Authority to organise a visit for her, and down she had gone, down in her protective overalls and helmet and waders, down through a manhole in the middle of Piccadilly, climbing down a greasy ladder to the underworld, wading through tissues and Tampax and orange peel, walking through the ancient red-brick Victorian arches . . . smelling the odours issuing from grand hotel kitchens and laundries. The dark tunnels, the mysterious network. (117)

The sewers, like Kate's aerial view of London, are an antihierarchical network whose odors forcibly remind one of the support systems of the grand hotels, the kitchens and laundries. The "red-brick Victorian arches" of the sewers link the disparate districts of the city. Although Kate is aware of the dangers and disease of the sewers, of Ted's view of the "insecticide-resistant cockroaches, water-borne meningitis viruses swimming their way through the heavily treated waters of London" (190), the mysterious network of connections overpowers the dangers and the disease for Kate.

In the same way, the image of the network of sewers gives Kate a partial answer to her concerns about her parents and about her career based on "women's issues." She even asks herself as she stands on the sewage bank, "Was this what she had come for, was this the window, the grille through which she should escape the prison of the present into the past, where dark spirits swam in the fast-moving flood? Well, no, nothing as simple as that, really. No revelations evoked by the smell, just memories" (117), and she laughs at herself. "She'd never read Proust, but she'd heard of Proust's *madeleine*. How typical of her to have chosen a sewage bank for such stirrings, instead of a nice little cake" (118). Those memories do make her think of her parents, but her vision of them now is benign: the "little clever man and the large idle woman, one suffering from paranoia, the other from agoraphobia," whom she can laugh at and admire and forgive. Her childhood memory of them, however, is still complex and powerful: "Yet what had laughter, admiration, or sympathy to do with the tangled roots in her heart? For she had loved these two terrible people, . . . in the dark before dawn, in the underground she had loved them" (118). The image of the underground network of sewers now combines with an image of underground roots. The idea of a network is still present in tangled roots, but the emphasis is on the dark underground nature of the connection and the power of its influence. Kate still does not enjoy visiting her parents and can barely conceal her disgust at the stewed fruit they serve for lunch. Nonetheless, she does go see them. She maintains the connections with the network of her past even if it is knotted and tangled.

The root image reoccurs as Kate meditates on her parents and her brother Peter, who writes her anonymous threatening letters which make her think he is mad:

> The dirty, tangled roots of childhood twisted back forever and ever, beyond all knowing. Impacted, interwoven, scrubby, interlocked, fibrous, cankerous, tuberous, ancient, matted. Back in the artificial pleasure ground, the dear, solitary, carefully nurtured groups of saplings stood and shivered in loneliness, straight and slim, sad and forlorn. Their roots in artificial loam, reared in artificial fibre pots, carefully separate. Tastefully arranged, fruitlessly deployed. (132)

Kate recognizes in her meditation that even if the network of her roots is interwoven and interlocked and even if it is rooted in "shit," that is better than the new suburb's lonely, fruitless saplings rooted in artificial loam.

As Kate thinks about her own roots, a case history pops into her mind: Sally Jackson, "one of those women who revert to eating their own shit in middle age. . . . Sally had taken the long journey back over the dark rivers of Lethe, Styx and Acheron, and crossed back to the other side of daylight and life. But for what, frankly? For what? Nobody wanted to know the resurrected adult Sally" (133). Kate does not draw her own psychological conclusions directly from these thoughts. Musing about the anal phase, she is glad Peter is not that mad, but in spite of her reservations about looking "to either side" on the "tightrope" that is sanity (134), her imagery indicates the psychological value of looking back. One should maintain connection with tangled roots and dark underground rivers. If one takes all the "shit" out of life, isn't one forced to replace it with artificial loam? If one tries to disentangle and clean up the matted network of roots, isn't one left with shivering fruitless saplings and bland personalities? Chodorow uses the language of object relations theorists rather than Freudian anal imagery, but she too focuses on the preoedipal issues of separation and connections. Chodorow acknowledges that the successful adult has to attain a sense of "confident separateness" or differentiation, she emphasizes that *"differentiation is not distinctness and separateness, but a particular way of being connected to others"* (her emphasis).[21] Kate maintains the network of connection to her past even though she has trouble understanding all of it and actively dislikes some of it because she recognizes that it has made her what she is. She has differentiated from her parents, but she retains the ability to be connected to others.

Still, however, she worries about her ability to connect to others. She thinks that her child self is not connected to her adult self and that she is unable to love. Yet another image of connection appears as she worries about this, the image of placental connection: "nothing in her conscious self, in her daylight self, had been able to love. . . . Those two selves, that prattling chattering journalist . . . and the child in its skimpy cotton dress, lonely, cast out, cut off—what had they in common? No blood flowed from one to the other, the cord was cut, she withered and grew dry" (118). In these musings Kate is intensely concerned with the connectedness of her past and present. Although the memories of her difficult childhood and the loss of her baby make her question her ability to love, she in fact does exhibit a variety of kinds of maternal love, love for her own children, for her friend Hugo (for whom she cuts up meat because he has lost an arm), for Mujid, and even for Hunt. When Kate argues with Hugo about remaining connected to one's children, she rejects his image of the placental cord that is cut. Hugo "had taken the line that it was not only natural but necessary for children to reject their parents; that it was dangerous, destructive, to try to preserve communion, to try to keep the blood flowing through the severed cord. She did not think that Hugo truly believed this" (121–122). Regardless of what Hugo really thinks, Kate clearly believes in maintaining connection. Kate also has had satisfying sexual love relationships in the past: for a short time with her husband, Stuart, with Ted, and even with a variety of other lovers. It is left open whether or not Kate's friendship with Hugo will evolve into an affair.

Kate, in spite of some of her present dislike of her parents and her buried anger at them, has turned out to be a rather well-adjusted adult. She can maintain a variety of adult relationships and mother her own children successfully without smothering them. Part of her ability to survive her parents, "these two terrible people" (118), is perhaps that Kate was as involved with her father as with her mother. All the sewage imagery connects to him. She even identifies with him in her doubts about her job: "I'm beginning to think I feel the same way about women that my father feels about the unions" (8). Kate's mother is potentially very incorporating; she is fat herself, a butcher's daughter who ate too much meat, and she cuts herself off from her neighbors, but Kate manages to escape her. Kate's mother does not hold the same power over Kate that Martha Quest's mother holds over Martha in Lessing's *The Four-Gated City*, probably because of the presence of Kate's father, that "little, undernourished, grey-faced man, self-educated, self-made" (14). Kate, freer of her mother than Martha Quest, is able to focus on networks rather than boundaries in her perception of the city because Kate has already set boundaries between herself and her mother. As Kate's mother becomes increasingly housebound, Kate becomes increasingly autonomous, running errands and creating her own network of school friends. She identifies with her father and thus escapes her mother. Kate of course recognizes that a father's power can be dangerous: she is aware of how her father treated Peter and how Ted treats his children. She thinks

that her own children are better off than Ted's "paradoxically
. . . because they didn't have a proper father as Evelyn's did.
Stuart . . . was a much less disturbing influence than Ted appeared to be" (42). Kate acknowledges her own father's limitations, his lack of comradely spirit with other men, his ter-
rorizing of Peter, his compliance with his wife's cold, upward
mobility; nonetheless, he was there for Kate and she often
defends him. Kate's "heritage of sewage, agoraphobia, and
women's magazine correspondence columns" (26) even if
dangerous in isolation, in combination have preserved her
sanity.

The same anal imagery recurs as Kate thinks about wom-
en's issues. Kate is angry at women who complain simplisti-
cally about women's lot and think their lives should be easy.
She is particularly offended by a "best-selling angry feminist
novel" [Marilyn French's *The Women's Room*],[22] in which it is
said women "spend their lives dealing with shit and string
beans" (58). Kate realizes after some thought that the statement offends her because

> her own father had indeed spent his life dealing with shit, real
> shit, whereas women only have to deal with nice clean yellow
> milky baby shit, which is perfectly inoffensive, in fact in its own
> way rather nice. Women do not have to wheel barrow loads of
> contraceptives, or crawl on their hands and knees through un-
> derground sewers, or wade thigh-high in torrents of effluent. No,
> most women's lives are a piece of cake in comparison. (58)

Kate is equally impatient with her dinner guest, Linda Rubenstein, who is married to an American and spends the evening
complaining about her marriage, her uncompleted studies,
the housework, and her husband's materialism. Kate, uncomprehending, suggests she give up marriage as Kate herself had
done. Linda responds, "It's different for you, you can earn
your own living." Kate, who has no university education herself, responds tartly: "So can anyone" (101). Kate has not
grown insensitive to women's lives and issues, however. She is
sympathetic to the women of Romley Riverside who she is
interviewing, and she is angry at Gabriel Denham, the pro-
ducer (reappearing from *Jerusalem the Golden*) whose pres-

ence intimidates the women. "*Damn*, thought Kate . . . *that's* why women go on about the need for women film crews and women's publishing houses, how bloody obvious . . . [Men] didn't like women talking straight about men, no men working in a group did, though they might agree individually . . ." (206). Kate refuses to let Gabriel Denham impose a pattern onto the interviews and oversimplify women's lives just as she refuses a simplistic thesis from a woman novelist and deplores reductive ads.

In spite of her many columns on women's issues and her ultimate support of women, however, Kate still has some ambivalence about her role as a woman and as a feminist. She doesn't like thinking negatively about men. When she asks herself, thinking of her ex-husband, why men never learn to cook vegetables, she rejects the thought, deciding it is "diminishing. . . . She knew some nasty women, who'd been what is called ruthless in their personal and professional lives, intent on getting to the top. Kate thought to do it all the nice way" (77). Although to Kate the "Stennett marriage confirmed her in her own dislike of marriage, in her own conviction that it was very bad for people, particularly children" (56), she still sometimes worries that Evelyn is the "proper woman" (115), the "real woman" who keeps a clean house, gives dinner parties, and cooks proper meals and that she, Kate, is not. Despite these misgivings, Kate is a strong and independent woman and an attentive and confident mother. She is sensitive to women's issues and sympathetic to individuals, although intolerant of self-pity. She quickly realizes that she cannot "afford to shut up [on women's issues]. She had to go on earning her living, and her living depended on peddling opinions. She had brought up three children on views" (108). Kate has to go on earning a living and speaking up on women's issues, but she refuses to let anyone impose oversimplified patterns on women's lives: "No wonder those women in Romley hadn't fitted into a pattern. Why the hell should they?" (229). Kate glories in the multiplicity and many connections of women's lives, though she doesn't deny the anger and the "shit" in women's lives. She acknowledges that her husband

Stuart "treated me like a shit and I treated him worse. . . . I hated him" (115), but she goes beyond her anger and at the end invites Stuart and all her ex–in-laws to her party. Kate's maternal virtues (to use Ruddick's classification) of "good humor," "clear-sighted cheerfulness," and "love"[23] for an eclectic variety of people and the city around her make Kate rise above her doubts and ambivalence. On her return home from interviewing the starlet Marylou, Kate thinks of her friends Mujid and Marylou: "How quite extraordinarily odd people are, Kate found herself thinking . . . and how interesting, and how diverse, and how lucky I am, . . . and how I love my job" (197).

Kate is reconciled to her parents and her job, and it is precisely the variety of her origins and her willingness to accept and connect with a variety of people that make her good at perceiving the urban milieu: "Her lower-middle-class origins, onto which she grafted the language and opinions of the artistic and articulate middle class, proved an invaluable asset; she could communicate with a large audience" (36). To her father's opinions on labor and unions and her mother's collection of women's magazines, Kate adds the Bohemian and artistic tastes of Hunt and her husband's family. Kate can thus recognize and analyze the variety of different classes and people of the city. When she goes down into the subway, she not only analyzes the ads and graffiti; she also notices the various contemporary urban characters: "Waiflike pallid Australian beggars dressed in yellow robes," one of whom was playing a flute and a "curious couple . . . dressed in a dirty variety of black leather, smelling even at this early hour of drink and pot. . . . Unlike the flautist, whatever they were doing, they were not playing at it. They were for real. A grim outline of jaw and a defiant slump of the shoulder revealed working-class origins" (104–105). Kate can also classify the girl whose dog she takes care of briefly: "a strange upper-class girl in a hacking jacket and trousers, a rare species in the district Kate inhabited" (67). Although Kate doesn't take in all the stray animals and people she meets, she takes in many of them; her own house is filled with an incongruous mixture of her own children, Mujid, Hunt, Joker James, and assorted teenagers. She doesn't enforce a pattern on her household but instead brings all the disparate visitors together into the network of a party.

While Kate ponders the vertical depths and networks of the sewers and subways, Evelyn progresses through the horizontal districts and paths of the city in her job as a social worker and thinks fondly of the variety of people who make up the city. The two women are quite different in personality and lifestyle. Kate is outgoing, aggressive, and free-thinking. Evelyn is quieter and more conservative; she is more traditional in trying to hold together her weak marriage. Nonetheless, both women see the connecting networks of the city, though in different ways: Kate sees connections in the vertical layers of the city and of generations. Evelyn responds to the city's breadth and diffusion. Evelyn is able to see the good in almost all of her clients and the beauty in all the districts of London, even in the run-down district of Finsbury Park. As she sits in a traffic jam, Evelyn contemplates the neighborhood:

> this had never been a good area, or not in her lifetime. The conglomeration of textures and surfaces, all glinting dully in the sun, had a certain beauty, and a varied richness: if hung on the wall of the Tate or the Serpentine, one would perceive them as beautiful. . . . Pockmocked sooty bricks, mica-chipped cement, corrugated-iron hoardings plastered with posters, peeling wooden doors, drainpipes dripping with green moss. Craters in the road . . . revealed greening copper taps and subterranean pipes covered with strange khaki grease-covered rags. Soft bulging plastic garbage bags stood side by side with rigid ribbed grey dustbins. The pavement was ornamented with grey-green cellar skylights of thick glass, with iron manhole covers, with a crazy mixture of paving stones and kerb stones, and the road itself, painted with hieroglyphs of road signs in white and yellow, was an interesting assortment of colours—black sweating tarmac, grey chips, against a background predominantly pink, a dark granitic dust pink. A delicate mélange, well weathered. (134–35)

Like the architect Robert Venturi, who sees color and vitality in the neon lights and signs of the Las Vegas and the urban strip,[24] Evelyn can appreciate the multiplicity of textures and colors in an urban neighborhood. She sees in Finsbury Park not a decaying urban area, but beauty. She also notices the multiethnic variety of contemporary London as she passes the small shops: "A Greek Cypriot grocer" speaking Greek, an "old-fashioned" English butcher, an "Indian supermarket," a "barrel of salted pigs' tails . . . outside the West Indian shop," an "Herbal Remedy Shop" and a "shabby Community Health Centre" (135). Evelyn sees the network of multiethnic shops as linking together diverse groups of immigrants.

Despite her ability to perceive its beauty, Evelyn is not sentimental or unrealistic about the city. As she looks at the outrageous advertisements and posters for rock groups, she worries about the children of these areas:

> What could one expect but delinquency, of children reared amidst such prospects? . . . No wonder they dressed in battledress, adorned with plate armour of badges on their bosoms and clinking chain mail of staples and safety pins and paper clips. Each day they went into battle, along their own streets. (136)

While sitting in a traffic jam, Evelyn wonders whether her sister Josephine's farm in Pembrokeshire would provide a valid respite for urban problems: "What would it be like to find one's daily imagery translated into trees and fields and sheep and hedges?" (136). But she knows this solution is false. Neither she nor Josephine really wants to escape the city. At a dinner party she and Ted, her other sister and husband, and Ayesha, Evelyn's Urdu teacher, with her Danish husband, all predict that Josephine "would not possibly . . . survive six weeks away from the comforts and distractions of the metropolis" (210). Evelyn's school friend Stella is shocked by the stories Evelyn's children, Vicky and Sebastian, tell about London school life, but she says that life in the West Midlands was no "Garden of Eden" for children: "The youth of the district might not look as bizarre as Vic [Vicky's boyfriend, a blond subway guard who wears one earring], Vicky, Puss and Sebastian, but their activities were no more innocent, and they were . . . more mercenary, for there was no counter-affectation of working-class culture to keep their aspirations in check" (140). Evelyn remembers her own childhood images of middle-class innocence:

> a luminous lamb, which had glowed with its pale yellow-white soft woolly light on her mantelpiece night after night . . . a little household god, symbol of a nice safe middle-class childhood. Though, of course, it had subsequently been discovered that these benign little darlings were full of lethal radioactivity. (154)

Evelyn worries about her own children and the children of the city, but she is under no illusion that another environment would protect them. Seeming innocence can be full of radioactivity.

Although Kate is the one who analyzes herself and goes down into the depths of sewers and subways and the basement of her old school, Evelyn does stop to think sometimes of her own motivations and her mother. Her discouragement with her work is summed up in her discomfort in dealing with an injured old woman she encounters standing outside a hospital; "the tiny woman with her large shabby shopping bag, lost, adrift in meaningless London" (60) made Evelyn feel helpless. Although Evelyn manages to get her back inside the hospital, she "could hear in her own voice the horrid inept middle-class interfering tones she so disliked in others" (61). Evelyn thinks to herself that she is "actually frightened of the old and the frail" because ever "since childhood . . . she had been frightened by visions of herself attacking them, hitting them, assaulting them. . . . [She] knew that she would never assault an old person, [but] . . . these horrid apparitions . . . frightened her" (61–62). With feelings like these, Evelyn wonders if she has mistaken her vocation, but she recognizes that such feelings also help her to understand others: "she was quite good with delinquent adolescents . . . [and abusive parents] partly because she seemed to have some insight into the impulse that makes the young and the violent turn upon the weak and the defenceless, and therefore did not regard this impulse with uncomprehending disgust" (62).

Evelyn is able to relate to and to connect so many different kinds of people because she can recognize the potential for good even in the most hopeless cases and the potential for violence in the good people. As Evelyn ponders how to approach the abusive mothers at the day-care center and wonders whether it is possible to get rid of the unsympathetic day-care worker, Mrs. Oakley, who force-feeds the children, she suddenly thinks back to her own mother, a good mother who was head of a well-known London school and brought up her three daughters "to stand on their own feet" (40).

> Suddenly Evelyn remembered her own mother, thirty years ago, washing her hair as she had done every Friday night, screwing the damp hair up into a towel turban, but tightly, tightly, till the small hairs at the nape of her neck tweaked and her eyes filled with tears. Punitive, satisfied. Leaden nipples, swaddling clothes, liberty bodices, strait-jackets. (150)

Evelyn recognizes this punitive potential in all kinds of relationships, but she affirms relationships nevertheless.[25] She even criticizes herself for her other negative image of her mother removing the luminous lamb with a "cautionary lecture." When she can't remember the lecture, Evelyn thinks "how mean of her [Evelyn] to have assumed the worst of her mother. On one thing professionals and amateurs agree: mothers can't win" (154).

Even if mother-child relationships are too complex to allow mothers to win,[26] maternal values and inclusive ways of thinking about the world allow Evelyn to continue her work and affirm her attitude toward London. Even if Evelyn feels helpless beside the old injured woman, she delights in her visit to one of her clients, Mrs. Meer, a "half-coloured widow" from South Africa whose Afrikaans husband died six months after they arrived in London, leaving her with four children to raise. Evelyn and Mrs. Meer discuss their recalcitrant teenage sons and share their moments of lapsing from sensibility and capability: "two women used to shaking their heads at the foibles of others, alarmed, ashamed, but in some small way reassured to find themselves as foolish as the next person, victims to common human silliness" (153). Evelyn uses this sense of the commonality of all human beings to affirm her attitude toward cities in spite of their dangers. She tells Hugo's daughter, Susanna, that cities are "made safe only by a conspiracy of faith. 'We ought to behave *as though* we trust one another, for the more often ordinary people walk across the Heath, the safer it is.'" Susanna absorbs Evelyn's definition: "This came well from Evelyn, thought Susanna, for Evelyn knew the dangers, the rough side, the seamy side, and continued to brave them. . . . one must trust . . . the train guard, the hitchhiker, the lost tourist . . . for how else can society function? Everyone must be extended faith, everyone must play a part in keeping whole the fabric" (224).

Evelyn manages to keep her faith in the city and in people even when she is nearly blinded during one of her visits to her clients—a scene that is nonetheless almost comic because of its colorful, outlandish, urban characters. Evelyn goes to Stoke Newington to visit Irene Crowther, a half-lesbian teenage mother from Bradford. Irene's lover, Joseph Leroy, a tall black Rastafarian Jamaican with long dreadlocks, arrives with a knife in a fit of jealousy. When Irene throws a pan of fat and ammonia at Leroy to stop him, the ammonia lands in Evelyn's face and Leroy trips on the paraffin heater and sets the apartment on fire. Rubia, an eight-year-old Pakistani girl from downstairs, manages to call an ambulance. Kate, recalling the prejudices of the women she has just interviewed and the terror and violence that can be in cities, thinks in discouragement: "Belfast, Beirut, Bagdad. And was this London, a bedsitter in flames, a girl from Bradford, an insane Jamaican, a child from East Pakistan? No, surely not, surely not" (228). Evelyn, however, lying in her hospital bed, waiting for her eyes to heal, thinks of Rubia Subhan as one of the people who can make cities work by assembling the disparate elements and people into a meaningful network:

> Rubia, who had done all she could do to handle adult tragedies, in an alien country, interpreter, messenger, go-between: Rubia, persuading her mother . . . to take the babies to the clinic . . . Rubia, who had learned from neighbourhood gossip which phone boxes usually worked, who had learned from television pro-

grammes about dialing 999: Rubia, who had found it hard to make the ambulance men believe her story: Rubia, child of Britain, child of Stoke Newington. How wonderful people are. (239)

Not only does her accident give Evelyn an appreciation of Rubia, the child of the city, but it also "restores" her son Sebastian "to a good nature he hadn't displayed in years. He became attentive, co-operative, affectionate. He started to attend his College of Further Education again" (240). Although mothers aren't supposed to "win," according to Evelyn, it seems as if she does here. She knows she's been overindulgent, but Sebastian seems to be able to move beyond her indulgence. He brings Evelyn little gifts and starts to make friends again and to date Hugo's daughter Susanna.[27]

It is as Kate stands in Evelyn's hospital room, looking out of the twelfth-floor window at London, that she has a vision of the city as a network and thinks of the connectedness of people:

London, how could one ever be tired of it? . . . The city, the kingdom. The aerial view. . . . The aerial view of human love, where all connections are made known, where all roads connect? (243–244)

The urban vision of connectedness reminds Kate of her own family and an old Russian fairy tale she had loved at school. She identifies herself and Peter with the two orphan children of the tale. The sister is enchanted by a witch and drowned, and the brother, who is turned into a lamb, comes to the river to call the drowned sister to save him from being slaughtered. The lamb doesn't appear again in her reverie; like Evelyn, who knows her little lamb lamp was radioactive, Kate has to let innocence go. She has accepted the fact that she can't save Peter, but she does think about herself: "The little sister is resurrected, dug up, dragged from the river, the stone that weighted her dissolves, she rises up. Perhaps, perhaps, thought Kate" (243). The city, with its aerial view of networks and the connectedness of human love, allows Kate to rise up out of the river, and out of her midlife crisis.

Kate celebrates her new commitment to life and to other

people by planning a party. Kate leaves Evelyn to go home, assemble her guest list, and clean her house. At this point of affirmation, one last sewage image occurs.[28] The garbage workers are on strike, but Kate with the help of her children can cope with the too heavy garbage bin. She bores a hole in the bottom of the bin with a corkscrew, "and out poured the most astonishing thick black liquid, the rotting sediment of ages: down into the drain it went . . . disgusting, putrid, but somehow not unpleasant, oddly satisfactory, to see the fluid ooze away" (253). Kate has learned how to drain off the negative part of the garbage so she can lift the bin and attend to the myriads of people she has invited to her party.

Evelyn too affirms all of life and all of the city, even the garbage. As she discusses the view of London with Kate, she says:

> I can't wait to get out into it, I want to see all the things I've never seen, I want to see the Rubens ceiling in Whitehall, I want to go to Greenwich, I want to go to Kew and see the aconites in February, I want to walk in Regent's Park, I want to walk down Bond Street and look at the amber-shop window, I want to walk over Westminster Bridge, I even want to go to Finsbury Park to look at the garbage. (244)

Evelyn, like Kate, enjoys all the districts of the city. And with her regained eyesight, she wants to go out like a tourist and see all the parts of London. Evelyn not only perceives the connections between Kew Gardens and Bond Street, the parks and wealthy areas of the city, but between the urban richness of run-down Finsbury Park and the art of Whitehall. Just as she sees Rubia as "the child of Britain, child of Stoke Newington" (239), she sees all the diverse and multiethnic urban inhabitants as children of London, and she glories in them all. Left alone, she recalls a passage from the medieval German mystic Meister Eckhart and refutes it:

> See to it that you are stripped of all creatures, of all consolation from all creatures. . . . But how could one strip oneself of all creatures when it was only through them that one could express one's love? . . . Meister Eckhart, he could wait. (250–51)

Evelyn, like Kate, rejects the separation of herself from other people. She too rejoices in connection with others.

In an article on Angus Wilson, Drabble quotes John Updike as saying that "writing fiction in the seventies, this global decade, becomes increasingly difficult."[29] Hugo, trying to write about the Middle East, ponders Updike's remark in the novel: "The 1970's, the global decade, as Updike said in an interview the other day. Will anyone ever again be able to write, with confidence, a book that assumes the significance of one culture" (173). Drabble said that she envies Angus Wilson's life as a writer with his "house in the country and the flat in town and he spends so many months of the year abroad, writing a book. . . . It also means you have a wider canvas. You can write about Cambodia or Morocco or Saigon or wherever. . . . I love travel [but] . . . I've not been able to do as much of it as I would like." Drabble contrasts Paul Theroux's traveling and writing with that of his wife's: "His writing life is free in a way that the life of a woman with two children as they have just couldn't be. And I can't think of any female writers who've had the freedom to travel, can you? Of course if you were single, but so many more women writers are married now. You can do both; you can write and have children, but you can't travel."[30] In spite of not traveling extensively, Drabble, perhaps because of her own "maternal thinking," has written a novel of a global city that has a multiplicity of districts and multiethnic and multicultural variety. In Kate Armstrong and Evelyn Stennett, Drabble portrays women who notice these districts, care for these people, and can see the urban network that holds them all together. Kate and Evelyn have assembled, in the words of Drabble's interpretation of the poet Adrian Henri, "a collage city" because they can "love what is there."

The Novels of Drabble's Middle Period

Although *The Middle Ground* is the novel which portrays the city in the most detail and most celebrates the city, Drabble's valuing of the city began to emerge in what are currently described as the novels of her "middle period"—*Jerusalem the Golden* (1967), *The Needle's Eye* (1972), and *The Realms of Gold* (1975). Joanne Creighton comments on the value of London in these novels: "Northern landscapes are rejected in each of these novels for the cosmopolitan environment of London; the characters 'by will and by strain' eject themselves from oppressive childhoods and create new selves and new worlds . . . a golden Jerusalem, a Bunyanesque holy city, realms of gold."[31] In all three works the city glitters with gold, and this positive perception is tied to characters' growing relationships with others. Although Clara Maugham in *Jerusalem the Golden* is only beginning to learn about relationships, she recognizes that it is only in London that she can do so. Clara is attracted to the affectionate, close community of the Denham family, so unlike her own in their easy show of affection for each other. Clara links herself to that community by having an affair with Gabriel Denham. Clearly, London is for Clara the golden Jerusalem of her childhood hymn, but much of her task in the novel is to come to terms with her past rather than to observe the city of the present.

Likewise, in *The Realms of Gold* Frances Wingate must come to terms with her origins in Tockley, a small northern village. Even if the setting of the novel is not primarily urban, cities for Frances are still Keats' "realms of gold" because she is an archeologist who has discovered an ancient city, Tizouk, and it has given her a valued professional status and fame:

> She had known that the city was there, she had gone out to dig for it, and she had found it. . . .
> Digging in the cold dawn, her city rising from its burial in the sand, a building in reverse. Walls, buildings. Stacked. Pots, beads, figurines. Gold bars even.[32]

Here the city is something immensely valuable, something golden that is recovered and revered. It stands for civilization itself: shelter, art, religion. It is a great city of the ancient world when the safety and elegance of cities contrasted sharply with the dangerous wilderness that surrounded them.

The recovery of Tizouk and this celebration of the city is a result of a woman's intelligence and imagination and perception. Frances meditates on the process by which she discovered Tizouk: "I imagine a city, and it exists. If I hadn't imagined it, it wouldn't have existed" (29). After connecting various bits of historical research, Frances imagines the city, digs for it, and finds it. It exists first in her imagination and then, because she has imagined it, it exists in reality. It was always there, of course, but it was buried under the sand, and no one could see it because no one until Frances had imagined it. It is this same quality of imagination and the same value system that allow Kate Armstrong and Evelyn Stennett to see the beauty of London in *The Middle Ground.*

Creighton contrasts Frances's value system with that of her male cousin by juxtaposing the element of human community in Frances's profession with the barrenness of her cousin's profession of geology: "The personal and professional alliance of David Ollerenshaw, Frances's cousin, with minerals, rocks and the larger processes of nature contrasts starkly with Frances's alliance with human evolution. While Frances studies human communities, David Ollerenshaw . . . seeks out uninhabited, arid, cataclysmic landscapes."[33] Both professionally and as a mother of four children, Frances Wingate focuses on community and relationship. Not all her relationships are successful; she is divorced and has lost contact with her lover, Karel Schmidt. Frances has to make a pilgrimage back to Tockley and learn about the Ollerenshaw family, but it is not surprising, given her interest in human community and human relationships, that she is able to reestablish relationships with her cousins, reunite with her lover, and integrate her career and family. In *The Realms of Gold* the concept of the city is celebrated as a "golden realm" in that an ancient city is imagined and rediscovered, but it is not until *The Middle Ground* that Drabble merges the portrayal of the contemporary city and the journey back into the past within a single and unusual "golden" image, the network of sewers where "shit" is turned into gold and the whole city rather than just the Denham or Ollerenshaw family becomes the immediate community of the protagonists.

The most urban of Drabble's middle novels is *The Needle's Eye,* which, Joyce Carol Oates writes, "makes poetic and pragmatic use of every possible aspect of [London]."[34] In this novel, Rose Vassiliou, an heiress, has given away her money and married a poor Greek with whom she has three children but whom she finally divorces on grounds of brutality. She remains in the lower-class neighborhood at the back of Alexandra Palace where "she built up brick by brick the holy city of her childhood, the holy city in the shape of that patched subsiding house."[35] Simon Camish, the male protagonist, who is a lawyer and Rose's friend, sees only the depressing aspect of Rose's neighborhood: "rows of identical houses, the endless curving streets, the ugly squat inelegantly-gabled terraces, the dark breath of urban uniformity, petty eccentricity and decay" (35). The different perceptions of the urban neighborhood match Simon's and Rose's approaches to life. Ellen Cronan Rose notes that long before Gilligan's work, *The Needle's Eye* contrasted "male and female concepts of morality. . . . rights versus responsibility, law versus love, Simon Camish versus Rose Vassiliou."[36] Rose can see the holy city in her rundown neighborhood because that neighborhood represents community for her. When she first moved there with her husband, Christopher, "the long drab streets, the hard-faced suspicious old ladies in the shops, the gas works, the bedding factory, the shabby children in the streets, the house itself" (52) frightened her. Gradually, however, she began to get to know the old ladies who came into the store to buy a single egg; she patched up her own old house; she shared babysitting with her neighbor, Mrs. Flanagan. The district became a community. Rose's attitude toward the neighborhood school sums up the process of her learning to love the city, to build up brick by brick a holy city:

> She walked past the school, a huge Victorian edifice that loomed up, complete with bell and weathercock, against the dirty sky, and felt some satisfaction . . . that all her children were safely in there, being educated. On the school windows, pasted from the inside, there were cut-out butterflies, and doily patterns, and

shoals of fish. . . . She remembered how the sight of this school had alarmed her, years before . . . and of how it had gradually transformed itself through connection and familiarity. (130)

Rose, like Evelyn Stennett, is able to see charm in shabby lower-class neighborhoods because she values connection and other people.

The familiarity of the neighborhood district gradually allows Rose to establish a network of relationships that can stretch even to include strangers. Rose admires "lovely Miss Lindley," the infant teacher at the school when she runs into her in the sweet shop; she sympathizes with old Janet down on her knees washing the floor of the sweet shop; she helps an immigrant from Ghana find a book when the librarian can't understand his accent. In responding to an essay by Monica Mannheimer on *The Needle's Eye,* Drabble herself emphasizes the importance of this kind of community:

> I have just read, for the first time, an account of Erikson's theory of the eight ages of man. It seems to me that to stop short at self-realisation, and the achieving of one's own identity, is to refuse to move into the eighth stage, in which (if I have got it right) one assumes responsibility for one's community and one's succeeding generations.[37]

Although Drabble actually seems to be referring more to Erikson's seventh stage of generativity versus stagnation,[38] her emphasis is accurate. It is only in reaching out to others, as Rose does, and in concern for children, which Rose has, that one can avoid stagnation both of the personality and of the city. It is community that Rose was so lacking in her isolated, wealthy childhood in the country, and it is the community Rose finds in the city that allows her to establish the network of relationships and familiar places that sustains her. Simon, a sensitive person whose contribution to society is to seek justice in labor relationships, tries to help Rose with the legal complications of child custody, but he lacks her sense of close community. He does not even have a close relationship with his own children, and he is unable to see the charm of city neighborhoods.

This male failure to observe and celebrate the city is even more conspicuous in Drabble's next novel, *The Ice Age* (1977), which has a male protagonist. Anthony Keating is a real estate developer who, before the recession that freezes all development, has been putting together property in London. He does not value the small, old-fashioned, family-run sweets factory in South London that he buys. He sees it only in terms of what he can build. Elaine Tuttle Hansen points out that Drabble criticizes the values which Anthony espouses as a developer:

> the specific kind of life Anthony imagines for himself when he becomes a developer entails the sacrifice of many of those culturally feminine traits and values he previously seemed to exemplify to a set of stereotypical masculine characteristics that Drabble, throughout her career as well as in *The Ice Age,* clearly indicts. . . .
>
> The personal is . . . replaced by the impersonal as London itself becomes a changed place for Anthony. . . . London was before a symbol of human connection and community, "a system of roads linking the houses of friends and the places of his employment . . . in his personal map" (26); after his conversion, it becomes merely "a dense and lively forest" of business possibilities.[39]

At first, Anthony had a more feminine vision of London as a network, "a system of roads linking houses of friends." When he turns to development, however, he sacrifices most of his close relationships with friends to concentrate only on his business associates, and he sees the city only in masculine terms as an urban wilderness that can be changed into concrete monuments.

Like Iris Murdoch's male narrators, Anthony now focuses only on the landmarks of the city. He takes special pride in the gasometer that is on one of the pieces of property his real estate company is assembling:

> It gave Anthony the most profound joy, to find himself in possession of a gasometer. He had always admired their delicate, airy, elaborately simple structures. . . . It was painted a steely gray-blue, and it rose up against the sky like a part of the sky itself; iron air. . . . It would have to come down, of course, for who

wants an obsolete gasometer? But while it stood, while the I.D. Property Company negotiated for the other parts of the jigsaw, Anthony would gaze upon it with . . . pride and . . . wonder. . . . A derelict gasometer, radiant with significance. One could see it from miles away, right across the Thames, from some directions. It lifted the heart.[40]

The tall, delicate gasometer, a phallic symbol, is for Anthony a landmark that stands for his power over the city. There are dangers in his fixating on the gasometer, however, because the very workings of the real estate company that lifted his heart by purchasing the gasometer also gave him a heart attack. In his focus on real estate, he has cut himself off from real relationships with other people, and now he constantly has to be on his guard lest his financial partner cheat him when he offers to buy Anthony out. Anthony does not really learn anything from the heart attack, however, because he is still happy to destroy all the neighborhoods and old factories in the city, and he still thinks only in terms of towering, phallic landmarks that symbolize man's achievement:

By their monuments ye shall know them. By the Pyramids, the Parthenon, by Chartres and the Hancock Building, by St. Pancras Station and the Eiffel Tower, by the Post Office Tower and the World Trade Center. All large buildings express both piety and pride: how could they not? Man's own achievement, they point to the skies. His own gasometer had enmeshed the skies. (200)

The women in *The Ice Age,* however, do not experience Anthony's and his colleague's real estate developments as great achievements. Maureen Kirby thinks of her Aunt Evie, who is to be moved to a Council flat when the district she lives in is redeveloped. Maureen knows that her boyfriend, Len Wincobank, who is in prison for financial mistakes he made in the development process, would not sympathize with Aunt Evie: "in principle he was always in favor of rebuilding, and nothing annoyed him more than stories about pathetic old ladies fighting lone battles to preserve their cherished crumbling homes. He was all for more ruthless powers of eviction" (87). Maureen, however, understands why Aunt Evie does not want to move:

> Aunt Evie had spent thirty years making herself one of the most respectable women in the neighborhood. Wherever she went—to the butcher, to the launderette, to the fish shop, to the Indian emporium—she received her due, the courtesy due to years of toil. And how had she done it? Through cleaning and washing dishes. It was a triumph, a careful slow laborious victory, over circumstance. . . . To have so much undone, by a council decision: all those patient years, all the rewards of old age— honor, love, civility, streets of friends. (88)

Maureen knows that her Aunt Evie has built up a network of friends and acquaintances who respect her for her hard work. Len Wincobank and Anthony Keating cannot understand the value of that network because they can think only in terms of concrete monoliths and landmarks.

Alison Murry, Anthony's girlfriend, is equally critical of the development projects. While Len frets in prison, anxious to return to the development of Northam (Drabble's name for Sheffield[41]), Alison actually experiences it when she tries to walk from the train station to buy Tampax and a present for her daughter. She can see the drug store, but there is no place for her suitcase and she has to carry it and cross an "enormous traffic circle, the beginning of an overpass, a road leading to a multistory carpark, and an underpass" (171). She thinks to herself: "So this was what people complained about when they complained about the ruination of city centers. How right they were. It was monstrous, inhuman, ludicrous" (172). As Rose says of *The Ice Age,* the "only eyes which continue to see Len Wincobank's projects clearsightedly are female. . . . Alison Murry . . . does not share Anthony Keating's phallocentric vision."[42] Len Wincobank and Anthony Keating see parts of the city, but their perception is limited by their masculine focus on achievement and development. The network that is the city emerges only in women's vision. *The Ice Age,* written in 1977, criticizes male approaches to urban issues. *The Middle Ground,* written three years later, gives the female viewpoint, and although it does not propose a solution to all urban problems, it provides a celebration of the city and a perspective with which to approach its problems.

The Radiant Way

After a hiatus of seven years, Drabble returned to the female viewpoint in another London novel, *The Radiant Way* (1987). Despite the title, the London of *The Radiant Way* is a darker city than that of *The Middle Ground*. Crime, squats, and the cutbacks of Tory politics come to the foreground. Nonetheless, the female protagonists of *The Radiant Way*, like those of *The Middle Ground*, view the city in terms of layers and connections. Liz Headleand, a psychotherapist who gets divorced during the course of the novel, is like Kate Armstrong in seeing the layers that compose the city, although she focuses more on the layers of time than the literal layers of city networks. Alix Bowen, like Evelyn Stennett, is married and working in social services. Alix, who teaches English to young female prisoners and works part-time for the Home Office on female offenders, sees the city in terms of the connections between people. In this novel, however, there is a third female protagonist, Esther Breuer, a single Jewish art historian, who adds the problematic view of the city. She is the one whose upstairs neighbor is discovered to be a murderer, and Esther is the one who at the end of the novel leaves London altogether.

Drabble's heroines have typically aged along with her, and these three women are older than Kate and Evelyn. Liz's children and Alix's son by her first marriage are grown. All three women have more time for reflection. As the novel opens, just before her New Year's Eve party, Liz speculates on this stage of their lives:

> How could one bear to be on the sidelines? Not to be invited to the waltz? Not ever again to be invited to the waltz? But now she could see the charm, could read the meaning, of the observer's role, a meaning inaccessible to a sixteen-year-old, to a thirty-year-old—for the observer was not, as she had from the vantage, the disadvantage of childhood supposed, charged with an envious and impotent malice, and consumed with a fear of imminent death: no, the observer was filled and informed with a quick and

lively and long-established interest in all those that passed before, . . . was filled with intimate connections and loving memories and hopes. . . . it was through the potency of the observer
that these children . . . took the floor.[43]

These women are the observers. They know the intimate connections of the past. Thus they can see the connections in the
city. John Updike, the novelist Drabble quoted in *The Middle
Ground* about the seventies as a global decade, entitled his
New Yorker review of *The Radiant Way*, "Seeking Connections in an Insecure Country," because, he explains, "the
sprawling, dazzling pluralism of her novel is meant to illustrate the glimmering interconnectedness of all humanity."[44]

Liz Headleand, Alix Bowen, and Esther Breuer are able to
see the interconnectedness of humanity partly because in
spite of their success, they have experienced what it is to be
on the margins of society. The narrator explains that this marginality is in fact what initially drew them together at Cambridge:

> They did not know then, were not to know for many years, were
> never fully to understand what it was that held them together—
> a sense of being on the margins of English life, perhaps, a sense
> of being outsiders, looking in from a cold street through a lighted
> window into a warm lit room that later might prove to be their
> own? Removed from the mainstream by a mad mother [Liz], by
> a deviant ideology [Alix's parents' Fabian socialism in a Yorkshire
> school], by refugee status and the warsickness of Middle Europe
> [Esther]? (90).

Like Doris Lessing's colonial Martha Quest (see Ch. 2, pp. 38–
39), they know what it is to stand slightly outside the dominant culture and to look in at it as if through a lighted window.
It is this experience that makes them perceptive observers of
the city.

Liz Headleand is the one who sees the layers of the city. In
this also she is like Lessing's Martha Quest, who sees the history of a house in the layers of wallpaper, or Janna Somers,
who sees the layers of a World War I house beneath her current office. Liz's first experience at seeing the layers of London is during the renovation of the big house on Harley Street

that she and Charles buy to raise Charles' three young sons and their two daughters. Partly it is Liz's experiences of marginality and motherhood that bring her to the renovation of the house. She had grown up poor herself, and she wants more for her children; "[her] own childhood had been lived on the margins: she had wanted theirs to be calm, to be spared the indignities of fighting unnecessary territorial and social wars" (18). As the old house is cleared out, Liz learns of its past, its margins, and layers and boarded-up cupboards:

> The most unpleasant discoveries were made during the process of clearance: cupboards full of urine-encrusted chamber pots, of ancient patent medicines, of dead mice, of moth-infested garments, of fossilized scraps of nineteenth-century food: Hogarthian, Dickensian relics of an oppressed and squalid past. In one room there was a plastic sack full of used sanitary towels. Liz had joked that they were sure, in the rafters, to discover a dead baby, and indeed they did find there a mummified cat, which a pathologist friend hazarded to be at least a hundred years old. . . . The untransformed house had contained treasures as well as horrors, including the portrait on the stairs, and the restored chandelier. (19)

Liz's discoveries are akin to Kate Armstrong's trip into the sewer and to Frances Wingate's discovery of Tizouk. Both find "gold" in the muck and the dirt.[45] Liz cleans up the house and allows a decorator to paint it white and gold. Liz now knows not only as a psychotherapist but also as a city dweller both the horrors and the treasures of the unseen layers.

Liz sees London, like her house, in layers, particularly her own district of Regent's Park and Harley Street, with all its historical architectural details:

> An almost full moon hung over Regent's Park. The familiar façades walked away towards the soft rising mound of green. Town houses, with that strange visionary little female gleam of grass at the end. The Post Office Tower rose amidst scudding clouds. Dutch gables, Adam pediments, Queen Anne windows, art nouveau cornices, blue plaques to dead statesmen and poets, brass plates to living consultants and royal institutions. This was her London, she felt at home here, its layers reassured her, confirmed her. (120–121)

Architectural details on a house in Harley Street, an historical district.

The landmark of the Post Office Tower is softened by the clouds and balanced by the female gleam of the park. Even more important to Liz than the landmark is the myriad of façades whose pediments, gables, cornices and plaques reveal the layers of time.

Liz finally has to sell the Harley Street house after her divorce, but she finds another house in St. John's Wood that also has historical charm, urban variety, and the presence of nature: "It was a house of character: it had one of those Edwardian glass canopies from front door to street, and pretty little romantic leaded windows with bits of dark fine art-nouveau stained glass. It rambled, eccentrically, with strange-shaped rooms, and alcoves" (257). Like the houses in Regent's Park, this one invokes echoes of past layers of city history in its architectural details. The new neighborhood also reflects the variety of an urban district. Liz and Esther tease the socialist Alix by saying she would surely approve of Liz's new house because its "undeniable attractions and the exclusivity of the neighbourhood were doubly modified, partly by a Family Planning Clinic next door . . . and partly by an extremely ugly block of luxury flats opposite, built in the 1960s from a horrible pinkish stone, and known vulgarly in the district as Menopause Mansions" (258). The variety is not just in the buildings. The garden in the back of the house brings nature into the city. When she lived in Harley Street, Liz used to go to Regent's Park. One of her strongest memories is her stepson Aaron "throwing crumbs for sparrows in the rose garden of Regent's Park" (123). Now Liz has that beauty in a garden of her own in St. John's Wood:

> The colours of the garden deepened in the evening light: a scent of rose and nicotiana and honeysuckle mingled. . . . [Beyond] stretched a small lawn, and . . . a small square pond, surrounded by bluish paving stones. (259)

Even at the end of the novel after she has learned of the murderer living above Esther, Liz is still euphoric about city life: "I *love* London. This is one of those days when I love London.

I love this restaurant, I love the restaurant cat, I love Notting Hill." (375–376). In the eighties, Liz Headleand can still celebrate London with its historical layers, its parks and gardens, and its varied districts.

Alix Bowen explores the breadth of people in London. Like Evelyn Stennett, Alix sees the humanity of all the various social classes. Brought up by old-fashioned, liberal parents, she values other people and is curious about the poor:

> As a child, she had always had secret yearning to enter the other city, the unknown city beyond and within the suburbs, where nobody, middle-class folklore declared, read books or washed or cooked proper meals. She had sometimes, even as a child, wondered if it could be as fearful as its reputation. She disliked . . . being made to feel fear of her fellow men and women. (103)

After the death of her first husband, Alix moves from wealth to "semi-comfortable squalor" (102) like Rose Vassiliou in *The Needle's Eye*: "In the streets of Islington, she observed poverty. She experienced it, also" (102). Once Alix experiences poverty, she realizes she has nothing to fear from others. As she walks her son down to "a little patch of grass, on the corner in front of the launderette and the pub," the row of drunks on the park bench accost her "not for money . . . but for company. 'Come and sit down for a minute, darling,' they would wheedle. And sometimes Alix sat down with them, in the feeble London sunshine, to pass the time of day. . . . They were past drunkenness. . . . Dirty, ragged, high-smelling, communing with the Lord. They told her not to worry, the worst would never happen" (104–105).

Not surprisingly, it is Alix who has a vision of humanity as a network, or a web. As she drives up the motorway on New Year's Day past the houses of Wanley to go to the female prisoners' pageant at Garfield Centre, Alix has a vision of a connecting network of people, a web that links the separate houses and districts and cities:

> She aspired to make connections. She and Liz, over supper together, often spoke of such things. Their own stories had

strangely interlocked, and sometimes she had a sense that such
interlockings were part of a vaster network, that there was a pattern, if only one could only discern it, a pattern that linked these
semi-detached houses of Wanley with those in Leeds and Northam, a pattern that linked Liz's vast house in Harley Street with
Garfield Centre. . . . [She saw] people perhaps more as flickering
impermanent points of light irradiating stretches, intersections,
threads, of a vast web, a vast network, which was humanity itself:
a web of which much remained dark, apparently but not necessarily unpeopled. (72–73)

Alix sees the connection between the districts of the city and
various peoples of cities as points of light in a huge network
or web. The darkness is there between the nodes of the web,
but in spite of the darkness the connection remains.

It is the sense of connection that helps Alix endure the dark
side of the city and her exile to Northam. The darkest aspect
of the city is the Horror of Harrow Row, a murderer who cuts
off the heads of young girls. His last victim is Jilly Fox, a girl
whom Alix taught at Garfield Centre. When Jilly's term is up,
Alix and the prison warden know she has no place to go, but
both the rules and commonsense prevent Alix from becoming
involved with Jilly "on the outside." Finally, after receiving a
strange letter from Jilly, obviously written while Jilly was in a
drug-induced high, Alix goes to see her. Jilly is living in a
squat off Harrow Road. The rooms are painted with lurid images of daggers, severed heads, wounds, and blood. Jilly
claims she is waiting for death. Alix finds she cannot reach
Jilly and leaves only to find her tires slashed. She runs to Esther's apartment. The next day Jilly's head is found in Alix's
car. The crime is a grim reality of urban life, and all Alix's
coping skills and goodwill have been powerless to help Jilly.
Alix thinks to herself: "I have courted horrors, and they have
come to greet me. Whereas I had wished not to court them,
but to exorcize them" (337).

Not all potential urban horrors materialize, however. Alix
worries about her older son, Nicholas, a painter who is living
"outside the system" (237), first in a squat and then in a condemned building with his girl friend, Ilse Nemorova. Alix goes

to see them, expecting "bare floor-boards, torn curtains, cracked windows, mattresses on the floor: inner city, cracking creaking, peeling squalor" (238). Instead, when she gets there she finds

> a fairy story, a Bohemian fairy story. The little room was illuminated by candles, by a paraffin lamp, by crackling packing-case twigs in a real fire in a real Victorian grate: its walls were painted a dark midnight blue, its floor was painted a deep red with a dark-blue and green patterned border, wooden painted chairs stood at a table covered with a white embroidered cloth. (238–239)

The lurid paintings of Jilly Fox's squat are not the only possible response to inner-city decay. Nicholas and Ilse have redeemed their housing, even if it is not to last. The building's owner is eventually found and it is torn down, but meanwhile beauty is created out of urban decay by human talent and work. Nicholas and Ilse, both talented painters, transform the city in positive ways, far beyond what Alice Mellings does in Lessing's *The Good Terrorist*. Even though Ilse and Nicholas finally move to the country to live in his grandmother's house, their story is a positive "fairy tale" of those who live on the edge of the city and transform it.[46]

Alix finally has to move to Northam when her husband Brian's College of Adult Education in London is shut down because of government budget cuts. Although Alix is depressed about the move away from London, she maintains her connections with the city. As she dines with Liz's sister in Northam, she thinks of Liz and her connection to London. Alix "was cheered . . . to think that selfish, bracing, energetic Liz existed, that she continued to inhabit the other world, the old world, the familiar London world. And the [Bowen] house in Wandsworth was only rented after all. Not sold" (377). Alix is discouraged about the politics of the eighties and her inability to save people like Jilly, but she maintains her vision of connection, of the city and all its people as a vast network, even if there are dark spaces, even horrors, in between the points of light.

Esther Breuer does not have as large a share of the story as Liz and Alix, perhaps because her vision of the city is a little different from theirs, a little darker. Esther, however, shares with them a basic enjoyment of city life. She actually spends more time than the other two walking the streets of London and enjoying the solitary freedom of her walks. She is much more aware than the others, though, of decay in the city and of the demolition of parts of the city. Before her own building is razed and she has to move to Somerset where some friends have a cottage, she explores even the back streets and run-down parts of London. She is comfortable in places where others might feel alienated.

When Esther is first introduced, she is walking from Ladbroke Grove to Harley Street to go to Liz's party:

> Esther Breuer has decided to walk to the intersection of Harley Street and Weymouth Street. She often walks alone at night. She walks from her flat at the wrong end of Ladbroke Grove, along the Harrow Road, under various stretches of motorway, past the Metropole Hotel where she calls in to buy herself a drink in the Cosmo-Cocktail Bar (she is perversely fond of the Metropole Hotel), and then through various increasingly handsome although gloomy back streets, until she arrives at the arranged corner. (3–4)

The name of the "Metropole Hotel" recalls the scene from T. S. Eliot's "The Waste Land" and the sinister Mr. Eugenides' invitation to "a weekend at the Metropole,"[47] but although the Metropole provides a layer of literary reference, it does not represent an alien place or illicit encounter. Esther likes to have drinks there, and Liz goes to a conference of Japanese psychotherapists there. Esther has created her own city haunts and is not afraid to walk down Harrow Road or up gloomy back streets.

Esther, an art historian, is bothered more by the ugliness of new buildings, the decay of city districts, and the neglect of nature in the city than by the danger:

> London has become difficult. Not impossible, but difficult. Even Esther, who likes urban life, is becoming slightly distressed by the visual impact of some stretches of Ladbroke Grove, by the apartment blocks of the Harrow Road, by the strange surreal landscape under the arches of the motorway. Her niece Ursula,

The Metropole Hotel.

who has a taste for the *louche,* likes it immensely . . . sits drinking cans of beer with impossible people in condemned and
boarded cottages in the middle of rubble wastes. (192)

Esther's niece can see these areas as places for adventure and
for meeting new people; Nicholas and Ilse can even transform
them; but for Esther this kind of surrounding has become
more a "landscape of nightmare, an extreme, end-of-the-
world, dreamlike parody of urban nemesis" (244). Sometimes, especially when she catches a glimpse of nature in the
city, the landscapes do not seem so bad, but even then it is
not the beauty of Liz's garden or Regent's Park: "she walked
beneath the great strutting legs and curved segmented under-
belly of the Westway, where a little herd of horses stood sadly
in a dry ring of sand, like an abandoned circus: she wandered
over waste grass near Wormwood Scrubs. . . . Alsatians
roamed, cats scavenged, buddleias grew from abandoned roof
tops" (243). Nature exists in this part of the city, but it seems
wistful and neglected.

Esther's worry about urban decay, like her dream of a severed head, has to be taken seriously because it is in a Lykewake Gardens[48] squat right around the corner from her flat
that Jilly Fox is killed, and it is in her own apartment building
on Ladbroke Grove during a visit of the three friends that the
murderer is found. Her very building itself is caught in the
demolition. Liz Headland tries to explain its disappearance
to a friend: "It's being eliminated. Utterly eliminated. As
though it had never been. Cut out of the city, like a cancer"
(376). Liz's comment is ironic; one cannot stop madness and
crime or stop urban decay by cutting it out like a cancer.[49]
The darkness of Esther Breuer's experience of the city remains as she moves on to Somerset and then Bologna. It is
not as grim as the vision in Doris Lessing's *The Good Terrorist,* however, where ordinary people have become unthinking
and dangerous, and it is not the only one presented in *The
Radiant Way.* Liz Headland still loves London with its layers
and varied districts, and Alix Bowen retains her vision of the
city as a vast network.

The Radiant Way ends with a radiant red sunset in Somerset when Alix and Liz visit Esther on her fiftieth birthday. Patrick Parrinder suggests that this sunset, following as it does the "horror" of the severed heads, is "a kind of Conradian nudge towards a vision of a future England as one of earth's dark places."[50] England, and certainly London, has some darkness within it, but it is not all dark as Liz's and Alix's vision of the city illustrates. Neither of course is it all radiant. In fact the title *The Radiant Way* is ironic. It was the title Charles Headleand chose during his early idealistic years for a documentary about education and class in England. As the Headleands look at it again in the eighties, they realize that it changed little. The title of the documentary was in turn based on the title of a primer from the 1930s which Liz finds in her mother's house after her death. Charles and Liz had learned to read from this primer, but its images of the traditional family have little relevance to Liz's own complex family of stepchildren and children or her discovery of the shabby past of her mysterious father (she has learned that he committed suicide after being accused of exposing himself to children). None of the ways has been radiant. Nor is London of the 1980s.

Radiance, however, can be a dangerous goal, whether it be the radiance of Evelyn Stennett's lamb-shaped radioactive lamp or a plan for cities. The French architect Le Corbusier planned a utopian dream city in the 1920s that he called the "Radiant City" (La Ville Radieuse),[51] a series of geometrical towers linked by highways and green spaces. The drawings were beautiful, but Jane Jacobs severely criticizes the social implications:

> Le Corbusier's Utopia was a condition of what he called maximum individual liberty, by which he seems to have meant not liberty to do anything much, but liberty from ordinary responsibility. In his Radiant City nobody, presumably, was going to have to be his brother's keeper any more. Nobody was going to have to struggle with plans of his own. Nobody was going to be tied down.[52]

Le Corbusier's machine-like towers might gleam with radiance, but without connection between people there can be no true urbanity. Much more livable is Drabble's vision of the city as a network, filled with people who make connection with each other. More than Conrad, Drabble's novels evoke E. M. Forster's *Howards End,* with its call for literature inspired by the town[53] and its epigraph "only connect." Drabble has created that connection and a portrait of London as a network that holds people together. It is an image of the city worth celebrating.

CHAPTER 4

The City as Labyrinth:
Iris Murdoch

Margaret Drabble in *The Writer's Britain* identifies Iris Murdoch as a "city lover." Noting that Murdoch in *The Sea, The Sea* even reverses the usual analogy of the city to nature by comparing the starry heavens to the lights of a city cinema, Drabble concludes that such valuing of the city over nature is "rare, rarer in literature than in life."[1] Murdoch not only compares nature to the city, however, she also describes the districts, streets, and landmarks of London with great particularity. Her London novels differ from those of Doris Lessing and Margaret Drabble because she uses primarily male characters, who focus on landmarks more often than female characters, and because she portrays the city as a somewhat dangerous labyrinth. In a relatively early novel like *Bruno's Dream* (1969), the landmarks can lead to a vision of the city as a place of redemptive love. In the novels of the 1970s, however, particularly *A Word Child* (1975), the potential for redemption becomes more problematic as the full image of the city as a labyrinth emerges. As in Drabble's *The Ice Age*, landmarks dominate the city and become signs of the male protagonists' obsessions. Not until Murdoch returns to a female protagonist in *Nuns and Soldiers* (1980) does the labyrinth of the city become clearly negotiable.

The Dickens Heritage and *Bruno's Dream*

Of all the contemporary urban writers, Murdoch provides the greatest variety of London scenes. The settings in her novels include scenes from all over London: the offices at Whitehall; the houses in Brompton Road, Chelsea, and Kensington; the flats in Earls Court, Bayswater, and Notting Hill. Her characters drink in the pubs in Fitzroy Square and Soho, walk through St. James's Park and Kensington Gardens, go to the Tate Gallery and Covent Garden, and ride the subway at Piccadilly Circus, Sloane Square, and Charing Cross. The variety and detail of the settings recall Dickens.[2] Louis Martz in 1970 identified Iris Murdoch as "the living writer who is, in her London novels [and 6 out of 10 of her novels since 1970 are set in London], the most important heir to the Dickens tradition."[3] Conradi, more recently, links her portrayal of the city to Dickens and Woolf: "London is a real presence in the books, indeed seems to figure sometimes as an extra character, and even when her people are having a hellish time there, which is often, the author's loving and patient apprehension of the city comes through. This is the more noticeable in that, Dickens and Woolf apart, London has lacked distinguished celebrants."[4] (See Ch. 1, pp. 5–7, on Woolf's influence.) Murdoch does celebrate the city, but more guardedly than Drabble and in a slightly different manner from Dickens. Martz explains how Murdoch's early novels up to and including *Bruno's Dream* are similar to those of Dickens: "The London novels of Iris Murdoch have their Dickensian quality of detail because they grow from a deep, instinctive affection for the London setting, whether sordid, shabby, or genteel. And that affection for the outward traces of man's habitation derives from the theme of love that constitutes the redemptive element in the novels of both writers."[5]

Murdoch does use a Dickensian quality of detail and she does use an image of the city as labyrinth which Dickens often used, but even in her most positive novels Murdoch's vision of love, although redemptive, is much tougher than Dickens's idealized domestic love. Murdoch shares with Dickens a view that self-centeredness and egotism are a source of evil in man, and she uses Dickens's word "muddle" to describe confused moral and social relationships. She does not, however, absolve her female characters from the struggle against selfishness as Dickens so often does in his sentimental portraits of innocent young women, with the exception of Bella Wilfer in *Our Mutual Friend*.[6] Furthermore, Murdoch sees romantic love, so idealized in Dickens, as being particularly susceptible to fantasy and selfishness. The love which functions as redemptive in one of Murdoch's early city novels, *Bruno's Dream* (1969), is not romantic at all but the selfless love which an ordinary, complacent, and emotionally greedy woman, Diana Greensleave, develops for her dying father-in-law, Bruno.[7] Martz is right, however, that in achieving this love, she is able to see the city. As

> she had come to love Bruno, to love him with a blank unanxious hopeless love. . . . familiar roads between Kempsford Gardens and Stadium Street seemed like those of an unknown city, so many were the new things which she now began to notice in them: potted plants in windows, irregular stains upon walls, moist green moss between paving stones. Even little piles of dust and screwed up paper drifted into corners seemed to claim and deserve her attention.[8]

Like Diana, her brother-in-law, the mild Danby Odell, who has been caring for his father-in-law, has an experience of redemption within the city. Although he succeeds in romantic love, his experience of beatitude comes as he plunges into the Thames after escaping injury in an absurd duel he tried to avoid:

> It did not seem cold. The still flowing tide took him gently with it. He felt a strange beatific lightness as if all his sins, including the ones which he had long ago forgotten, had been suddenly forgiven. The mist had lifted. . . . A little pale sunlight began to glow from behind him, and he saw that a perfect rainbow had come into being, hanging over London. . . . (240)[9]

Stadium Street, the setting for Murdoch's *Bruno's Dream*.

Even though the Thames still floods after the rainbow over London and the sinful, shabby city still contains the sterile bourgeois houses of Kempsford Gardens and the desolate basement flats observed by Nigel, the city in *Bruno's Dream* is primarily a positive place in which the theme of human love combines with the love of the city.

This affirmation of the city and the possibility of human redemption are suggested by the unusual landmark that presides over the city: the "trinity of towers of Lots Road power station" (34).[10] These towers unite the disparate districts portrayed in the novel, Danby's house on Stadium Street, the printing works in Battersea, and the Kempsford Garden suburbs, in that from each place Bruno or Danby looks up to see if he can see the towers. The towers themselves are like the city and like the river Thames: grimy, black, and shabby, but providing light and a sense of protection, and even, when viewed by Danby from a cemetery, seeming to suggest redemption. In the opening of the novel they are linked to the city and to the Thames as Bruno thinks of "the chilly spring sun, casting a graceless light upon sinful London and the flooding Thames and the grimy ringed towers of Lots Road power station"(1). When Danby looks at them, they seem "suitable extensions of that murky infertile earth"(19) of his well-loved little yard surrounding the house on Stadium Street. Later, Danby's associations imbue the towers with greater significance. As he looks up at them from Brompton Cemetery, where the black towers are outlined against "mist-green budding lime trees," a Biblical verse springs into Danby's mind: *"Ye are come unto Mount Zion and the city of the living God"* (133). Even though the mist can hide Danby's view of the towers from the printing works and the power station can be flooded by the Thames, the towers are associated with the protective qualities of "the city of the living God." The muddy, smelly, littered river can produce in Danby a sense of forgiveness; the grimy, black, man-made towers can produce light and a reassuring sense of protection; the "sinful city" is pierced by spring sunlight and warm lamplight. In

Bruno's Dream, redemption can occur under the towers of the Lots Road power station within a city that is celebrated and affirmed. After *Bruno's Dream,* however, the assurance of redemption and the affirmation of the city disappear. Elizabeth Dipple emphasizes: "Murdoch will allow this felicitous conclusion. . . . in *Bruno's Dream,* but thereafter the darkness of man's squalid limitations will give a resounding 'no.'" Dipple summarizes, "she will never again allow herself the cakes and ale of *Bruno's Dream.*"[11] The landmarks that dominate the vision of Murdoch's later male observers of the city are not so benign. They match the observers' own rigidity and problems with interrelationship.

For the six London novels written in the 1970s, there is no moment of insight and only the barest hint of redemption, or of "fairly honourable defeat." In these novels Murdoch's characters do not experience the heady liberating freedom of the city as Lessing's Martha Quest and Janna Somers do or the joyous network of connections that Drabble's Kate Armstrong, Evelyn Stennett and Alix Bowen do. Furthermore, in the decade, and seven novels, that separate *Bruno's Dream* (1969) from *Nuns and Soldiers* (1980), no female character attains significant insight as Diana does in *Bruno's Dream.* Male characters dominate the novels of the seventies, and they almost never break out of their prison of ego. The city in these novels is a labyrinth, and the self on which the male protagonists are so desperately focused can easily become lost in its twistings and turnings.

Feminism and Murdoch's Theory of Attachment

Although Murdoch has written half a dozen novels with a male first person narrator,[12] she never has written a novel purely from a female point of view. When asked about this in a 1978 interview, she replied:

Lots Road power station with its two towers, as seen from Stadium Street.

Well, I don't really see there is much difference between men and women. I think perhaps I identify with men more than with women, because the ordinary human condition still seems to belong more to a man than to a woman. . . . if one writes "as a woman," something about the female predicament may be supposed to emerge. And I'm not very interested in the female predicament. I'm passionately in favor of women's lib, in the general, ordinary, proper sense of women's having equal rights. . . . [but] I'm not interested in the "woman's world" or the . . . "female viewpoint." . . . We want to join the human race, not invent a new separation.[13]

Even though Murdoch claims she is not interested in the "female predicament" or "women's world" or the "female viewpoint," her philosophical writings are seen by several feminist theorists as illustrative of female thinking. Both Sara Ruddick and Carol Gilligan have been influenced by Murdoch's discussion of love, with its emphasis on love as attention to others and love as a capacity for attachment. Murdoch's concept of love appears as one of the key qualities in Ruddick's definition of "Maternal Thinking": "The identification of the capacity of attention and the virtue of love is at once the foundation and corrective of maternal thought. The notion of 'attention' is central to the philosophy of Simone Weil and is developed, along with the related notion of 'love' by Iris Murdoch."[14] What Ruddick especially values in Murdoch's concept of love is its attention to "the other." This focus appears in an early philosophical essay, where Murdoch writes, "Freedom is exercised in the confrontation by each other, in the context of an infinitely extensible work of imaginative understanding, of two irreducibly dissimilar individuals. Love is the imaginative recognition of, that is respect for, this otherness."[15]

Carol Gilligan uses Murdoch to link the concept of morality to love. She quotes from Murdoch's philosophical work, *The Sovereignty of Good* (1970): "Iris Murdoch observed that philosophers seemed to have 'forgotten' or 'theorized away' the facts that an unexamined life can be virtuous and love is a central concept in morals."[16] In that work Murdoch defines love as a capacity for attachment. Attachment is a particularly important concept for Gilligan: she finds both in other psychologists' studies and in her own experiments that men's adult development focuses on separation and achievement whereas women focus more on attachment and intimacy or love.[17] In one of her experiments, Gilligan found that men responded to pictures of intimacy by writing stories of violence. Women might fear success, Gilligan points out, but men see "danger more often in close personal affiliation. . . . Thus, it appears that men and women may experience attachment and separation in different ways and that each sex perceives a danger which the other does not see—men in connection, women in separation."[18]

It is precisely in separation and its extremes of selfishness and egotism that Murdoch sees moral danger and in attachment that she sees a potential for redemption. Murdoch's egotistical male narrators, like Bradley Pearson in *The Black Prince* or Hilary Burde in *A Word Child,* often reside in a city among many people, but they are completely separated from others. In fact, they often use the labyrinth of the city, as in *A Word Child,* to hide from others. In *The Sovereignty of Good* Murdoch says that ordinary "human conduct is moved by mechanical energy of an egocentric kind. In the moral life the enemy is the fat relentless ego."[19] The way out of this egocentricity that has separated itself away from everything else is attention to something outside the self. Murdoch explains that

> we can all receive moral help by focusing our attention upon things which are valuable: virtuous people, great art . . . the idea of goodness itself. Human beings are naturally "attached" and when an attachment seems painful or bad it is most readily displaced by another attachment, which an attempt at attention can encourage. (56)

Paradoxically, the only way to detach oneself from the prison of the isolated ego is by attachment to another. It is also the only way out of the labyrinth. Murdoch ties attachment to love, but she does not sentimentalize love: "Love is the general name of the quality of attachment and it is capable of infinite degradation and is the source of our greatest errors; but when it is even partially refined it is the energy and passion of the soul in its search for Good" (103). Peter Hawkins, a theologian, comments that

> Murdoch's central interest lies in the possibility of self-transcendence, a breaking out of the dream of solipcism [*sic*] into the cold light of external, shared reality. There is the chance . . . that we can break through the prison of egocentricity to discover suddenly the existence of other people and their entirely independent claims. . . . In her lexicon it signifies nothing less than the beginning and end of wisdom, this ability to cast a just and loving eye on another individual reality.[20]

Although Murdoch says she is not interested in the "female viewpoint," she reveals a morality that in its focus on others and the capacity for attachment matches very closely what Ruddick, Gilligan, and others have found typical of women.

Murdoch sees the capacity for attachment as good, but she does spend much time on good characters in her novels. In *The Sovereignty of Good,* she explains: "Goodness appears to be both rare and hard to picture. It is perhaps most convincingly met with in simple people—inarticulate, unselfish mothers of large families" (53). Dipple notes that in all Murdoch's novels "only one person is clearly identified as a saint by a genuinely trustworthy reporter: the priest Brendan Craddock in *Henry and Cato* calls his mother one. . . . but she is not a character who lives and speaks in the book."[21] Even of her novel entitled *The Nice and the Good,* Murdoch says, "no one in the book is good."[22] Murdoch identifies unselfish mothers as potentially good, but she, unlike Drabble, does not portray them in her novels. Up to *Nuns and Soldiers* (1980), the closest she comes to characters who are good throughout the novel and not just transformed at the very end, like Diana, are male characters who have female virtues. Dipple identifies only three "good" characters in Murdoch's first nineteen novels: Bledyard in *The Sandcastle,* Tallis Browne in *A Fairly Honourable Defeat,* and Brendan Craddock in *Henry and*

Cato. All three of these men are non-assertive and have the female virtues of humility and interest in others. Both Bledyard as a schoolmaster and Tallis Browne as a social worker have traditionally feminine occupations, and Brendan Craddock has removed himself from male sexuality by the skirts of the Roman Catholic priesthood. Although Murdoch finds that goodness can be achieved in mothers and in men who have the female capacity to pay attention to others and to attach to them, she does not focus on good characters, and they are not the ones whose perception records the city.

Instead, the vivid portrayal of London in Murdoch's novels of the 1970s is conveyed by egotistical male characters. Murdoch says that she uses male narrators because "the ordinary human condition seems to belong more to a man than a woman," but in *The Sovereignty of Good,* she describes the ordinary human condition as that of the "fat relentless ego" (52). The male narrators are thus negative moral examples, and the city at this stage of Murdoch's career is portrayed by these men who are self-absorbed and afraid of others. Men like Bradley Pearson in *The Black Prince* and Hilary Burde in *A Word Child* do not see the variety or the other people in the city. They in fact use the city to escape others, seeing only the phallic landmarks that dominate their city. As the psychoanalyst Jessica Benjamin theorizes, "the idealization of separation and the idealization of the phallus go together."[23] In *The Black Prince,* Bradley Pearson is obsessed with sexuality; his London, which is analyzed in Freudian terms by Peter Wolfe, is dominated "by the serene austere erection of the Post Office Tower."[24] Hilary Burde in *A Word Child* is fixated on the past, and his London is dominated by a symbol of time, Big Ben. For all such male protagonists, the city is a dangerous place because there is often the potential for bumping into others. In their desperate attempts to avoid others, the protagonists walk anxiously up and down the labyrinth of city streets. For them the labyrinth then becomes doubly dangerous because there is the possibility of losing the self as well in its intricacies.

The Image of the Labyrinth

The image of the labyrinth, the dangerous maze for which only a woman, Ariadne, has the thread of survival, is a familiar image in the novels of male writers. The image of the city as labyrinth dominates Dickens's novels, especially *Oliver Twist*, and it pervades the works of contemporary male novelists like Samuel Beckett and Alain Robbe-Grillet.[25] For these novelists the labyrinth is a wholly negative image. In Murdoch, however, it is more complex and relates to several other images, such as the net in *Under the Net*[26] and the spider webs in *Bruno's Dream*. The images of net and web, according to Gilligan, are female images, as opposed to men's images of hierarchy:

> The images of hierarchy and web, drawn from the texts of men's and women's fantasies and thoughts, convey different ways of structuring relationships and are associated with different views of morality and self. But these images create a problem in understanding because each distorts the other's representation. As the top of the hierarchy becomes the edge of the web and as the center of a network of connection becomes the middle of a hierarchical progression, each image marks as dangerous the place which the other defines as safe. Thus the images of hierarchy and web inform different modes of assertion and response: the wish to be alone at the top and . . . the wish to be at the center of connection.[27]

The labyrinth, although it shares a spatial configuration with nets and webs, has a dangerous center, the Minotaur.[28] Thus the image connects Murdoch's male narrators to Gilligan's analysis of imagery in reflecting the male fear of the female "safe place."

In contrast, Drabble's image of the network suggests an unambiguously safe center. Even Virginia Woolf's use of web imagery in *Night and Day* is positive. Squier points out that in *Night and Day*

> London is . . . a maze to Mary Datchet, yet . . . she finds it "won-
> derful" because she knows exactly where she belongs—"at the
> very center of it all". . . . In an image that mythologizes Mary's
> work in the Suffrage Office, Katherine sees her and her co-
> workers . . . "flinging their frail spiders' webs over the torrent of
> life which rushed down the streets outside" (ND, 93, 94).[29]

Woolf, using female characters like Drabble, finds safety at the
center of the maze, the web. Murdoch, in her morality of attachment and criticism of selfishness, clearly rejects the male
imagery of being "alone at the top," but the labyrinth is ambiguous as a female image because the center may not be a
safe place. At the center of the labyrinth is the Minotaur, and
even spiderwebs in Murdoch's works might well have poison-
ous spiders at the center. However, when Murdoch extends
the image of the labyrinth to relationships as well as to the
city, she illustrates that her labyrinth is nonetheless related
to Drabble's network and Woolf's web. The network, which
implies that all relationships are supportive, is too easy a solution for Murdoch, but Murdoch does sometimes allow her
labyrinths to be negotiated safely. Her image of the labyrinth
is partly a projection of her male narrators' fear of relationship, but partly an acknowledgment by Murdoch that relationships and human love can sometimes be selfish and bad.
In *The Sovereignty of Good,* Murdoch writes:

> Ignorance, muddle, fear, wishful thinking, lack of tests often
> make us feel that moral choice is something arbitrary, a matter
> for personal will rather than for attentive study. Our attachments
> tend to be selfish and strong, and the transformation of our loves
> from selfishness to unselfishness is sometimes hard even to con-
> ceive of. (91)

There is an answer to the dilemma, however, even if it is hard
to conceive of, and that answer lies in continuing to value
attachment and love. There is thus a way through the labyrinth if one can be attentive and kill the devouring Minotaur
of selfish bestial love, but success requires the thread of female virtues, of unselfish attachments. Murdoch's male narrators are often not capable of facing this Minotaur, but when
the image is associated with a female character, as in *Nuns*

and Soldiers, the labyrinth is still tricky, but the female protagonist can work her way through the labyrinth of the city
and of relationships by holding on to the thread of female virtues. Gilligan too uses the imagery of the thread, noting that
in one of her studies a girl sees a dilemma as "a fracture of a
relationship that must be mended with its own thread."[30]

The image of the city as a labyrinth is built up in several of
Murdoch's novels. It conveys a portrait of a city as a place of
intricate pathways and blind alleys, as a dark maze of streets
and a darker underground maze of subways. It occurs twice
in Murdoch's first novel, *Under the Net* (1954). Jake Donaghue, the narrator, describes Hammersmith Mall as "a labyrinth of waterworks and laundries with pubs and Georgian
houses in between, which sometimes face the river and sometimes back it."[31] Later Jake and Finn and Lefty look for the
Thames: "We turned . . . into a dark labyrinth of alleys and
gutted warehouses where indistinguishable objects loomed in
piles. Scraps of newspapers blotted the streets, immobilized
in the motionless night. The rare street lamps revealed pitted
brick walls and cast the shadow of an occasional cat" (119).
Jake knows his way around parts of the labyrinth, but he
never really gets out of it because he is afraid of relationships;
he loses Anna, the woman he idealizes. Although Jake can
describe the labyrinth that is the city, he is not sufficiently
self-aware to recognize its dangers. The dangers are specific
in Murdoch's second novel, *The Flight from the Enchanter,*
which begins with Annette Cockeyne's listening to an Italian
lesson on Dante's description of the Minotaur in *The Inferno.*
The naive girl feels sorry for the Minotaur and does not realize
its dangers. Soon she runs away from school to London, there
to experience herself the urban dangers of the labyrinth and
Minotaur. Dipple points out that "the allusion to the Minotaur
with its suggestion of labyrinth and its present, hellish, physical fury serves as a good introduction to the characters who
thread their way through tortured lives and the peculiar physical brutalities of civilized London."[32] In *Henry and Cato,* the
image is first used to describe the filthy slum which contains
the condemned house in which Cato, a doubting priest, lives:

the north end Ladbroke Grove "becomes seedy and poor. . . . a mass of decrepit houses let out in single rooms. A small terrace house in this melancholy labyrinth off the Grove was Cato Forbes's destination. . . . the street ended in a wasteland of strewn rubble."[33] Here the "seedy" quality that so charmed Danby Odell in *Bruno's Dream* becomes filthy and dangerous in the enclosed labyrinth. Later the image becomes even more ominous when "Beautiful Joe," whom Cato loves, locks him in the basement of the house and demands ransom. Cato, however, does not know he is in his own basement and fears he is in a dark underground "labyrinthine" prison:

> Then he thought he heard a faint brief distant rumbling, perhaps simply a vibration. A machine? The underground? . . . he was *somewhere*, hidden, caught, somewhere in London, in some fantastic, perhaps huge and labyrinthine hideout, in somebody's terrible private prison. (227)

Cato has become imprisoned in the labyrinth of the city and of his own tortured love for Joe.

Although Murdoch does not use the specific word "labyrinth" in either novel, the depths of an underground air raid shelter or sewer in *The Nice and the Good* (1968) and the subway station in *A Fairly Honourable Defeat* (1970) evoke the image of the underground labyrinth. In both cases, the London that is portrayed is London in the summer, enveloped in close, suffocating heat. In *The Nice and the Good,* Murdoch implies that it is precisely during such times of heat and moral laziness that evil can enter:

> There is a pointlessness of summer London more awful than anything which fogs or early afternoon twilights are able to evoke, a summer mood of yawning and glazing eyes and little nightmare-ridden sleeps in bored and desperate rooms. With this ennui, evil comes creeping through the city, the evil of indifference and sleepiness and lack of care.[34]

The evil that appears comes in an underground labyrinth. When Ducane descends into the basements of Whitehall to investigate the suicide of a colleague named Radeechy, he

finds not cool relief from the summer's heat but sinister, cob-
webbed corridors. As Ducane descends, the flashlight reveals
"a short flight of steps sheeted over with a fungoid veneer of
damp dust. There was a pattern of footprints in the centre and
tangles of black thread at the side" (207). He thinks uneasily,
"These passages can't lead to more air-raid shelters, we've left
the air-raid shelters behind, we're at much too low a level now.
It's more likely that this is some disused part of the Underground or something to do with sewers" (208). In a small
room that recalled for Ducane "dug-outs and guard-rooms . . .
something to do with the war, something secret and unre-
corded and lost" (209), he finds the remnants of Radeechy's
celebration of a Black Mass: a silver chalice, dead pigeons,
incense, a reversed cross, black thread, bottled poisons, and
a whip. Ducane gladly retreats from these depths, aware that
they contain evil.

In *A Fairly Honourable Defeat,* the depths of London are
less exotic but even more sinister in their realism. As Murdoch has said, the " 'fairly honourable defeat' is the defeat of
good by evil."[35] The city is again enveloped in heat: "London
in July with the sun for once continually shining had become
a mad place, stifling, enclosed, dry, whose rows of unreal and
shimmering houses seemed to conceal something quite else,
some more than Saharan desolation."[36] This desolation is felt
even more strongly by Morgan, the egotistical female linguis-
tics professor, when she enters Piccadilly Circus subway station and sees a pigeon trapped underground: "The idea of the
bird trapped in that warm dusty electric-lighted underground
place filled her heart with pity and horror" (291). She tries to
save the pigeon, but fails and loses her purse. In a panic, she
thinks she sees her estranged husband Tallis, but he is travel-
ling on a down escalator and she on an up. When she runs to
get his help, she cannot find him:

> She came out into the main station and began to run again. The
> station was very strange, it was dark. . . . The huge cast iron
> vaults were not glowing with light, they were obscure and yellow
> as if filled with steamy mist, and below them it was as dim and

> murky as a winter afternoon although the air was hot. . . She fled
> up a long flight of stairs and down another and came out under
> the sky which was misty and sulphurous and overcast. (295)

The subway station is a labyrinth of confusion for Morgan in
which she cannot find her purse or her husband and from
which she cannot save a pigeon or herself. The sulfurous smell
makes the whole city a hell.

A Word Child

The image of the labyrinth is most fully developed in Murdoch's later novel, *A Word Child.* As in *A Fairly Honourable
Defeat,* the underground labyrinth pervades much of the
novel. The subway is the favorite hiding place of Hilary Burde,
but for him London above ground is also a labyrinth in which
he hides and in which he tries to keep each district of the city
separate from the next like a dead end or walled-off turn of
the labyrinth. *A Word Child* has the most vivid, even if most
pessimistic, portrait of London. Hilary Burde, the narrator, is
the "word child," a linguist and a grammarian who loves the
rules and logic (the qualities Gilligan finds that males use to
make ethical decisions) of grammar but who misses the
meaning not only of poetry but of relationships. Laura Impiatt
accuses Hilary of using "words as a hiding place."[37] In the
past, Hilary has had an adulterous affair with Anne Jopling,
his mentor's wife. After Anne is killed in a car driven by Hilary, words alone are not a good enough hiding place. As Hilary
explains, he went "to London, as criminals and destroyed
people do, because it is the best place to hide. And I hid"
(128). Hilary has to hide not only from Gunnar Jopling and
his Oxford colleagues, but from himself and his own consciousness and memory of guilt. He is able to hide, at least
partially, in his routine job as a minor official in Whitehall,
itself a maze of offices and mindless, ridiculous bureaucrats,
and in a careful rule-bound grammar of dinners in which he
numbs his evening hours by eating with different people in
different districts of the city on different days of the week.

Hilary carefully tries to separate his life into discrete units of time to avoid facing his own past. When the separation of his life into units of time does not work, Hilary seeks oblivion and further hiding places in the subway. Given Hilary's obsession with hiding and with time, it is not surprising that his London is dominated by the subway stations and the landmark, Big Ben.

The "underground" or subway system in *A Word Child* is a subterranean labyrinth extending underneath all of London. Whenever Hilary's routine is broken and he might have to come to terms with himself, he seeks oblivion by descending into the subway; he would "get onto the Inner Circle and go round and round until opening time and then go to the bar either at Liverpool Street [Station] or Sloane Square [Station]" (138). For Hilary the appeal of the subway is that there is no way out, only the continuous circling that provides momentary distraction from reality. The circling trains allow Hilary to stay in the outside rings of the labyrinth. In this novel there is no facing of the Minotaur as there is in the underground Black Mass of *The Nice and the Good* or as is hinted at in Morgan's panic and confusion in *A Fairly Honourable Defeat*. Dipple comments that "Murdoch's use of the London Underground, especially the Inner Circle route, is marvelously apropos of this character, who rides round and round the Circle route just as his mind circles and circles the routes so often travelled, which he, in despair, acknowledges to be absolutely his and infinitely repeatable."[38] The subway does not just reflect Hilary's own character, the self-proclaimed underground man, it also reveals for Hilary the essence of London. It is here in the darkness that Hilary feels a "profound" sense of "communication with London":

The concept of the tube station platform bar excited me. In fact the whole Underground region moved me, I felt as if it were in some sense my natural home. These two bars [Liverpool Street and Sloane Square] were . . . the source of a dark excitement, places of profound communication with London, with the sources of life, with the caverns of resignation to grief and to mortality. . . . one could feel on one's shoulders as a curiously

The site of the tube station platform bar in Sloane Square. It no longer operates as a pub.

soothing yoke the weariness of toiling London, that blank released tiredness after work which can somehow console even the
bored, even the frenzied. The coming and departing rattle of
trains, the drifting movement of the travellers . . . presented a
mesmeric and indeed symbolic fresco. . . . (37) I was not the
only Circle rider. There were others, especially in winter. Homeless people, lonely people, alcoholics, people on drugs, people in
despair. We recognized each other. It was a fit place for me, I was
indeed an Undergrounder. (38)

Hilary's "communication with London" is of a limited kind,
however, for although the "undergrounders" recognize each
other, they do not really communicate. Hilary talks to no one
in the station pubs. There is an irony in Hilary's perception of
the subway stations in that they are what Lynch calls "nodes,"
the ultimate places of connection, places of juncture and concentration, "a convergence of paths."[39] But in spite of the
concentration and convergence of people, Hilary perceives
only "blank released tiredness," "drifting movement," and "a
mesmeric . . . fresco," all states of oblivion, not really of communication.

The only place Hilary really conveys excitement is in his
description of the trains themselves which take on an almost
sexual dimension:

Then once upon the train that sense of its thrusting life, its intent
and purposive turning which conveys itself so subtly to the trav-
eller's body. . . . The train of consciousness, the present moment,
the little lighted tube moving in the long dark tunnel. The inevi-
tability of it all and yet its endless variety: the awful daylight
glimpses, the blessed plunges back into the dark; the stations,
each unique, the sinister brightness of Charing Cross, the mysterious gloom of Regent's Park, the dereliction of Mornington
Crescent, the futuristic melancholy of Moorgate. . . . I preferred
the dark however. Emergence was like a worm pulled from its
hole. (38)

Hilary's excitement about riding the train is falsely achieved,
however, because it replaces a real sexual relationship with
Tommy, his mistress (with whom he avoids having sex).
Furthermore, even on the train the aim is "the blessed
plunges back into the dark." For Hilary the value of the under-

ground is still oblivion and darkness, not destination or communication. Hilary's descent into these subways is no *via negativa* in which the self is purged of ego and emotion. Hilary Burde's subway is like Eliot's in "Burnt Norton"; it does not have "darkness to purify the soul . . . Only a flicker/ Over the strained time-ridden faces/ Distracted from distraction by distraction . . ./ Tumid apathy with no concentration/ Men and bits of paper, whirled by the cold wind."[40] To reach the path of the *via negativa,* one must "descend lower," as "Burnt Norton" makes clear, but Hilary is not interested in that; he is only interested in having the "train of consciousness" plunge "back into the dark" labyrinth of the subway tunnels.

When Hilary does ascend to the streets to walk around London, the weather in the city and his walks around it create the same labyrinth above ground that Hilary so valued below. Hilary's movement on the surface of London conveys the same impression of the city as his descent into the nodes of the tube stations. The city itself is mostly dark, enveloped in fog or haze, and the entire novel takes place in winter. Most days, if it is not actually raining or snowing, are "those yellow days which are so very Londonish, not exactly foggy, but pervaded from late dawn to early dusk by a uniform fuzzy damp cold dirty yellowish haze" (68). On other days fog sweeps over London "like a sea mist, greyish, not brown, and carrying suspended in its gauzy being cold globules of water which lightly covered the overcoats of early Londoners with a spider's web of moisture" (105). If one is not caught in the subterranean labyrinth of the subway, one is in the web of fog above ground. A blackout even occurs for two days during an electricians' strike. Occasionally the gloom is pierced by the stars, but however brilliant they shed no light on the city below: "The stars were so crowded together, they formed the segment of one golden ring. Yet the light they gave was to each other, they seemed not to know of us, and there was no brightness here below" (110). It is through this darkness and the maze of London streets that Hilary walks. He says: "I knew my London blindfold" (110). He walks "a special kind of metaphysical sad London walking . . . with an almost ritualistic intensity"

(137). This ritual serves the same purpose for him as riding the underground; the repetition erases meaning and lulls him into a desired oblivion.

Hilary cannot remain forever an Underground Man or a ritualistic walker of the streets, however, because he recognizes that it is madness to give up consciousness entirely. When he learns Gunnar Jopling has come to London, he thinks to himself: "I must do everything in order as I had always done. I must go regularly to work. I must keep to my 'days.' I must not become a madman walking about London and living on the tube" (150). Hilary realizes that he cannot always escape to his underground labyrinth, but he makes his above ground travel through London a rigid separation of districts and time like a rat going through only certain variations of a maze. Hilary's "days," which also function as the structure of the novel, are his way of compartmentalizing the people in his life and the districts of London as well as an attempt to control time.

Each day of the week Hilary has dinner with a different friend in a different district of London. The varied districts of London are vividly portrayed, but unlike Philippa Palfrey in P. D. James' *Innocent Blood*, Hilary makes no connection between districts. He prefers to keep them separate. The novel opens on Thursday when Hilary has dinner in a large, stylish house on "Queen's Gate Terrace" with an office colleague, the Impiatts. On Friday he goes to his mistress, Tommy, who "lived in a lost region on the confines of Fulham and Chelsea . . . in a little neat flat in a little neat house in a terrace of little neat houses, each with its tiny ornate portico and . . . its smelly basement full of dustbin litter" (37). Hilary mocks Tommy's neighborhood by contrasting its neat houses with the smelly basements, but he does not mind shabby neighborhoods themselves. On Saturday, Hilary eats a plain supper with his sister Crystal, who lives "in a bed-sitter flat in one of the shabby little streets beyond the North End Road. . . . The stucco of the fronts, once painted different colours, had faded into a uniform grime and fallen off in patches to reveal ochre-coloured brick beneath. Here and there a gaping or boarded window or a doorless doorway proclaimed the abandonment of hope" (13). Hilary intends to transform Crystal's life, but in fact he likes to have her in his control in her shabby bed-sitter. He is afraid of her love for his clerk, Arthur. On Sundays Hilary goes to the cinema, and on Mondays he dines with an-other office colleague, Clifford Larr, whom he had known at Oxford. Clifford Larr is a sophisticated homosexual who lives in Lexham Gardens in a flat "like a museum, a temple" (77). On Tuesdays Hilary eats with Arthur in his "two-room flat over a baker's shop in Blythe Road" (86), and on Wednesdays he goes home to his own "small mean nasty flatlet in Bays-water, in a big square red-brick block in a cul-de-sac" (1). Hilary has tried to impose a tight form on his life that will keep all his relationships in their own little corner of the maze, but as Murdoch emphasizes, "Morality has to do with not imposing form, except appropriately and cautiously and carefully and with attention to appropriate detail."[41] Hilary imposes control over his life, but not appropriately. His con-trol is only for the purpose of avoiding thought of his past.

Given Hilary's fascination with the imposition of form and ability to control, it is not surprising that he is interested in landmarks in the city. Landmarks represent the manmade world of work and achievement and these, according to Gilli-gan, are the areas that men particularly focus on. Lessing's Martha Quest laughs at landmarks, and for Drabble's Kate Armstrong they are no more important than the little streets and backyards. Only Drabble's male protagonist, Anthony Keating, shows an interest in landmarks. For all Murdoch's male characters, even the feminine Danby Odell, landmarks are very important. After the benign power station towers in *Bruno's Dream*, however, Murdoch undercuts the symbolism of the landmarks. Although Bradley Pearson in *The Black Prince* is obsessed with the Post Office Tower, he fails disas-trously to communicate with anyone. Hilary is fascinated by form and control, but when he notices landmarks he reduces them to mysterious, almost unreal places: His own offices at Whitehall become "fairy pinnacles" (93). The House of Com-mons, seen through the fog, becomes only a "line of bright-ness[,] . . . a very faint impression" (167). Sometimes he notices them, but they make no impression upon him at all. In his wanderings around London, he finds himself "at the foot of the Post Office tower" (149) or "as far as St Paul's" (199), but even these do not seem to be able to break the daze created by his "mindless wandering." Once or twice, while walking with women, Hilary notices a different kind of more natural landmark, but these too are endowed with mystical imagery. Hilary does not automatically see nature as a part of the city as P. D. James's or Maureen Duffy's characters do. While walking in Kensington Gardens with Tommy, Hilary thinks of the Round Pond as that "mysterious and holy place, the omphalos of London" (177). In Kensington Gardens with Biscuit, Kitty Jopling's Indian maid, he associates "the mysterious stone garden at the end of the lake. . . [with] a camouflaged entrance to some strange region (Acheron?)" (54–55). A contemplation of mystery brings Hilary's mind quickly back to his search for unconsciousness in the underground. Even Acheron will suffice to submerge "the train of consciousness."

The most significant, and the most ironic, landmark for Hilary is Big Ben. It is symptomatic of Hilary's obsession with time and his attempt to control it by his "days" that he focuses on the landmark of Big Ben. It is different from the other landmarks for him in that it is not unreal in its mystery but magical. Hilary's office at Whitehall has "a sort of bay window from which, through a cleft in an inner courtyard, one could see Big Ben" (30). Almost every day Hilary looks out to see whether its face is visible or whether it is hidden in the fog. Hilary gives Big Ben an almost talismanic aura. He even gets Biscuit to swear by Big Ben that she will return (56). With Biscuit, Hilary walks across Westminster Bridge and looks through the fog at "the moon face of Big Ben far above" (167). The irony of Hilary's obsession with Big Ben is that for all his efforts to hide in the labyrinth of London and all his attempts to control time, time in fact controls him. Hilary is fixated by that one event in the past which dominates his life: his adultery with Anne Jopling and her subsequent death.

Hilary realizes that he and Anne "had created a maze and

Big Ben and the Houses of Parliament, famous London landmarks. Hilary in Murdoch's *A Word Child* is fixated upon Big Ben. Lessing also refers to Big Ben in *The Four-Gated City*, P. D. James mentions them in *A Taste for Death*, and Duffy mocks them in *Londoners*.

The Chelsea Embankment is an example of an "edge," a boundary between the river and the district of Chelsea. The Lots Road power station is in the background.

were lost" (121). At Anne's death Hilary locks himself into the maze by avoiding Gunnar, leaving Oxford, and hiding in London, cutting himself off from all intimate contact except his sister Crystal, whom he bullies and treats as merely an extension of his own ego. Hilary hides himself in the labyrinth of the London underground and London streets, circling repetitiously to avoid thinking of the event that ruined his life. That event, that "monstrous thing . . . [imprisoned in] the sealed sphere which composed my consciousness and Crystal's" (111), is the Minotaur at the center of his labyrinth. Since Hilary never faced it, he creates it anew when he falls in love with Gunnar's second wife, Lady Kitty, and she meets clandestinely with Hilary in hope of alleviating Gunnar's obsession with that event.

In falling in love with Lady Kitty, Hilary crosses both social and class boundaries. After the death of Anne Jopling, Hilary had been careful not to cross any boundaries; he kept all the people and the times of his life separate. He also avoided places in the city which Lynch calls "edges[,] . . . the boundaries between two kinds of areas."[42] Unlike Martha Quest in *The Four-Gated City*, who explored boundary issues in her own psyche and sought out these edges, Hilary is afraid of boundary areas because he cannot separate them, confine them, and control them. Sure enough, another death occurs when Hilary crosses these social boundaries and the characters congregate on an edge, the Chelsea Embankment. It is here that Hilary causes Kitty's death. Gunnar appears on the embankment where Kitty and Hilary are meeting and in the ensuing fight between the two men, Kitty falls into the frigid Thames and later dies of exposure. Hilary dives in after her but to no avail: "in an awful jumbled darkness, the Thames rushed me onward, squeezing me with its icy coldness, squeezing the remaining warmth out of my body, whirling me about and hurrying me onward and trying to kill me, to crush me to death in its cold embrace" (376). Hilary cannot save Kitty, and this cold immersion in the Thames offers no insight and no rainbow as the swim in the Thames in *Bruno's Dream* did. Hilary remains as locked in the repetitive patterns of the maze he created as he ever was.

There is a hint, however, of how to negotiate this maze. Hilary is obsessed by one event in his past, but he tries desperately to avoid it by focusing on an "eternal present," losing himself in a rigid, time-bound routine under the shadow of Big Ben. This routine is broken by the death of Kitty Jopling and the suicide of Hilary's friend, Clifford Larr. After he learns of Clifford's suicide, Hilary goes to St. Stephen's church and looks at Eliot's grave, mourning Anne and Kitty and Clifford, to whom in his obsession with Kitty, Hilary had not reached out: "Clifford had been carried away by the cold river and I had not stretched out my hand to him, not even touched his fingers. . . . it felt to me as if I had killed him in a fit of anger, as I had, in a fit of anger, killed Anne. And where there might have been the relief or reconciliation . . . there was blankness and solitude" (378–79). Hilary realizes that he "lured Kitty to her doom" (380) and even failed his former schoolmaster, Mr. Osmond, the one person from his childhood he cared about. Mr. Osmond had in desperation sought out Hilary, but Hilary had not reached out to him either. In his obsession with one bad and selfish attachment, Hilary has ignored all the opportunities for selfless attachment. As he looks at a memorial tablet for T. S. Eliot, Hilary stops hiding in words and grammar and turns to poetry, quoting the lines from "Burnt Norton": "If all time is eternally present all time is unredeemable" (384). Hilary in his fixation on Anne made that one event into an "eternal present." By hiding in an eternal present, Hilary cannot redeem the past; he in fact can only repeat it. As Conradi puts it, Hilary has "refused any healing surrender to history."[43]

The only way to redeem the past is to face it, to come to the center of the labyrinth and grapple with the Minotaur of self-love, to struggle with ego, to ask forgiveness, and to reach out to others in unselfish attachment. Earlier, Arthur tried to get Hilary to face his past by going to Gunnar to ask forgiveness. Arthur tells Hilary: "you mustn't have muddles and secrets, and—and excitement—you must only have faithful sort of—good will and—truthfulness. . . but you're just running away from it into a sort of complicated—" (290), but Hilary cuts him off and indeed does run away into complicated and disastrous meetings with Kitty Jopling. And when Crystal[44] urges Hilary to forgive Gunnar, saying, "If you forgive him then there'll be—a kind of open space—and he'll be able—" (306), Hilary stops listening to Crystal and thinks of an absurd LSD trip that he had been tricked into the previous night when he thought he had "the secret of the universe. Forgiving equals being forgiven. Now in sober daylight it seemed just a piece of verbal nonsense" (306–7). Finally, as he sits in St. Stephen's, Hilary begins to face his past and realizes all that he needs to be forgiven for. The novel ends ambiguously on Christmas Day: Hilary, divested of his routine, leaves Crystal and Arthur's wedding with Tommy. Earlier, Tommy promised that she would give him "forgiveness" for Christmas, and she begs Hilary's forgiveness for writing to Gunnar Jopling to tell him that Hilary was seeing Kitty. She then says that she plans to marry him. Although Hilary does not answer, there is the possibility that he can get through his maze by seeking forgiveness and real love, not the fantasies of Anne and Kitty or his egotistical domination of Crystal, but perhaps in the real attachment of a human relationship, Hilary can find forgiveness.[45] Tommy is Hilary's Ariadne and has offered him a thread of hope. Whether he faces his Minotaur, uses the thread, and goes to Ariadne or whether he abandons her remains unanswered, but Murdoch illustrates how her labyrinth can be a positive image of relationship like Gilligan's nets and webs, if only one can avoid egotistical love and achieve selfless attachment.

Nuns and Soldiers

Nuns and Soldiers (1980) is not as pessimistic as *A Word Child* or the other novels of the 1970s dominated by male narrators. In *Nuns and Soldiers* there are in fact two ways through the labyrinth: a way like the one that Tommy offers Hilary, through ordinary but unselfish human love, and another way, through a higher unselfish love of God. The muddle and jumble of relationships still occur, but in this novel they are transcended. The successful negotiation of the labyrinth is tied to the fact that although the narration is omniscient, several of the major characters are female and Murdoch spends more time in the female mind than in any other novel. It is also the first time since *An Unofficial Rose* (1962) that a major female character, Anne Cavidge, the nun, has been a seeker of the good.[46] As Deborah Johnson writes, "*Nuns and Soldiers* . . . gives female characters a new freedom of thought and action."[47] It is also in this novel that a female character, Anne Cavidge, picks up the image of the city as labyrinth and compares relationships to it. Anne wonders whether Peter, the Count, whom she loves, would marry Gertrude: "Perhaps Gertrude would simply not want Peter after all. Perhaps she would marry Manfred . . . or somebody quite else. . . . All these thoughts were so familiar to Anne from sleepless nights that they were before her like a physical place, a labyrinth with paths, a city with streets."[48] The city with its streets is a labyrinth with paths, and it is a place where tangled relationships take place.

Although the familiar image occurs, London is not as strongly evoked in this novel as it is in *A Word Child*. *Nuns and Soldiers*, like *The Nice and the Good*, is divided in setting between London and a vividly rendered natural setting, in this case a rural district in Southern France where Gertrude Openshaw has a house. It is in this almost mystically rendered setting of great rocks and pools and fields and canals that Gertrude, a widow, falls in love with Tim and where he experiences a near drowning that allows him to resolve his muddled love relationships and reconcile with Gertrude. Nonetheless, Gertrude says, "our reality lies there, Tim, over in London" (210). Thus even if London does not contain the most memorable scenes of the novel, it is the real world where relationships must survive if they are going to. Furthermore, the London of *Nuns and Soldiers,* even if still a labyrinth and even if less vividly portrayed, has a charm that it lacks in other novels. The weather is benign both in winter and summer. There are no murky depths. A few characters ride the subways, but neither the rides nor the stations are described. In place of the subways as impersonal convergings of people are the pubs as jovial gathering places like those in Lessing's *If the Old Could* . . . . The landmarks mentioned are mainly those associated with art or nature: the British Museum, the National Gallery, Hyde Park, and Kensington Gardens. There are no ominous, dominating towers, and the characters take nature within the city for granted. Mystical experiences occur in the parks, but the parks are observed as ordinary parts of the city. Varied districts are portrayed, but these are districts without squalor that contain gathering places like houses or pubs. There is, however, one parallel with *A Word Child*: it is the ordinary man, Tim Reede, who is most associated with the city. Tim is not a monster of selfishness like many of the male narrators, but he does have lessons to learn about the nature of a labyrinth. Anne Cavidge, one of the seekers of the good, walks through the city and understands the nature of the labyrinth, but she notices less about the details of the city than Tim.

The weather in Murdoch's novels often reflects something about the narrator or main events of the novels: for instance, the cold dampness in *A Word Child* reflects Hilary's character; the sulfurous heat reflects the demonic in *The Nice and the Good* and *A Fairly Honourable Defeat*; the rain and flooding, Bruno's death in *Bruno's Dream*. In *Nuns and Soldiers,* even though the opening London scenes focus on Guy Openshaw's dying, neither the winter nor the summer is oppressive. Unlike in many of the other novels, the action takes place over a whole year, from November to November, and all the seasons are represented. Even in the opening scenes of winter, whenever snow or fog are mentioned, they are paired with light that glitters or sparkles or has a shining iridescent quality: "Ebury

Street, quiet now, glittered in the lamplight. The recent snow had covered the foot-prints on the pavement" (45). Even when the snow begins to melt, the luster remains: "Outside the sun was shining on the melting snow, smoothing it over, yellowing it and making it glow and sparkle. . . . A strange mystical light pervaded London" (48). Nor does rain change the quality of the light: "It was raining outside, and a cold east wind was making the rain run rippling across the streets of north Soho, which glittered like rivers under the street lamps" (72). Summer in *Nuns and Soldiers* has none of the glare that it does in other Murdoch novels: "There was a pale dawn light over Ebury Street, descending from above over the dim street lamps like a pearly mist. Soon it would be June and midsummer" (264).

The varied London districts are also benign and pleasant. The Openshaws' house in Ebury Street, elegantly and comfortably furnished, serves as a gathering place for the Openshaw clan both before and after Guy's death; the "solitary" Count and Anne Cavidge are drawn into the Openshaw group. In contrast to this wealth and comfort are Tim's studio, "a sort of loft, over a garage just off the Chiswick High Road" and his mistress Daisy's "one-room-with-kitchenette place in the dusty confines of Hammersmith and Shepherd's Bush" (83). Tim and Daisy do not spend much time in their cheap flats, however; they mainly frequent the pubs, especially one called "The Prince of Denmark" near Fitzroy Square. Despite poverty, which Tim and Daisy as artists consciously embrace, there is a gathering and connection. Even if the people in "The Prince of Denmark" sometimes misjudge and malign others, this pub is nonetheless a place of food and warmth and human connection:

> Tim and Daisy loved all pubs the way some people love all dogs. The pubs were innocent places wherein they were innocent children. They returned to the Soho pubs which had been their original home, where they had spent every evening . . . when they were young. This sort of urban life suited Tim, pub-crawling, wandering, looking in shop windows. He loved the charm of noisy

Ebury Street, the setting for the Openshaw house in *Nuns and Soldiers*. Virginia Woolf also uses it.

messy changing London, pedestrian bridges and roads on stilts,
the magic of Westway, of modern pubs beside noisy roundabouts.
Soho in summer was his South of France. (83)

The unambitious, unaggressive Tim loves and celebrates
"noisy messy changing London" for its vitality and variety.
When Tim falls in love with Gertrude, he introduces her to
the charm of London. Then, after they return from the real
South of France, they live together secretly for a while, enjoying the city:

> they vanished into London every day. They had a festival lunch
> and a festival dinner. . . . They went to museums and art galler-
> ies. . . . Tim took her to funny out-of-the-way pubs. They ex-
> plored obscure seedy places along the river. (258)
>
> . . . .
>
> There remained the vast pleasure-palace of London and fitfully,
> wandering there together like people on a holiday, they had felt
> happy. (270)

Even when their love runs into problems and they part, the
city and chance return them to one another: "they both kept
returning compulsively to places where they had been together. . . . Once they visited the same pub in Chiswick on
the same day but at different times. . . . They met finally in
the British Museum, when Tim found Gertrude one morning
sitting on a seat near the Rosetta Stone" (277). Even more
than in *Bruno's Dream*, London in *Nuns and Soldiers* is a
place of cakes and ale and love.

However, even in this London there are twists and turnings
in the labyrinth and potential for confusion in relationships.
Tim never told Gertrude about Daisy. Someone from the
Prince of Denmark told an Openshaw relative about Daisy;
the story was then related to the Count, who consulted Anne,
and Anne went to meet her. The lighthearted holiday atmosphere of the pubs does bring people together, but these connections can result in jealousy and negative emotions as well
as positive ones. Also Tim was clearly at fault for not telling
Gertrude the truth and sticking rigorously to it as Guy Openshaw and Peter, who represent the good, both do. The joke
that Tim and Daisy once expressed in the pub of marrying

someone wealthy to support them now comes back to Gertrude to create a maze that neither Tim nor Gertrude knows how to negotiate. Tim cannot deny lying about Daisy, and Gertrude will not believe Tim has really left Daisy. When Gertrude throws him out, Tim in despair takes some money from Gertrude and his account and does go back to Daisy. When Gertrude communicates to him through Peter, Tim is too proud in his guilty remorse and despair to say the words of defense Gertrude offers to listen to. Miserable in his guilt and in the loss of Gertrude, Tim starts to walk through London. It is now the paths and edges of London and the parks that he haunts. He eventually stops going to the pleasant district pubs:

> During the day Tim walked, he walked down the Finchly Road, through Maida Vale along the Edgeware Road to Hyde Park, or else through St John's Wood to Regent's Park. Sometimes he went to Kilburn or to his old haunts in the Harrow Road. More often he made for central London, always on foot, and walked in the parks or as far as Whitehall and the Embankment. Walking was now his task. (It was Anne Cavidge's task too, and they nearly met head-on once in St James's Park. . . .) (371)

Immersed in the complex labyrinth of muddled relationships, Tim's task is now to walk the streets and paths that represent the labyrinth of the city. Depressed, Tim walks through the labyrinth of the city streets, thinking about the labyrinth of relationships. Unlike Hilary Burde, he does not walk ritualistically to seek oblivion. Tim wanders, lost in a maze, reproducing his own emotional state in his actions.

Finally Tim decides to leave Daisy. He is nostalgic about the relationship, saying to her that it "felt like innocence" as they roamed the pubs and wandered together. Daisy, more realistically, replies: "We've remained children, we've retarded each other" (382). They both recognize that it is a kind of death to sever their relationship, but Daisy praises Tim for having the pluck to end the attachment which has become negative for them both. After ending that relationship Tim continues to walk through London and sit on the park benches. There he twice has a mystical experience. Sitting in the park, he focuses on the London summer and finally escapes the prison of self:

> The weather was golden, London was dazzlingly beautiful. The huge long-armed plane trees were dreaming of autumn. . . . Leaves sailed slowly down and laid themselves quietly at Tim's feet. He felt as if he were being transmitted into some other spiritual state. . . . Everything seemed to vanish including his own personality. . . . He was an atom, an electron, a proton, a point in empty space. He was transparent. It was this transparency which made him feel invisible. (385–86)

The second time, he is meditating on the death of his relationship with Daisy and feels he needs open space. He takes a taxi to Hyde Park and walks across the grass: "He could see in the distance the line of the lake and the Serpentine bridge. Then suddenly his knees gave way, he knelt down and lay prone on the grass. Like an orgasm, like a birth, something wrenched his body. . . . A warm wave had broken over him and now flowed on and on. A wave of pure thoughtless happiness which made him . . . moan with joy" (388). In contemplating death, even if just of a relationship, Tim is forced to get out of himself.

Before Guy's death, Tim had learned a Greek word from him, *lanthano,* "I escape notice," and Tim decided to take it as his motto. Now Tim goes a step further to experience "invisibility" and a momentary joy of egolessness. In *Henry and Cato,* Brendan Craddock, Murdoch's most articulate spokesman for the good, identifies invisibility as a quality of a saint when he speaks of his mother as "the sort of saint that no one ever notices or sees, she was almost invisible" (335). Tim experiences this invisibility only briefly, but it allows him to return to his art and his teaching and to decorate a church for a harvest festival, piling up autumn leaves and berries under a banner saying "Jesus pardons, Jesus saves." Tim at this point has not completely subdued his Minotaur of self-centeredness and self-pity; his "thoughts about Gertrude were darker and more agonizingly and tightly knotted" (402) than ever, and it will take his own near-death experience in the watery tunnel in France to enable him to go to her, but in achieving this sense of invisibility in the London parks, he learns how to face the Minotaur and to pick up Ariadne's thread. After his reconciliation with Gertrude and their return to London, Tim resumes his "solitary London walks" (474) because he deems them necessary perhaps to remind himself of the labyrinthine potential of reality and relationships and to keep himself from forgetting how to deal with them.

The other character who walks through the labyrinth of the city's paths and edges is Anne Cavidge. She is morally much further developed than Tim. She had sought out the seclusion of a nunnery to preserve her innocence: "The convent had been for her an indoor place, a hiding place: her little cell, the chapel, the dark corridors smelling of bread" (376), but as her sense of God changed, she felt "a *duty* . . . [to] move away to *some other place*" (60). Even after leaving the nunnery, she still wants to be alone, "with no plan and no vision, homeless and invisible, a wanderer, a no-one" (63) in order to figure out her experience of God and discover her mission. Later in London, however, she worries whether she has gained invisibility instead of innocence: "Was invisibility the gift she had been given by a discerning and just God, in lieu of the *great* gift which she had sought . . . Innocence" (141). At the outset of the novel, she does not quite recognize what this invisibility means, but others like Manfred Openshaw, who silently falls in love with her, see it and value it: "A nun's invisibility. I worshipped it" (487). Anne's "invisibility," however, does not protect her from the muddle of her own thoughts and the muddle of relationships in the world. When Gertrude goes to France, Anne goes alone to Cumbria to experience her first Easter outside the convent:

> The Abbess had warned her, and she had warned herself, of a black time to come, a dark night, a night of fruitlessness. . . . She had not conceived of a dry despair wherein, as with a trick of vision, odd and awful things flickered at her. . . . She returned to London sooner than she had intended. Here she walked the streets daily till she was thoughtless with weariness. (237)

This time Anne does not retreat to "the hiding place" of her enclosed convent, but goes out into the labyrinth of the city to face her thoughts.

It is in the city, in her two-room flat in Paddington, that Anne experiences her visitation from Christ. She still wants "to be made good . . . to be made innocent" (293), but her tall, thin, blond visitor dressed in plimsolls and an open shirt says gently to her: "You must be the miracle-worker, little one. You must be the proof. The work is yours" (293). When she asks "to be washed whiter than snow," he tells her to wash at the sink. She scrubs for some time before she grasps his meaning that he will not make her innocent, that she is the one who must work the miracles in the world. Neither will he let her romanticize suffering;[49] in fact, his hands have no wounds. He explains that "pain is a scandal and a task, but it is a shadow that passes! Death is a teaching. Indeed it is one of my names" (291). Tim progressed morally in facing the death of a relationship and his own near-death; Anne approaches death first in her conversation with Guy Openshaw and now theologically in her discussion with Christ. Murdoch explains in *The Sovereignty of Good* that "acceptance of death is an acceptance of our own nothingness which is an automatic spur to our concern with what is not ourselves" (103). Anne is given her spur in this conversation. As Christ leaves, Anne reaches out to touch him and receives a burn on her finger that does not heal for a long time after the experience. It is no mere vision or dream.

Anne still remains in her labyrinth, however, for even before the visitation occurred she discovered she was in love with Peter. She feels she is "back in the hell of the personal, the very place I ran away from to God" (302). At this point for Anne personal love and spiritual love are muddled together:

She had wondered earlier whether belief in God would ever return, sweep over her one day like a great warm wet cloud. . . . Yet her earlier morning visitor, was he not something? . . . And it came to her that he was real. (304)

No sooner does she acknowledge the reality of her visitation, than she realizes again that she loves "not Christ but Peter" (304). She goes out again to walk through the city to sort out her thoughts. Intellectually Anne understands, but emotionally she is caught in the maze. Her task now, like Tim's, is to go out and walk through London. Anne, at the border of doubt and uncertainty, walks especially along the edges of the city: "She walked so much now, especially at night, especially along the river" (304). Anne, unlike Hilary, is tolerant of edges and ambiguity, and the edges hold no dangers for her. When Peter, who is in love with Gertrude, comes to Anne in despair because Gertrude is marrying Tim, Anne talks him out of suicide. Although Anne is disciplined enough never to tell her love, she does follow Peter through the city: "She was literally following him now along the Chelsea Embankment. . . . There had been a little rain and then a little sunshine. It was Sunday and London was full of church bells. . . . She felt as she walked this silent watchful walking a kind of happiness that was like her best days in the convent" (441).

When Gertrude is reconciled with Tim, Anne thinks she might have a chance for ordinary happiness with Peter, but then Gertrude, worrying about Peter's loneliness, draws him in to the circle of her new marriage, promising to be his friend. When Anne comes to Ebury Street, she sees a laughing, calm, and joyful Peter, and she realizes that "Gertrude has made a love-treaty with the Count. He was not to be miserable or to go away. He was to stay forever as her courtier, within the light of her countenance. Tim would not mind. It was, for Gertrude, easy" (460). Anne's renunciation is made for her. The next day at lunch she tells Gertrude that she will go to Chicago to join the Poor Clares as a camp follower. She will remain in the new city and not go "back inside," but she explains to Gertrude that she must leave because "I am given to religious life . . . and I have got to be alone" (470). Murdoch's characters, Dipple emphasizes, can have either happiness or the good, but not both.[50] Murdoch explains why in *The Sovereignty of Good* when she says that "human love is normally too profoundly possessive and also too 'mechanical' to be a place of vision. There is a paradox here about the nature of love itself. That the highest love is in some sense impersonal is something which we . . . cannot see clearly, except in a very piecemeal manner, in the relationships of human beings" (75). Anne's aloneness, however, is not the same as Hilary's selfish solitude, the kind of separation from other people and denial of connection that Jessica Benjamin and others have said is typical of male forms of individuality.[51] Anne's journey toward the good includes unselfish love, and it will include serving other people when she works for the Poor Clares. In her renunciation Anne is seeking egolessness. She still values intimacy, but she is seeking intimacy with whatever form of God she can believe in. She still clings to the doctrine that "only God can be perfectly loved. Human love, however, behovable, is hopelessly imperfect. . . . Happiness sought anywhere but in God tends to corruption. . . . she had been irrevocably spoilt for the world by God. . . . Anne felt now that she . . . could pray . . . in her utmost need, calling upon the name of the nonexistent God" (499).

Anne spends her last evenings in London at the pub, the Prince of Denmark, looking for Daisy, whom she felt she had judged too quickly. Anne feels a new sympathy for the outspoken feminist Daisy, who is also now a wanderer on her own, but Daisy's feminism and morality are shallow. In art school Daisy was friendly "with a group of vociferous American Women's Liberationists" (77–78), and she defends women to Tim. Her only real action occurs every night at the Prince of Denmark, and it even brings people from other nearby pubs to hear her. When the bartender announces, "Time gentlemen," Daisy bangs her glass on the table, saying, "There are ladies present!" Finally Anne overhears that Daisy has left for America. "She's another wanderer," Anne concludes, "And so she was seeking innocence. It was a quest suited to human powers" (503). The profane Daisy is far behind Anne and may never achieve innocence, but she too is starting out where Anne began. Anne feels a kinship with her because Anne too wondered about her own role as a woman in the church: "Would the priesthood have lifted her above some level where she felt at times that it did not matter what she thought or did because she was a woman?" (107). She had agreed with Gertrude earlier that women should be priests if they wanted to (50), but when Guy Openshaw seems as if he wants to confess to her, she cuts him off in panic, thinking, "I am not a priest. With me it would be muddled and personal. I have no role here . . . no authority to touch his soul" (69–70). Anne nonetheless learns through her experiences in the city of London to deal with the muddle and the personal. Gertrude thanks her for taking care of Peter: "He says you held his hand like a priest" (463). Anne denies that she ever took his hand and recognizes that it was out of a very personal muddled love that she helped him. It was undeniable, however, that she had helped him and not avoided him. She thinks: "in an odd way . . . if Daisy ever terribly needed her they would perhaps meet again" (504). As she walks out of the Prince of Denmark into the snowy streets, Anne has a transcendent vision in the dark London sky:

> It was still snowing and the roads and pavements were dark with running water and brown slush. . . . The snow, illuminated by the street lamps, was falling abundantly, against the further background of the enclosing dark. . . . It looked like the heavens spread out in glory, totally unrolled before the face of God, countless, limitless, eternally beautiful, the universe in majesty proclaiming the presence and the goodness of its Creator.
>
> Anne stood there for a while. Then she began to walk through the snowy streets at random, feeling lightened of her burdens. (505)

It is in the city, as the lamplight shines through the falling snow, that Anne has her final vision of the goodness of the universe and of the Creator. Both she and Tim continue to walk the streets of the labyrinth that is the city, but both of them have grappled with their Minotaurs and know that the threads of "invisibility" and "egolessness" will lead them through the maze. For Anne, the dangerous multicursal labyrinth has evolved into the unicursal labyrinth of the church floor that leads one to a spot symbolic of Jerusalem.[52] Anne has followed her labyrinth to a vision of God in the city.

Gertrude remains secure in her network of intimate love and intimate friendships. She has married, like her namesake, "with mirth in funeral and dirge in marriage" (279), but her mental quotation of these words is not ironic like Claudius's original pronouncement in *Hamlet*. She felt genuine love for Guy and mourns him, but she also feels real love for Tim, even if he is not as "good" a man as Guy. Gertrude does not go out into the city or see the image of the labyrinth. She experiences "muddle," as all who live in the world do, but her solutions are the simple female solutions of human attachment.

Murdoch in this novel portrays two female characters who search out two different ways of existence: Gertrude's way of human love and attachment and Anne's striving for the greater good of an intimacy with an unknown God. T. S. Eliot is not quoted directly here as he is in *A Word Child* or referred to as he is in Murdoch's article, "T. S. Eliot as a Moralist,"[53] but the two ways echo Eliot's *The Cocktail Party,* where Sir Henry Harcourt-Reilly, the psychiatrist and Christ Figure, explains two ways of salvation. Harcourt-Reilly first offers Celia the ordinary choice, which the other couple in the play, like Gertrude and Tim, have taken:

> I can reconcile you to the human condition,
> The condition to which some who have gone as far as
> you
> Have succeeded in returning. They may remember
> The vision they have had, but they cease to regret it,
> Maintain themselves by the common routine,
> Learn to avoid excessive expectation,
> Become tolerant of themselves and others,
> Giving and taking, in the usual actions
> What there is to give and take. They do not repine;
> Are contented with the morning that separates
> And with the evening that brings together
> For casual talk before the fire
> Two people who know they do not understand each
> other,
>
> . . . .

Celia: Is that the best life?

> Reilly: It is a good life. Though you will not know how good
> Till you come to the end. . . . .
> The second is unknown, and so requires faith—
> The kind of faith that issues from despair.
> The destination cannot be described;
> You will know very little until you get there.[54]

Like Anne, Celia chooses the second way, although for Celia it is martyrdom in Africa. Just before the last cocktail party, Reilly explains her choice to the others in terms of the labyrinth image:

> But such experience can only be hinted at
> In myths and images. To speak about it
> We talk of darkness, labyrinths, Minotaur terrors.
> But that world does not take the place of this one.[55]

Murdoch differs from Eliot, however, in seeing the labyrinth with all its moral complexities and dangers not only in "that world," the realm Anne and Celia choose, but also in the real world of the city and in the everyday moral realm of human relationships. The trip through the labyrinth is possible for men and for women, but the Minotaur of self-centeredness must be killed, and Ariadne's (and Gilligan's) thread of the female virtues of intimacy and attachment, whether to human beings or to God, must be picked up. Then the labyrinth of the city becomes a benign place, not dominated by towering landmarks, but reflecting the "universe in majesty" in the lamplight and falling snow.

Murdoch's next three novels of the eighties are not set primarily in London. The setting of *The Philosopher's Pupil* (1983) is "Ennistone," which Murdoch describes as a town in south England not far from London. *The Good Apprentice* (1985) has some London scenes, but the primary setting is "Seegard," a country estate. *The Book and the Brotherhood* (1987) opens with a scene in Oxford, and important sections occur at "Boyars," a country estate. There are a few London scenes in characters' houses in Notting Hill and Shepherd's

Bush, but not the detailed description of the city found in *Nuns and Soldiers*. The plots and the characters' relationships are still "labyrinthine" in these three novels, but it may be the nineties before Murdoch returns to the labyrinth of the city and the positive ending of *Nuns and Soldiers*.

CHAPTER 5

The City as Mosaic:
P. D. James

A strong sub-genre of urban fiction is the detective novel. Throughout the twentieth century, women writers have infiltrated this seemingly "masculine" genre. Among contemporary writers, P. D. James, in particular, presents a complex portrait of the city as a mosaic in her detective stories and her novel *Innocent Blood*. The city in these works is an intricate picture built up out of many small pieces. But the mosaic is not only an image of the city in these works; it is also the method of a detective or mystery novel. From the point of view of the detective, it is not just a question of putting together pieces of a puzzle, because the picture has not yet been created. The detective must create it by fitting together the small pieces available. The pieces which P. D. James' detectives must use to create their picture of the city are London's "villages,"[1] all the districts of London that must be connected together to form a coherent whole.

The concept of London as a collection of villages echoes throughout P. D. James' works. In *Unnatural Causes* (1967), the male detective Adam Dalgleish refers to the district of Soho as "a cosmopolitan village tucked away behind Piccadilly with its own mysterious village life."[2] In *Skull Beneath the Skin* (1982), a character who is a drama critic explains: "No one has all the London gossip. London, as you very well know, is a collection of villages, socially, occupationally, as well as geographically."[3] In *Innocent Blood* (1980) Norman Scase, who is tracking the heroine, thinks of London as a place, "which asked no questions, kept its secrets, provided in its hundred urban villages the varied needs of ten million people."[4] In her most recent work, *A Taste for Death* (1986), it is a female detective, Kate Miskin, who sees the mosaic of city, the linking of all the villages into an overall pattern. As she looks from the balcony of her Lansdowne Road flat, she thinks to herself:

> The world stretched out below her was one she was at home in, part of that dense, exciting conglomerate of urban villages which made up the Metropolitan Police district. She pictured it stretching away over Notting Hill Gate, over Hyde Park and the curve of the river, past the towers of Westminster and Big Ben.

Kate Miskin not only sees the individual villages and landmarks, she also sees the pattern that links them:

> This was how she saw the capital, patterned in police areas, districts, divisions and sub-divisions. And immediately below her lay Notting Hill, that tough, diverse, richly cosmopolitan village.[5]

The image of the connectedness of the urban villages belongs to P. D. James' female characters, and it reflects their ability to connect to other people. Kate Miskin, unlike the traditional detective, is willing to get involved with others, and it is she who has the vision of London as a pattern, a mosaic. This is an image of London which Philippa Palfrey in *Innocent Blood* learns to see when she learns to connect with other people. Furthermore, it is the female characters, Kate Miskin, Philippa Palfrey and Cordelia Gray, another untraditional detective, who recognize the beauty of the city and celebrate it. There is nonetheless a hint in *A Taste for Death* that Adam Dalgleish, in the earlier works a typical uninvolved male detective, may start to see the beauty of the city as he gets to know Cordelia Gray.

The Tradition of the Detective Novel

The urban mystery or detective story began to appear in England in the late nineteenth century. Raymond Williams notes that it emerged as a "predominant image of the darkness and poverty of the city . . . became quite central in literature and social thought."[6] If the image of the city is that of darkness, then the urban hero becomes the one who can penetrate that darkness and make sense of the city. Williams explains:

> the urban detective, prefigured in a minor way in Dickens and Wilkie Collins, now begins to emerge as a significant and ratifying figure: the man who can find his way through the fog, who can penetrate the intricacies of the streets. The opaque complexity of modern city life is represented by crime; the explorer of society is reduced to the discoverer of single causes. . . . [Sherlock Holmes' London is] : the fog, the gaslight, the hansom cabs, the street urchins, and through them all, this eccentric sharp mind, this almost disembodied but locally furnished intelligence, which can unravel complexity, . . . the clear abstract system beyond all the bustle and fog.[7]

The tradition of the detective novel clearly deals with the questions and darkness of the city, but from Williams' description, it seems to do so in a particularly masculine way: the rational abstract intelligence, elevated and separated from others, which isolates and differentiates until it identifies a single cause.

Feminist critic Carolyn Heilbrun, however, finds that the British tradition of detective novels is not as strictly masculine as it first appears. She points out that British detective novels contain autonomous and well-developed female characters and sympathetic male characters. Even if Sherlock Holmes is the "quintessential male" in his excessive ratiocination, his female clients and antagonists are strong and resourceful women. Heilbrun also sees a clear difference between the violent, gory "tough-guy" tradition with limited roles for women that evolved in American detective novels and the British tradition of "effete," "charming," and "tender" male detectives: "Manliness . . . was left for the Watsons in the outfit. The British in their detective fiction from Holmes on, were the first, and perhaps the last, to equate manliness with stupidity."[8] Although ratiocination remains a prominent trait in British male detective heroes, the macho quality admired in American fiction does not appear. Heilbrun links the tradition of sympathetic male detective heroes to the success of many of the women writers who took over the British detective story in the 1920s and 1930s; furthermore Heilbrun notes a "special phenomenon" in these British women mystery writers. They start out with a charming, gentlemanly male detective, but then they bring in a woman character who begins to take over whole books: Sayers' Harriet Vane, Marsh's Agatha Troy, and Christie's Miss Marple.

Heilbrun hails P. D. James as the inheritor of this tradition.[9] After creating a successful male police detective in Adam Dalgleish, James wrote *An Unsuitable Job for a Woman* (1972) and created private detective Cordelia Gray,[10] to whom she returned in *Skull Beneath the Skin* (1982). In *A Taste for Death* Cordelia Gray appears briefly, and the female police officer Kate Miskin is introduced. In 1980, Heilbrun praised James as the best detective novelist of the tradition of Sayers and Tey in the past two decades: "The best of P. D. James' detective novels raise the genre to new heights. . . . [They] preserve all the glories of the earlier detective fiction while adding a modernity of detail and setting, and a concern with contemporary problems that does more than resurrect a past genre: it both recreates and strengthens it."[11] Furthermore, P. D. James' works portray a city as not just a place of darkness. The dark alleys and corners are there, especially in the early Adam Dalgleish novels, but Cordelia Gray and Kate Miskin see light and change in the city as well as darkness.

P. D. James' portrayal of contemporary problems reveals a woman's viewpoint, particularly in the Cordelia Gray and Kate Miskin novels and in *Innocent Blood*. Although P. D. James creates the traditional uninvolved, rational male detective in Adam Dalgleish, she creates female detectives in Cordelia Gray and Kate Miskin who are not only autonomous and strong, but also exhibit some of the qualities of involvement with and concern for other people that the psychologists Carol Gilligan and Jessica Benjamin particularly associate with women.[12] P. D. James too identifies these qualities as female. In a 1977 interview James said: "I believe . . . that women are as intelligent as men and in many ways as able, but women have got other qualities as well. These are qualities of sympathy and of understanding (an instinctive wish to look after people who are weaker than themselves) and of less aggression. This is what the world *wants!*"[13] SueEllen Campbell even thinks that the women characters cause a "generic shift" in these detective novels which, like Sayers' *Gaudy Night,* have a "thematic richness" that is "at least partly a response to the presence of a heroine . . . for whom there is no established formula."[14] This shift created by the focus on female characters and female concerns becomes even more pronounced in P. D. James' *Innocent Blood,* with its young, developing heroine.

The Early Detective Novels: Adam Dalgleish and Cordelia Gray

P. D. James' awareness of the differences in qualities associated with men and women is evident in her portrayal of her male and female detectives. Adam Dalgleish is a typical British male detective: although he is a published poet, he is still analytical and non-involved whether he is observing the streets or interrogating people. Yet even in an early novel, *A Mind to Murder* (1963), he feels guilty about this detachment:

> His job, in which he could deceive himself that non-involvement was a duty, had given him glimpses into the secret lives of men and women whom he might never see again except as half-recognized faces in a London crowd. Sometimes he despised his private image, the patient, uninvolved, uncensorious inquisitor of other people's misery and guilt. How long could you stay detached he wondered, before you lost your own soul?[15]

In *Unnatural Causes* one of the suspects sums up Dalgleish's professional detachment, saying, "Doesn't being a policeman protect your privacy? You have a professional excuse for remaining uninvolved. . . . I think you are a man who values his privacy" (117). Although this sense of privacy and uninvolved rationality places Dalgleish in the tradition of male detective heroes, P. D. James makes clear the cost of his non-involvement. All his personal relationships are sacrificed to this stance. In some period before the series began, he had a wife, but she and their baby died in childbirth. Another woman is in love with him, but at the end of *Unnatural Causes* she leaves to take a job in New York because she can "no longer bear to loiter about on the periphery of his life" (236). P. D. James said in a recent interview with Dale Salwak that she is conscious of these qualities in Adam Dalgleish. She did not want to create a character so perfect that he would be boring: "I do have to remind myself there are things about his character which I don't admire. He's so almost completely detached at times, even a little cold, and I wouldn't have thought easy to work for at all."[16] Only his writing poetry, like Holmes' playing the violin, shows his potential for sensitivity.

Cordelia Gray does not have to feel guilty about detachment because although she is strong and autonomous, she does allow herself to get involved. At the beginning of *An Unsuitable Job for a Woman,* her openness to involvement almost undermines her professionalism. Cordelia Gray is faced with keeping a detective agency open all by herself after the suicide of her partner, who had cancer. Her first case, the seeming suicide of Mark Callender, takes her to Cambridge, where she almost succumbs to the undergraduates' offer of camaraderie. She had not been to the university herself; her mother died at birth, and her father, a revolutionary, took her out of convent school at sixteen so she could join him on the continent. When the Cambridge undergraduates take her for a picnic and a ride in a punt, she is almost lulled into giving up her case and agreeing that Mark Callender's death is suicide. Cordelia Gray, however, is more independent and plucky than the undergraduates, and she perseveres, enduring threats and even an attempt on her life. Finally, she does get involved after she has solved the mystery of Mark's death. When Miss Leaming, Ronald Callender's secretary, kills him upon learning that he grotesquely murdered their son, Cordelia protects the woman, not really for her own sake, but because Miss Leaming is Mark's mother and Cordelia grew to respect Mark during her investigation. She also hated Ronald Callender for desecrating Mark's body and setting Mark up as an object of contempt. Cordelia carefully helps Miss Leaming to make it look as if Sir Ronald committed suicide. She manages to stick to her story even under Adam Dalgleish's questioning, although she knows he suspects the truth. In spite of the supposed detachment required of a detective, Cordelia is not afraid of sympathy for and involvement with people. She was genuinely fond of her partner, Bernie Pryde, and at the end of her questioning by Dalgleish, she bursts into tears, partly of relief, but mostly for Bernie, whom Adam had fired even though Bernie idealized him. She lashes out at Adam, "after you'd sacked him, you never enquired how he got on. You didn't even come to the funeral."[17]

In both *An Unsuitable Job for a Woman* and *Skull Beneath the Skin*, it is Cordelia, with her acceptance of involvement and connection, who walks around London. Even though both novels in which she appears are set primarily outside London, they both open with Cordelia walking down Kingly Street, just past Oxford Circus, to her office. She has kept Pryde's detective agency solvent by taking cases searching for lost cats and dogs. She has even trained her inefficient elderly secretary, Miss Maudsley, to help look for cats: Miss Maudsley "managed to conquer her timidity when in pursuit of cat thieves and on Saturday mornings walked purposely through the rowdy exuberance and half-submerged terrors of London's street markets as if under divine protection, which no doubt she felt herself to be" (*Skull* 6). Also in *Skull Beneath the Skin* she gets involved even at risk of her own life by trying to save the young murderer, who is terrified into trying to drown himself. In response to the monstrous selfishness of the real villain, Ambrose Gorringe, Cordelia cries in anger, "You killed him [the young murderer], and you tried to kill me. . . . Not even in self-defense. Not even out of hatred. My life counted for less than your comfort, your possessions" (*Skull* 324). After dealing with Ambrose, Cordelia finds it reassuring to get a call from Miss Maudsley, who urges her home to find a Siamese cat because it belongs to a girl who is just out of the hospital after a leukemia treatment. The city has room for detectives with compassion.

In P. D. James' early detective novels, her male detective, Adam Dalgleish, does not see the city as a positive place where missing cats can be found. When Dalgleish walks through Soho in *Unnatural Causes,* he correctly identifies it as a village, but it fills him with disgust:

> It was difficult to believe that he had once enjoyed walking through this shoddy gulch. . . . It was largely a matter of mood, no doubt, for the district is all things to all men, catering comprehensively for those needs which money can buy. You see it as you wish. An agreeable place to dine; a cosmopolitan village tucked away behind Piccadilly with its own mysterious village life, one of the best shopping centres for food in London, the nastiest and most sordid nursery of crime in Europe. . . . Passing the strip clubs, the grubby basement stairs, the silhouettes of bored girls against the upstairs window blinds, Dalgleish thought that a daily walk through these ugly streets could drive any man into a monastery. (154)

Some of the same aspects of the city are portrayed in *Innocent Blood.* The city is seen as reflecting an observer's mood. Although a district is vividly portrayed as a "village" within the city, here, from a male point of view, it is a grim district with no redeeming qualities. The same disgust is present in *Shroud for a Nightingale* (1971), when the male Sergeant Masterson goes into London to interview an informant and ends up at a macabre dance contest at the Athenaeum Hall. The urban districts are there, but are not yet seen as part of the glittering tiles of a mosaic.

The same difference is evident in male and female observation of architectural change and renovation. Bernard Benstock, writing primarily about the Dalgleish novels, notes that almost "every important building that serves as the central stage of her tragic dramas has been converted from something else, and each is either in the process or in potential danger of being reconverted or abandoned or torn down in turn."[18]

This awareness of architectural change is especially vivid in the city where the male observers, as in Dickens, are disgusted by the change, but the female observers, as in Lessing, can delight in it (see Ch. 2, pp. 34–36). In *Unnatural Causes,* Adam Dalgleish goes to London to search for a suspect and walks through a mews which has just been renovated:

> The cobbled entrance was uninviting, ill-lit and smelt strongly of urine. Dalgleish . . . passed under the archway into a wide yard lit only by a solitary and unshaded bulb over one of a double row of garages. The premises had apparently once been the headquarters of a driving school. . . . But they were dedicated now to a nobler purpose, the improvement of London's chronic housing shortage. More accurately, they were being converted into dark, under-sized and over-priced cottages soon, no doubt, to be advertized as "bijou town residences" to tenants or owners prepared to tolerate any expense or inconvenience for the status of a London address and the taste for contemporary chi-chi. (170)

The darkness of the houses and the snob appeal of the district recall Dickens' description of the Barnacle house in *Little Dorrit,* an ill-smelling, cramped house located on the fringes of a fashionable neighborhood:

> Mews Street, Grosvenor Square, was not absolutely Grosvenor Square itself, but it was very near it. It was a hideous little street of dead wall, stables, and dunghills, with lofts over coachhouses inhabited by coachmen's families, who had a passion for drying clothes and decorating their window-sills with miniature turnpikegates. . . . Yet there were two or three small airless houses at the entrance end of Mews Street, which went at enormous rents on account of their being abject hangers-on to a fashionable situation.[19]

In *Shroud for a Nightingale,* the renovations Dalgleish encounters in North Kensington are less chic and even grimmer than those in *Unnatural Causes:*

> Number 49 Millington Square,W.10, was a large dilapidated Italianate house fronted with crumbling stucco. There was nothing remarkable about it. It was typical of hundreds in this part of London. It was obviously divided into bed-sitting rooms since

every window showed a different set of curtains, or none, and it exuded that curious atmosphere of secretive and lonely over-occupation which hung over the whole district. (218)

In *Skull Beneath the Skin,* however, the renovation of Cordelia Gray's flat off Thames Street is seen in a positive light:

as she moved from the single large sitting room to her bedroom she could see spread below her the glittering streets, the dark alleyways, the towers and steeples of the city, could glimpse beyond them the necklace of light slung along the Embankment and the smooth, light-dazzled curve of the river. The view, in daylight or after dark, was a continual marvel to her, the flat itself a source of astonished delight. . . . No building society had been interested in a sixth-floor apartment at the top of a Victorian warehouse with no lift and the barest amenities. . . . But her bank manager, apparently to his surprise as much as hers, had been sympathetic and had authorized a five-year loan. (47)

The buildings Adam Dalgleish sees throughout London have been thoughtlessly chopped up into small bedsitters or carelessly renovated with a false attempt at chic. Cordelia, who has done some of the renovation herself, is rewarded by a glorious view of London that sustains her after her sorties out into the countryside to solve murders. Although both detectives go into the city of London in the course of these early novels, it is Cordelia Gray who is portrayed as the lover of London.

Not only Cordelia but even one of the female murderers has a more positive view of the city than Adam Dalgleish. *A Mind to Murder* is set in London in a psychiatric clinic located in a Georgian Terrace house on an imaginary London square with a mews to the rear. Occasionally the story follows characters to their London residences, such as Nurse Bolam's flat in a narrow terraced house at 17 Rettinger Street N.W.1. The ground floor smells of "frying fat, furniture polish and stale urine," but in summer evenings she could "watch the sun setting behind a castellation of sloping roofs and twisting chimneys with, in the distance, the turrets of St. Pancras Station darkening against a flaming sky" (121–2). In P. D. James' early detective novels, it is only the women, whether they be detectives or murderers, who see the beauty of London.

A Taste for Death

In James' most recent detective novel, *A Taste for Death* (1986), which is set entirely in London, there is some hint that Dalgleish can change. A friend mentions that Dalgleish was seen dining with Cordelia Gray (203); perhaps he is beginning to learn from her. In *A Taste for Death*, the victim is for the first time someone Dalgleish knew, however briefly, Sir Paul Berowne, a government minister, and Dalgleish worries whether he is too involved. Dalgleish is less sure of himself in this novel. He is no longer writing poetry and is somewhat "disillusioned" with police work. He asks himself: "And if I tell myself that enough is enough, twenty years of using people's weakness against them, twenty years of careful non-involvement, if I resign, what then?" (296). This time, though, he recognizes that he is involved. After a difficult interview in which he tries to get information from the Special Branch, Dalgleish thinks:

> what depressed him most and left him with a sour taste of self-disgust, was how close he had come to losing his control. He realized how important it had become to him, his reputation for coolness, detachment, uninvolvement. Well, he was involved now. Perhaps they were right. You shouldn't take on a case if you knew the victim. But how could he claim to have known Berowne . . . a three-hour train journey, a brief ten-minute spell in his office, an interrupted walk in St James's Park? And yet he knew that he had never felt so great an empathy with any other victim. (313)

In spite of feeling empathy for Berowne, Dalgleish still remains a rational man. Upon hearing a priest suggest that he thought he saw the stigmata on Berowne's hands shortly before the minister was killed, Dalgleish is shocked and even feels "revulsion" towards "the bizarre intrusion of irrationality into a job so firmly rooted in the search for evidence . . . demonstrable, real" (55). When two assistants discuss Dalgleish, one says to the other, "AD likes life to be rational. Odd for a poet, but there it is" (285). Even if Dalgleish remains rational and is depressed by his involvement, he nonetheless has a vision of London in this novel similar to those experienced by female characters in P. D. James' other novels. While an Assistant Commissioner looks into a file, Dalgleish looks out over the city of London and contrasts Manhattan, whose "spectacular soaring beauty always seemed . . . precarious," with the gentler panorama of his own city:

> London, laid out beneath him under a low ceiling of silver-grey cloud, looked eternal, rooted, domestic. He saw the panorama, of which he never tired, in terms of painting. Sometimes it had the softness and immediacy of watercolour; sometimes, in high summer, when the park burgeoned with greenness, it had the rich texture of oil. This morning it was a steel engraving, hard-edged, grey, one-dimensional. (341)

Here Dalgleish actually stops to observe the city below him and draws an analogy between the variety of London and styles of painting.

P. D. James introduces a new female character, Police Inspector Kate Miskin, in *A Taste for Death*. Kate, an illegitimate child whose mother died in childbirth, was brought up by her grandmother in a "meanly proportioned, dirty, noisy flat . . . of a post-war tower block" (156) and attended a multi-racial state school, Ancroft Comprehensive. Kate has no nostalgia for her childhood. She is delighted with her new job and her flat in an old Victorian building near the corner of Lansdowne and Ladbroke Roads because it allows her to escape the past: "She had little feeling for the past; all her life had been a striving to struggle free of it" (155). When asked why she chose police work, Kate thinks to herself: "I thought I could do the job. I was ambitious. I prefer order and hierarchy to muddle" (326). Kate says she prefers order and hierarchy and freedom from the past, but she naturally involves herself with people, and during her first case, she comes to terms with her past. When she and Adam Dalgleish go to visit Berowne's mistress,

Carole Washburn, the male detective admires Kate's feminine ease with people:

> It was typical of her, thought Dalgleish, this unsentimental, practical response to people and their immediate concerns. Without hectoring or presumption, she could reduce the most embarrassing situation to something approaching normality. It was one of her strengths. Now, above the tinkle of kettle lid and crockery, he could hear their voices, conversational, almost ordinary. (258)

Listening to them, Dalgleish suddenly feels that they "would both get on better without his male, destructive presence" (258).

When Carole Washburn has some information to give the police, it is Kate she asks to see. She and Kate meet in Holland Park, and she tells Kate about a letter Berowne received from a girl who committed suicide. As Kate talks to Carole about Berowne's wife, Carole bursts into tears. Kate's first impulse is to invite Carole back to her flat for coffee. Kate at first checks herself, then submits to her own feelings of sympathy:

> suppose Carole were required to give evidence in court, then any suggestion of friendship, of an understanding between them could be prejudicial to the prosecution. And more than to the prosecution; it could be prejudicial to her own career. It was the kind of sentimental error of judgement which wouldn't exactly displease Massingham if he came to hear of it. And then she heard herself saying:
> "My flat is very close, just across the avenue. Come and have coffee before you go." (325–326)

Kate knows she should be careful not to be "sentimental" and become involved with people while investigating a case, but she does anyway. She met her lover, a theology librarian, when she went to investigate a stolen book. This time, when she sees how distraught Carole is, her sympathy for people and, as P. D. James says of women in general, her "instinctive wish to look after people who are weaker"[20] than she is, take precedence over her "better" judgment.

In this novel Kate also comes to terms with her past in the person of her aging grandmother. Kate doesn't want her grandmother to move in with her because she cherishes her freedom and is committed to her job. Nonetheless, when her grandmother is mugged, Kate takes her in and realizes that personal relationships are even more important than her job:

> Nothing is more important to me than my job. But I can't make the law the basis of my personal morality. There has to be something more if I'm to live at ease with myself. And it seemed to her that she had made a discovery about herself and about her job which was of immense importance, and she smiled that it should have happened while she was hesitating between two brands of tinned pears in a Notting Hill Gate supermarket. (424)

Kate Miskin comes to terms with her past, and it is not surprising that someone who can come to terms with her own past and who values involvement with other people above the law can, like Maureen Duffy's characters, see the past in the city and recognize that nature is part of the city. Like Dalgleish, Kate too can see the panorama of the city; from the balcony of her flat, she looks out over London past "the great limes [lindens] lining Holland Park Avenue" (156):

> To the south the trees of Holland Park were a black curdle against the sky, and ahead the spire of St John's church gleamed like some distant mirage. . . . Far below to her right under the high arc lights the avenue ran due west, greasy as a molten river, bearing its unending cargo of cars, trucks and red buses. This, she knew, had once been the old Roman road leading westward straight out of Londinium; its constant grinding roar came to her only faintly like the surge of a distant sea. (156)

Kate meets witnesses in Holland Park, and every night she looks out at the lime trees and the plane trees that line the great rivers of avenues. She learns to deal with her own past, and she can connect London and Londinium. She can see the mosaic of the city.

Innocent Blood

P. D. James' most vivid portrayal of London is not in one of her detective novels, although *A Taste for Death* comes close, but in *Innocent Blood* (1980). Several reviewers call *Innocent*

Blood a "straight" novel, but Nancy Joyner points out that it still includes many elements of the traditional mystery form: two violent deaths described in detail; two amateur detectives, Philippa Palfrey and Norman Scase; clues that lead up to a final revelation, and the London setting.[21] It is in this novel, as Philippa Palfrey tries to put together the pieces of her past to find her identity, that London and its many districts and neighborhoods are presented in great detail and that the image of London as mosaic emerges most strongly. It is particularly important because it is reflected in the novel's detective structure as well as its theme.

Philippa Palfrey is younger than the protagonists of Lessing's, Drabble's, and Murdoch's novels and her task is the establishment of identity and the development of the ability to love. Unlike most teenagers, who break with their past or at least strain against it to find their identity, she is an adopted child who must discover her past and connect with it. Philippa is like Cordelia Gray and Kate Miskin in being intelligent and independent, but unlike them she has not yet learned to be concerned for others. Although she has achieved for her adoptive parents, she has no real love for them nor does she think they really love her. Maurice Palfrey, and his second wife Hilda, had adopted Philippa after Maurice's first wife and son were killed in an automobile accident. Philippa has almost no memory of her first eight years before she was adopted. Her fantasy, aided by Hilda, has been that she is the daughter of a lord and his serving maid because she has a memory of the rose garden and the library of Pennington, a country manor house. Now she must let her fantasies evaporate and slowly, piece by piece, build up her real past. She does this by moving around London, where each district is like a small village or piece of mosaic tile that, put together, is the larger reality of London.

The city cannot create an identity for Philippa; like the small glittering tiles of a mosaic or the mirrors that Philippa and Norman Scase look into, the city can only reflect back what is before it. When Philippa goes out to find an apartment for herself and her natural mother, she sees the city as a mirror for the observer's mood:

> She came to know a different London and she saw it through different eyes. The city was all things to all men. It reflected and deepened mood; it did not create it. Here the miserable were more miserable, the lonely more bereft, while the prosperous and happy saw reflected in her river and glittering life the confirmation of their deserved success. (94)

Ultimately the city can only reflect, but that quality offers Philippa two things, a reminder of physical reality and the freedom of anonymity. When Philippa first discovers her parents' names, she takes the train from Liverpool Station out "through the urban sprawl of the eastern suburbs; rows of drab houses with blackened bricks and patched roofs" (15). The train passed "wastelands rank with weeds" (16) and finally arrived at Seven Kings Station near Bancroft Gardens where her parents lived. There in the "leafy privacy and cosy domesticity" (17) of Church Lane with its "identical semi-detached houses . . . architecturally undistinguished, but at least . . . on a human scale" (17), she learns from neighbors that Martin and Mary Ducton were the rapist and murderess of twelve-year-old Julie Scase, and that her father died in prison. Her earlier fantasy about her past bursts like an iridescent soap bubble and she feels faint and sick.

Philippa regains her sense of self by concentrating on a piece of shiny paving stone that evokes the image of a mosaic tile: "she opened her eyes and made herself concentrate on the things she could touch and feel. She ran her fingers over the roughness of the wall" (20). After Philippa grounds herself in reality by feeling the texture of the wall, she is able to see the paving stone:

> It was pricked with light, set with infinitesimal specks, bright as diamonds. Pollen from the gardens had blown over it and there was a single flattened rose petal like a drop of blood. How extraordinary that a paving stone should be so varied, should reveal under the intensity of her gaze such gleaming wonders. These

> things at least were real, and she was real—more vulnerable, less durable than bricks and stones, but still present, visible, an identity. (20–21)

Physical reality isn't much of an identity; Philippa has much to learn, including the meaning of the rose petal, red as blood, but at least she starts with one piece of identity, her physical existence. The paving stone glittering with bits of reflected light is itself a piece of mosaic revealing wonder and variety. It foreshadows the many villages that make up London and the pieces of the picture Philippa must put together of her past. Philippa pulls herself together enough to take the train back into London, but she spends "the rest of the day walking in the City" (29). The city reflects her mood in the grey rainy sky, and even the "pavement stones were as tacky as if . . . [rain] had fallen heavily all day, and a few shallow puddles had collected in the gutter into which occasional dollops dropped with heavy portentousness from a sky as thick and gray as curdled milk" (29). This time the paving stones reflect no gleam of light. Philippa will have to discover that on her own.

The city also offers Philippa the freedom and anonymity in which to get to know her natural mother, Mary Ducton, whom she brings to London after her mother's release from prison. By moving out of her adopted parents' house and renting a flat in another district, Philippa achieves anonymity for herself and her mother. They glory in it as Martha Quest did in *The Four-Gated City:*

> Their freedom did, indeed, seem to be limitless, stretching out in concentric waves from those three small rooms above Monty's Fruit and Veg to embrace the whole of London. The freedom of the city—of the lumpy grass under the elms of St. James's Park, where they would search for a spare length of grass . . . and lie on their backs, staring up through a dazzle of shivering green and silver and listening to the midday band concert. (178)

The city offers Philippa and her mother the anonymity of the crowd, but it does not offer escape from their own past. As Hilary Burde discovered in Iris Murdoch's *A Word Child,* the past can find them in the city even if they come to the city to try to escape it. Norman Scase recognizes the opportunity that London offers but he, in his vow to avenge the death of his daughter, represents the past that haunts Mary Ducton. Norman Scase loses Philippa and Mary Ducton when they first get off the train from the prison in York, but he knows he can find them in spite of the city's anonymity:

> He didn't believe for one moment they were in the country. It was in the vast anonymity of the capital that the hunted felt most secure. London, which asked no questions, kept its secrets, provided in its hundred urban villages the varied needs of ten million people. And the girl was no provincial. Only a Londoner would have stridden with such confidence through the complexities of King's Cross Underground Station. (134)

London may be secretive, but Norman Scase has a map, and like a good detective he can fit the pieces of a puzzle together and discover which urban village Philippa has chosen.

These villages, or districts, are described in even greater detail in *Innocent Blood* then in P. D. James' other novels. When Maurice Palfrey, Philippa's adoptive father, thinks back to his first wife and their selection of a house, he remembers that they tried to decide which district had the character they wanted: "All districts of London were apparently impossible for her. Hampstead was too trendy, Mayfair too expensive, Bayswater vulgar, Belgravia too smart" (24). Finally they find Caldecote Terrace in Pimlico. After the death of his first wife and her son Orlando, Maurice marries his dowdy secretary Hilda, not really because he loves her, but because she weeps for Orlando. Hilda is not a society woman like his first wife; she prefers to keep house and cook. Pimlico becomes Hilda's village, and when Norman Scase loses Philippa and Mary Ducton on the subway, he finds the Palfreys' address, Caldecote Terrace, which "lay on the fringes of Pimlico, southeast of Victoria and Ecclestone Bridge" (144). When Norman goes there he discovers "a cul-de-sac of converted but unspoiled late eighteenth-century terraced houses which lay off the wider and busier Caldecote Road" (144). Although he feels "like an interloper entering a private precinct of orderliness, culture, and comfortable prosperity" (144), he is on his mission as a detective and has trained himself to observe carefully. At first he imagines what the district is like:

> They would, he imagined, affect to despise the smartness of Belgravia; would enthuse about the advantages of a socially mixed society, even if the mixing didn't actually extend to sending their children to local schools; would patronize as a duty the small shopkeepers in Caldecote Road. (144–45)

He soon gives up his reverie and starts to observe the area carefully:

> The street had an impressive uniformity; the houses were identical except for variations in the patterns of the fanlights and in the wrought-iron tracery of the first-floor balconies. The front railings guarding the basements were spiked and ornamented at the ends with pineapples. The doors, flanked with columns, were thoroughly intimidating; the brass letter boxes and knockers gleamed. (145)

Kevin Lynch notes in *The Image of the City* that a "city district in its simplest sense is an area of homogeneous character, recognized by clues which are continuous throughout the district. . . . The homogeneity may be of spatial characteristics . . . of building type . . . of style or of topography. It may be a typical building feature. . . . Where physical homogeneity coincides with use and status, the effect is unmistakable."[22] In Pimlico, as P. D. James describes it, the eighteenth-century terraced houses have an "impressive uniformity," varying only in the shapes of fanlights and the patterns of wrought-iron tracery. Although Maurice Palfrey is the professional sociologist, Norman Scase's intent focus on detection and eye for details give him accurate "preconceptions" of the upper-middle-class liberal inhabitants of this district. The physical boundaries of the district are reinforced by its visual characteristics, and together they clearly delineate the "urban village".

Pimlico is a well-defined district with clearly differentiated public and private paths. Norman Scase knows that he cannot

Eaton Terrace near Sloan Street illustrates the wrought iron
balconies and ornamental pineapples that P. D. James describes
on her fictional street.

watch the Palfreys' house from Caldecote Terrace because he would be noticed. In Caldecote Road, the public area, however, he is safe:

> The road was in marked contrast to the terrace, a disorderly muddle of shops, cafes, pubs, and the occasional office, typical of an inner London commercial street from which any glory had long departed. It was a bus route, and small, disconsolate groups of shoppers, laden with their baskets and trolleys, waited at the stops. . . . Here, if not in Caldecote Terrace, he could loiter in safety. (146)

Although Norman at first mistakes the plain, unassuming Hilda for a maid, he finally identifies her and trails her, hoping for a lead to Philippa:

> Pimlico was her [Hilda's] village, and it became his, bounded by Victoria Street and Vauxhall Bridge Road, two flowing thoroughfares like unnavigable rivers over which she never ventured to pass. (168)

Pimlico's clearly marked public and private paths and the unmistakable boundaries of the two thoroughfares define the district. Within it are not only housing and shopping facilities but even recreational areas. It has its own park, Embankment Gardens, with a view of the Thames. Hilda goes there to eat lunch on summer days and to lean on the parapet, staring "at the gritty fringes of the Thames, plumed with gulls, at the great barges as they grunted upstream, slapping the tide against the embankment wall" (169). The Thames functions not only as an edge for the district, but also as a link with the rest of London, as the barges go upstream. In spite of the specific boundaries, Hilda is content to stay within the confines of Pimlico because she already knows other parts of London; she grew up as the only child of working-class parents "in a small terraced house in the poorer part of Ruislip" (200). Philippa, however, feels that Pimlico is part of the "charade" (42) of a fabricated past. She thinks her reflection in the mirror of her room in Caldecote Terrace is inaccurate and unreal. She "had half expected the image to fudge and quiver like a reflection seen in a distorting mirror" (39–40). The district of Pimlico alone, no matter how well defined in and of itself, cannot reflect back to Philippa a complete identity. To get that she must go out into the city of London and get to know other districts.

To discover her past, Philippa needs to see the other districts of London anew. As she looks for her own apartment in the city, she gains a new perspective:

> Once, from the security of Caldecote Terrace she would have seen the meaner streets of north Paddington, Kilburn, and Earls Court as fascinating outposts of an alien culture, part of the variety and color of any capital city.
> Now with disenchanted and prejudiced eyes she saw only filth and deformity; the bursting bags of uncollected rubbish, the litter which choked the gutters . . . the walls defaced by the scribbled hate of extremists of the left and right. (94)

Philippa also feels uncomfortable with the people of the district:

> The alien shrouded bodies crouching on the curbside, watching from the open doors, threatened her with their strangeness; the prevailing smells of curry, of herded bodies, of scented women's hair, emphasized the sense of exclusion, of being unwanted in her own city. (94)

Philippa learns to accept strangeness and finally even to be concerned for others when she moves into her apartment on Delaney Street with her mother.

P. D. James describes Delaney Street as being "at the Lisson Grove end of Mell Street" (100) near Praed Street and Edgware Road, but Delaney Street is a made-up name, as are Mell Street and Caldecote Terrace. Although P. D. James uses real main streets like Praed Street and Edgware Road, Victoria Street and Vauxhall Bridge Road, she often makes up street names for residences in her novels. Frequently these names are very close to real street names. For instance, there is a Caldecot Road (without the final *e*) in another part of London. There is no Delaney Street, but there is a Delancey Street.[23] Mell Street, as Nancy Joyner notes, is "clearly modelled on London's Bell Street."[24] In *A Taste for Death,* the most urban of all her traditional detective novels, James adds an author's note when she uses real street names for residences: "My apologies are due to the inhabitants of Camden Hill Square for my temerity in erecting a Sir John Soane house to disrupt the symmetry of their terraces and to the Diocese of London for providing, surplus to pastoral requirements, a Sir Arthur Blomfield basilica and its campanile on the banks of the Grand Union Canal" (5).

Delaney Street first gives Philippa the anonymity that she needs to put together her past. Safe in her newfound anonymity, she can get to know the district. Delaney Street becomes her new "village":

> the core of their joint life lay in Delaney Street and Mell Street. Philippa told herself that she couldn't have found a better part of London in which to be anonymous. The district had a life of its own, but it was one in which the sense of community was fostered by seeing the same familiar faces, not by inquiring into their business. Delaney Street was a quiet cul-de-sac inhabited chiefly by the middle-aged or elderly living above their small family shops. It had something of the atmosphere of a self-sufficient, ancient, and sleepy village, a sluggish backwater between the great surging rivers of the Marylebone Road and the Edgware Road (178).

Like Pimlico, Delaney Street has clearly defined boundaries and identifiable, homogeneous physical features. It fits Jane Jacobs' definition of an ideal city neighborhood in that it offers privacy and yet some degree of community and contact.[25] Philippa and her mother have the anonymity they need. Although they deliberately do not drink at their local pub, the Blind Beggar, in order to maintain their privacy, still "they felt accepted in the street" (179). No longer "unwanted in her own city," Philippa can relax and begin to learn from the district.

Philippa begins to celebrate the variety and festive quality of the district as she and her mother go out into the crowds of Mell Street on marketing day:

> It was a small, intimate, bustling market, cosmopolitan but at the same time very English. . . . Early in the morning the seller of second-hand rugs and carpets wheeled up his great wooden bar-

row and patterned the road with his wares. . . . The tarmac itself became festive. Later the market took on something of the atmosphere of an eastern souk when the brass seller arrived to set out his jangling pots, and a Pakistani who sold cheap jewelry hung across his stall a swinging curtain of wooden beads. (179)

The shops also set the tone of the district:

> Behind the stalls were the small shops: the old-fashioned draper where one could still buy woolen combinations and sleeved vests . . . the Greek delicatessen smelling of syrup and sharp Mediterranean wine; the small general store, clean, sweet-smelling, perpetually dark . . . the half-dozen junk shops. (180)

No longer does Philippa feel threatened by strangeness and difference. She can perceive the festivity of market day and enjoy the variety of shops and people.

Having come to know the "village" of Delaney Street, Philippa can branch out to get to know some of the people of various classes that make up the city. Previously she knew only her private school friends and her adoptive father's academically and socially distinguished acquaintances. Now Philippa learns to get along with some lower-class women when she and her mother take jobs as waitresses at Sid's Plaice, a fish-and-chip shop off Kilburn High Road. There they share waiting on tables and washing up with Black Shirl, who knifed her mother when she was twelve; with Marlene, who has bright orange spiked hair and tattoos on her arm; and with waif-like, pale Debbie. When Debbie holds a knife to Marlene's throat, Philippa is not as calm as her mother, who, "undisturbed by the irrational explosions of violence" (174), merely persuades the girl to give her the knife. The incident makes Philippa, however, aware of the economic injustice of the city:

> Two vivid and contrasting mental pictures came frequently into her mind: Gabriel calling for her . . . swinging himself out of his Lagonda, running up the steps of number 68, his cashmere sweater slung from his shoulders; Black Shirl humping to a corner of the kitchen the great bag of washing for her five children which she would wheel in a pram to the launderette on her way home. Perhaps Maurice's [Palfrey, her adoptive father] mind was patterned with equally vivid images, contrasts which had made him a Socialist. (176)

Philippa has still not developed as much of a concern for others as her mother, who feels guilty that she and Philippa talk about the three women "as if they're objects, interesting specimens." Philippa says that it doesn't matter as long as they do not know, but Mary Ducton replies, "Perhaps not to them. It might to us" (177). Philippa still regards others objectively, from the outside, filing people away in her subconscious to use someday when she becomes a writer, but at least as she gets to know a greater variety of people, she becomes more aware of economic injustice. She starts to connect Pimlico and Delaney Street.

It is the connection of districts that for Lynch makes a mosaic of the city. When "regions are close enough together and sufficiently well joined . . . [they] make a continuous mosaic of distinctive districts."[26] Lynch explains that the districts can be connected in different ways: "District may join to district, by juxtaposition, intervisibility, relation to a line, or by some link such as a mediating node."[27] In *Innocent Blood* the links that connect the "villages" and make them into a city are not only in the mind of Philippa, but also physically present in the forms of the underground and the trains, which function as the mediating nodes. Lynch defines a node as a place of "junction" and "convergence of paths."[28] The underground and the trains represent "junction" not only in themselves, but as they connect the various districts. It is also by means of the underground that the various characters connect with each other. All the characters use the trains and the underground; there are numerous references to Liverpool Street Station, King's Cross Station, Piccadilly Circus, and the stops on the Circle Line. Even though both the "villages," Pimlico and Delaney Street, have strong boundaries in the heavily-traveled thoroughfares, these boundaries can be crossed. They function as "seams" rather than as "barriers," to use Lynch's terms,[29] and the districts are connected into a mosaic. It is via the underground that Norman Scase first tracks Hilda and then Philippa and her mother. Although Pimlico is Hilda's "village," she leaves it once a fortnight to serve as a juvenile magistrate, a job she takes to please Maurice.

Norman Scase trails her from Victoria Station, to her change at Oxford Circus to the Bakerloo line, and out at Marylebone Station (198). It is on this trip that Hilda leads him to nearby Delaney Street, where she stops on her way home. Once Norman Scase has found Philippa and her mother, it "was simple enough to trail them on the underground. They usually went from Marylebone, the nearest station" (227). If Norman Scase doesn't know districts, he doesn't worry. The underground and his map of London connect the city for him: "On his larger map he traced the route of the Circle line. Bloomsbury, Marylebone, Bayswater, Kensington. The districts were unfamiliar to him, but he would get to know them" (135). Norman's approach to the city differs from Philippa's. Although an observant detective and able to use the connecting underground system, he still needs his map to get to know the city. She, however, goes into the districts of the city, lives there, and comes to understand the people of the city. Her ability to connect becomes more powerful than that of the purely rational detective because it eventually becomes an ability to connect emotionally and value other people. She is the one who will see the mosaic.

Philippa is comfortable riding the underground, and she begins to think about connection between districts and economic policies, but before she can connect fully and learn to love others, she must come to terms with her past. At first she thinks she can get rid of the past that is merely a blur in her memory. After Philippa and her mother first get to London, she takes her mother to Knightsbridge to buy some expensive new clothes. Then they pack up everything that her mother had brought with her from prison into an old battered case and throw it into the Grand Union Canal. As the case submerges under the "greasy surface" of the canal,

> Philippa felt an almost physical relief, as if she had flung away something of herself, of her past—not the past which she knew and recognized, but the formless weight of unremembered years, of childhood miseries which were not less acute because they lurked beyond the frontier of memory. They were gone now, gone forever, sinking slowly into the mud. (153)

In her relationship with her mother, Philippa tells herself that "L.P. Hartley was right; the past was another country and they could choose whether to visit there" (180). Philippa, who often thinks in literary allusions, is comfortable with an intellectual past, but not a personal and emotional one. When she thinks back to life with the Palfreys, and Maurice bringing her morning tea, an allusion flits through her mind, slightly misquoted from Marlowe's *Jew of Malta:* "But that was in another country and, besides, that wench was dead" (150).[30] The "wench" that she was with Maurice and Hilda Palfrey, however, is no more dead than the first eight years of her life with her mother. The only "wench" who is dead is Julie Scase, and even she lives on in her father's determination for revenge.

Philippa also attempts to ignore the past when she watches TV. On their days off from Sid's fish-and-chip shop, Philippa and her mother watch a family drama, and Philippa thinks that the "convenient ability to live for the moment with its subliminal message that the past could literally be put behind one had much to recommend it" (184). But even that innocuous TV show intersects with the past when they turn on the TV early and see Maurice Palfrey, supposedly an atheist, debate with a bishop. As they listen to the show, Mary Ducton reveals that she understands both her past and the nature of belief. She observes of Maurice: "Your father knows and hates what he knows. I believe, but I can't love anymore. He and I are the unlucky ones" (186). Mary Ducton explains that she cannot love because she has to feel contrition for the murder of Julie Scase in order to receive God's forgiveness, but contrition is now impossible because she has spent her time in prison convincing herself that she wasn't responsible. The crying child reminded her of her little brother who was often beaten by their father; she had to quiet it lest more beatings occur. She says to Philippa:

> I can't spend ten years explaining to myself that I wasn't responsible, that I couldn't have prevented myself doing what I did, and then when I'm free . . . decide that it would be pleasant to have God's forgiveness as well. (187)

Mary Ducton understands that she must accept the past. This conversation leads to Philippa's questions about baptism, and she learns that she was christened "Rose."

Behind the name "Rose" and Philippa's relationship to it lie a series of references to roses throughout the novel. They all relate to the idea of human connection and compassion. As the novel opens, Philippa looks at a bowl of roses in the social worker's office, not "scentless, thornless . . . florist's" roses, but garden roses (3). Philippa thinks of her fantasy of a lord and maid meeting in the rose garden at Pennington. The social worker urges that Philippa trace her father through an intermediary, warning: "We all need our fantasies in order to live. Sometimes relinquishing them can be extraordinarily painful, not a rebirth into something exciting and new, but a kind of death" (14). Relinquishing her fantasies will lead to a death for Philippa, not her own, but her mother's. Still Philippa will learn from relinquishing her fantasies even though the social worker's warning exhibited valid human concern and compassion. Other roses occur throughout the novel. There are small pink rosebuds on the curtain surrounding the hospital deathbed of Norman Scase's wife. Norman Scase does not really love his wife anymore; she had given up everything to grief and a desire for revenge, but he does sit at her deathbed and hold her hand. The punk waitress Marlene has a tattoo of hearts and roses on her arm. When Hilda, sitting on the juvenile magistrate's bench, looks down at a young girl whose baby has been taken from her for fear she or her husband beat the child, she notices a metal brooch in the shape of a rose dragging on the young mother's flimsy cotton top: "She yearned to lean over the bench and stretch out her hands to the girl, to get out from her seat and fold the rigid body in her arms" (204). And it is when he sees Hilda clumsily trying to arrange a bowl of roses that Maurice Palfrey blurts out that he is the one who is infertile, not she: "Because of a bowl of ruined roses, because of a moment of futile compassion, he had blurted it out. Not the whole truth . . . but a part of the truth, the essential truth. A secret he had kept for twelve years" (218). Although such compassion seems futile to Maurice, it lifts a burden from Hilda and makes her realize that she "needn't spend her life making up to him for a deprivation which was nothing to do with her" (221). She can resign from the juvenile magistrate bench where she cannot help anyone; she can fulfill her long-held wish for a dog. Reacting against the fragility and messiness of real roses, Maurice decides suddenly that he doesn't like them anymore:

> They were an overpraised flower, soon blowzy, their beauty dependent on scent and poetic association. One perfect bloom in a specimen vase placed against a plain wall could be a marvel of color and form, but flowers ought to be judged by how they grew. A rose garden always looked messy, spiky, recalcitrant bushes bearing mean leaves. And the roses grew untidily, had such a brief moment of beauty before the petals bleached and peeled in the wind, littering the soil (216).

Richard Gidez points out that Maurice and Hilda are really talking about Philippa in their comments on roses.[31] Maurice had thought that he could take Philippa out of the messy, spiky garden of ordinary life and rear her as a perfect specimen, but now Philippa has gone back to ordinary life. Suddenly it occurs to Maurice that the roses parallel the human condition. People, like roses, cannot be judged in isolation, but rather must be perceived as growing in a garden. The messiness, the thorns, the briefness of the beauty, and the disintegration are all a part of the real human condition.

This cluster of images is tied to the city and to the central action of the novel when Philippa, who is with her mother, sees Norman Scase on an outing in Regent's Park with the blind clerk from his hotel, Violet Tetley. All the roses are in bloom: "In Queen Mary's rose garden the roses, plumped by the rain, held the last drops between delicate streaked petals: pink Harriny, bright yellow Summer Sunshine, Ena Harkness, and Peace (193)." For Philippa, Queen Mary's Rose Garden brings back memories:

> There was one rose garden which she could remember, but that had been at Pennington and her imagined father had been there. . . . Odd that so clear a memory, scent, warmth, and mellow afternoon light, recalled with such peculiar intensity, almost

Queen Mary's Rose Garden in Regent's Park, with the Post Office Tower. Since the foliage has grown up, the Nash Terraces are no longer visible from the Rose Garden. This scene provides both an illustration of nature within the city and an example of a contemporary landmark, the Post Office Tower. The turning point of P. D. James' *Innocent Blood* takes place in this park. Regent's Park is also referred to in Drabble's *The Middle Ground* and *The Radiant Way* and Lessing's *The Diaries of Jane Somers*. The Post Office Tower is referred to in Murdoch's *A Word Child* and Drabble's *The Ice Age*.

with pain, should be nothing but a childish fantasy. But this garden, this park were real enough, and Maurice was right about architecture. Nature needed the contrast, the discipline of brick and stone. The colonnades and pediments of John Nash's terraces, the eccentric outline of the zoo, even the technical phallus of the Post Office Tower soaring above the hedges, contributed to the park's beauty, defined it, and set its limits. (193–194)

Nature and the rose garden are not some idyllic place away from human life and the city, but rather need the city, and not only the old colonnades, but even the new Post Office Tower. Philippa, thinking back to Maurice, connects the city and the rose garden. Like the architectural critics Jacobs and Lynch, James presents nature and the city not as contrasting elements, but as parts of a coherent whole (see Ch. 1, pp. 25–27). Even when Norman Scase climbs out the lavatory window of the pub into the "wasteland" of junk and backyards on Delaney Street, there are flowers on the waist-high weeds: "They looked so fragile with their small, pink flowers, yet they had forced their way through this impacted earth, in places splitting the concrete" (213). Plane trees (sycamores) grow all over London, not only in Bancroft Gardens and Caldecote Terrace, but even in Delaney Street. Backyards have beautiful weeds and plane trees and the city has public rose gardens. It is in the rose garden that Philippa unwittingly makes contact with her mother's past as she smiles at Norman Scase and Violet Tetly.

Philippa had thought that she could ignore her own past life as Rose Ducton, and even as Philippa Rose Palfrey, but she cannot. Mary Ducton's past intersects with Philippa Palfrey's when they meet Gabriel Lomas at an exhibit of Victorian paintings at the Royal Academy. With some underhanded lies to Hilda, Gabriel learns of Philippa and Mary Ducton's apartment and sends a reporter there. Philippa manages to intimidate the reporter, but she and her mother decide to leave London for the Isle of Wight. Philippa even suggests that her mother change her name. Mary Ducton replies, "I couldn't do that. That would be defeat. I have to know who I am" (261). Although Mary Ducton wants to avoid contaminating Philippa's past with her own, she does not deny her past. Philippa decides to take some of Maurice's antique silver and pawn it to finance their trip. It is at this moment that Mary Ducton for the first time calls Philippa by the name Rose: "Suddenly her mother called her back. She said, 'Rose! You won't take anything that isn't yours?'" (261).

When Philippa arrives at Caldecote Terrace, she finds Maurice in bed with one of his graduate students. After the graduate student is dismissed, Maurice and Philippa talk, feeling an intensity between them. Philippa says that she will give up going to Cambridge and just live with her mother. Maurice finally says to her, "it's time you stopped living in a fantasy world and faced reality" (271). He reveals the significance of her name, Rose Ducton. He points out that Philippa assumed that she was adopted after the murder, but in fact she was adopted before the murder because her mother had abused her. Her mother had been unable to stand the screaming, unloving child who had inherited her violent temper. Her mother herself had put Philippa in a foster home, and both her natural parents consented to her adoption. Philippa goes back to Delaney Street in a daze and confronts her mother angrily. Mary Ducton finally asks, "Is what I did to you so much more difficult to forgive than what I did to that child?" Philippa responds, "I don't want to see you ever again. I wish they'd hanged you nine years ago. I wish you were dead" (284), and she flees out of the apartment into the city streets.

As Philippa runs through the city, experiencing the death of the last of her fantasies, the city reflects her anguish. Earlier, Maurice says to her that if his adoption order "lacks the emotional charge of the blood tie, hasn't your family had enough of blood?" (275).[32] Being Rose Ducton had meant abuse from the mother who had fractured her skull and drawn her blood. The city reflects her mood: "The city was streaked with light, bleeding with light. The headlamps of the cars dazzled on the road and the crimson pools of the traffic lights lay on the surface like blood. The rain was falling in a solid wall of water." (285). Philippa runs away from the Warwick Avenue Underground station, along a "wide road, lined with

Italianate houses and stuccoed villas" (286), to the Grand Union Canal and there takes off the sweater her mother just knit her and throws it into the canal, trying one last time to jettison her past. She walks until she is completely exhausted and looks for a place to rest when suddenly a gang of youths start to chase her. She only barely escapes by ducking behind a gate and going into a "dark, evil-smelling area, almost colliding with three battered dustbins" (288). As she sits in this cramped, stinking space,

> [t]here came to her in the darkness no blinding revelation, no healing of the spirit, only a measure of painful self-knowledge. From the moment of her counseling she had thought of no one but herself. Not of Hilda, who had so little to give but asked so little in return and needed that little so much. . . . Not of Maurice, as arrogant and self-deceiving as herself, but who had done his best for her, had given with generosity even if he couldn't give with love, had somehow found the kindness to shield her from the worst knowledge. Not of her mother. (288)

The thought of her mother makes Rose aware of her true feelings:

> She knew, too, that what bound her to her mother was stronger than hate or disappointment or the pain of rejection. Surely this need to see her again, to be comforted by her, was the beginning of love; and how could she have expected that there could be love without pain?" (288–289)

Sitting in the alleyway, Philippa at last, though painfully, learns to accept her past and think of others. The city reflects her pain: "In her mind the city seemed to stretch forever, a silent half-derelict immensity, palely illumined by the recurrent moon. It was a dead city, plague-ridden and abandoned, from which all life had fled except for that band of scavenging louts" (289). Just then the city reveals that it is not dead and abandoned; across the street she sees an elegant young woman in an evening dress. Philippa crosses over to her to ask directions. She tells Philippa that she is in Moxford Square and explains to her how to get home. Philippa hurries home to Delaney Street, which was "sleeping as quietly as a village street . . . [while the] rain-washed air smelled of the sea" (290) to tell her mother that she loves her. But she is too late for her mother; Mary Ducton has already committed suicide. Philippa can still save Norman Scase, however, who has crept into the apartment and stuck his knife into the corpse. Philippa finds Norman sitting there, saying over and over to himself, "she won't bleed" (291). Although Philippa reads the note from her mother which says "I can die happy because you are alive and I love you" (292), she does not spend her time on the dead. She turns to Norman saying, "[the] dead don't bleed. I got to her before you" (292). Philippa acknowledges her past and her deed, then forgets her focus on self and exhibits concern for others by helping Norman escape. She holds his head as he vomits into the sink, dismisses him, and puts her fingerprints on the knife.

After saving Norman, she calls Maurice, realizing that she too needs human connection and help. Maurice, for whom all the graduate students had been only a substitute for Philippa, arrives quickly and embraces her with "a clasp of possession, not a gesture of comfort" (296). He takes care of the details with the police, takes her home to Caldecote Terrace, and tucks her into her own bed. Philippa learned to love her natural mother; she also needs to come to terms with her relationship to her adopted father. At the beginning of the novel, Philippa thinks she is searching for her real father whom she supposes is an earl at Pennington. She learns early that her natural father is dead and later that he was a weak man unable to protect her from her mother. After her mother's death, Philippa turns to Maurice, her adoptive father. All through the novel, even when with her mother, Philippa thinks of Maurice. She remembers how he taught her to appreciate good wine; she quotes to herself his opinion on architecture and buildings; she thinks about why he became a socialist; and she even recalls how he used to bring her tea in the mornings. When she goes back to Caldecote Terrace and finds him in bed with his student, Philippa wants to hear him say that he has missed her (271), but he doesn't say it. After he tells her how her real mother had abused her, she angrily asks him what motive he had for adopting her. Maurice finally responds, "Perhaps what I hoped for was love" (276). As he thinks back to when he first saw Philippa, he reveals that her memory of the rose garden at Pennington was real, but that it was not an earl or any natural father whom she met there as a child, but Maurice.

In the epilogue Philippa reveals that she has a new relationship with Maurice. At Cambridge, she meets Norman Scase as she comes out of church. She reassures him that she will not reveal his past to his new wife, the blind Violet Tetley, but what she does not say echoes in her mind, "I used my mother to avenge myself on my adoptive father" (308). Those feelings, however, are forgiven as Philippa and her father reestablish their relationship. Philippa explains to Norman:

> "My adoptive father arranged everything; he's a great fixer. Afterward he took me on a long holiday to Italy. We went to see the mosaics at Ravenna."
> She didn't add, "And in Ravenna I went to bed with him." . . . What, she wondered, had it meant exactly, that gentle, tender, surprisingly uncomplicated coupling; an affirmation, a curiosity satisfied, a test successfully passed, an obstacle ceremoniously moved out of the way so that they could again take up their roles of father and daughter, the excitement of incest without its legal prohibition, without any more guilt than they already carried? That single night together . . . had been necessary, inevitable, but it was no longer important (310).[33]

Having accepted her past, gotten to know her mother, and reestablished connection with Maurice, Philippa has put together the mosaic of her past. Watching Norman Scase go down the path, Philippa hopes that in marrying the blind Violet Tetley, "he would find his patch of rose garden. . . . If it is only through learning to love that we find identity, then he had found his. She hoped one day to find hers. She wished him well. And perhaps to be able to wish him well with all that she could recognize of her unpracticed heart, to say a short, untutored prayer for him and his Violet, was in itself a small accession of grace" (311). Philippa now understands the meaning of her name, "Rose," although she doesn't use it because it "didn't suit" her (306). She does not think she has completely learned to love yet, but she recognizes what it is and values the grace that allows her a prayer for Norman's happiness.

The references to the mosaics at Ravenna bring to an end a pattern that has run throughout the novel. Wherever mosaics or similar images have appeared, they have been associated with churches and with characters who have learned how to love. Hilda goes to Westminster Cathedral, passing through Lady Chapel, "gleaming with gold mosaics" (171); Mary Ducton's request to go to church raises in Philippa's mind images of London churches including "Margaret Street, in a dazzle of mosaics, gilded saints, and stained glass" (192). Philippa discusses several times the possibility of going to Ravenna to see the mosaics, but she only goes after she has learned to love her mother and to reconnect with Maurice. The mosaics stand for the value of human connection, given only perhaps by grace as their association with the churches implies. They are like Philippa's closing spontaneous prayer for Norman Scase. As Philippa's peace of mind and awareness of grace illustrate, she has been able to put together the pieces of her life. It is a similar knowledge that has allowed her to put together the mosaic of the city and see the connections that link the urban villages.

CHAPTER 6

The City as Archeological Dig:
Maureen Duffy

Whereas P. D. James' characters search out individual pasts in order to put together the mosaic of the city, Maureen Duffy in *Londoners: an Elegy* (1983) and *Capital: a Fiction* (1976) goes further back in time to portray the city as an archeological site. In *Capital,* where one of the characters searches for evidence of fifth- and sixth-century life in London, there is literally an archeological dig; it appears more figuratively in *Londoners,* in which Al, the narrator, connects modern-day London with medieval Paris while translating the poetry of François Villon and writing his biography. Maureen Duffy, like Doris Lessing, is a close observer of modern-day London who looks behind the varied details of contemporary life to depict a strong awareness of history and the city's past. The protagonists of her novels are loners, people who have to dig carefully to uncover any relationships. For them, unlike Margaret Drabble's characters, there is no easy descent into a rich network of complex relationships. Instead, Duffy's narrators are analyzers of the past and observers of the fluid, changing life of the present. The stream-of-consciousness point of view and the experimental, often lyrical style of these novels differ from the realistic modes of Lessing, Drabble, Murdoch, and P. D. James, partly because Maureen Duffy is also a poet, but also because in these novels, unlike some of her other realistic ones, the emphasis is on the relationship between the historical past and a fluid present. *Capital* is a layered text that alternates the story of an amateur archeologist, Meepers, with the letters of a professor of eighteenth-century history and with vignettes from prehistoric time to the present. *Londoners* is in a stream-of-consciousness style set entirely in the mind of Al and loosely structured around nine days in Al's life as Al tries to concentrate on the translation and biography of Villon and also to meet the professional commitments of a practicing writer.

London as Archeological Dig

Duffy uses the image of the archeological dig or mine to define British urban writers' relationship to London: "We come to her, literally and metaphorically, as to a mine or a many layered image we can all as writers quarry or unravel and yet the riches and complexity will remain."[1] In *Londoners* it is Al who first identifies the city as an archeological dig. From the vantage point of a basement flat, Al first calls an Earls Court house an "archeological site," but it becomes clear that in Al's mind the whole city is an archeological dig with a changed, hardly recognizable, top cosmopolitan layer that echoes Villon's question "where are the snows of yesteryear?":

> I've become as much a stranger as Jemal [a Muslim from Northwest India] or Wolfgang [a German], more because they don't expect to be at home in my native city. They are the true Londoners, denizens of cosmopolis. My hometown was danced away round a VJ bonfire while yesterday's snows turned to slush and piddled off down the drain. . . .
> For it's gone. As I lie here with the house like an archeological site staged above me I know my dad, sharp as he was, would barely have understood this grave new world.[2]

London is a cosmopolitan city harboring people from numerous countries, but beneath that layer is the London of World War II, the familiar London of Al's childhood that Al's father knew. Later Al merges the pre–World War I London of Marie Lloyd's music halls with medieval Paris: "It's perverse to be at heart a mediaevalist in the computer age, to have an imagination with a five-hundred-year time warp, to see the Paris of Joan of Arc and the London of Marie Lloyd as one eternal city so that the snows of yesteryear slop over the tops of my track shoes . . . when I step over my threshold into Oliver Gardens and trudge through to Fulham Road" (15). It is this imagination, mining the layers of London's past and juxtaposing it with a vivid cosmopolitan present, that dominates the urban novels of Maureen Duffy. Social scientists and planners emphasize that this connection to the past is an important one in cities. In "The Kind of City We Want," Margaret Mead writes: "The need to be bound to the past is, I think, a basic human need."[3] Kevin Lynch reinforces Mead's idea: "[it] is the sense of depth in an old city that is so intriguing."[4] It is precisely this sense of time and of depth that Maureen Duffy presents in her novels.

In the 1982 preface to her first novel, *That's How It Was* (1962), Maureen Duffy said that she has "written again and again out of my long love affair with London which is one of the main themes of *That's How It Was*."[5] That novel, which is autobiographical, is set in World War II London. The young girl, Paddy Mahoney, although often evacuated during the bombing of London, nonetheless identifies herself as a Londoner:

> For the first time I had a feeling of belonging in a place. That I remembered the sea . . . meant nothing. This was where I belonged, in these dirty streets with the railway close by, the street markets, the lighted shop windows, the pavements that splashed with mud and sodden papers, cartons, tissue paper from the oranges around Christmas-time; that blew like a sandstorm in the summer, with grit and dust . . . and whirling bus-tickets . . . in August. These were her [Paddy's mother's] streets where all the legendary family had lived and dared, and I was one of them. I was a Londoner, an East Ender. . . . I would always belong. (42)

In spite of Paddy's identification with London, the city itself is not vividly portrayed in this early novel because the setting soon shifts to the town of "Wortbridge."[6] Paddy's mother had gone there after marrying a widower in order to live in an area where Paddy can win a place to high school. Paddy's early sense of belonging in London, however, sets up the "love affair with London" that emerges in later novels.

The Matrilinear City

The city in Duffy's fiction is not only many-layered, but also closely connected to the idea of the mother, and the exploration of a many-layered city becomes the exploration of the relationship with the mother. As Duffy comments, "My identification of and with the city was matrilinear, intense and instinctive."[7] Duffy's interest in the mother figure pervades her fiction. In the preface to *That's How It Was,* she writes:

> The core of my first book, the relationship to the mother which John Fowles has singled out as the basis of all fiction,[8] I have mined repeatedly in later work. *Love Child* [in which a child's actions contribute to the suicide of the mother's lover] can be read as a myth which is the *déclassé* mirror image of that earlier theme; mother and child effectively open and close *Capital;* they are recurrent figures in *Wounds* and *I Want To Go To Moscow* where Scully's [sic][9] mother is the presiding goddess as is Mrs Bardfield in *Gor Saga.* All nativities are the Nativity. (xi)

Particularly the working-class mothers in *I Want To Go To Moscow* and *Gor Saga* and the black mothers in *Capital* and *Wounds* are nurturant and concerned for their children, even against great odds, like Paddy's mother in *That's How It Was.* In *Londoners* there is no specific mother figure, but London itself is defined as a mother. Returning to London on the train, Al muses: "London begins to draw round me in my small cubicle, running up against the windows just as it did when I was a child coming home for a holiday from evacuation in a lull in the bombing. It will always be there, great nurse, grand mother" (232).

If London is associated with the mother, then an exploration of the city as an archeological site is like an exploration of the relationship with the mother that has been built up in layers over time. Nancy Chodorow says: "Throughout their development . . . women have been building layers of identification with their mothers upon the primary internalized mother-child relationship."[10] Duffy mines the layers of the relationship with the mother throughout her fiction. Since her identification with London is "matrilinear," it is not surprising that in her "long love affair with London" ("Preface," *That's How It Was*, x) the city should be portrayed in all its layers throughout time. Even more often than Doris Lessing, Maureen Duffy explores the layers of the city in time as she carefully presents each segment of city life and sees the preceding ages behind it. *Capital* is concerned with the continuity of London: if only Meepers can prove that London's existence has been continuous even after the Romans left, then he can prove that the city survived once and that it will again. Continuity, like layers of identification, also characterizes the female psyche, according to Chodorow: "growing girls come to define and experience themselves as continuous with others."[11] Both concepts, of layering and of continuity, are thus characteristic female concerns as well as archeological issues.

For Duffy, the relationship to the mother is also important because it explains the origins of her own lesbianism. She writes in the preface to *That's How It Was:*

> I wanted to celebrate my mother but I also wanted to show how a personality and a relationship that in the world's eyes were brave and fine could produce a psychological result which, also in the world's eyes at the beginning of that socio-sexual revolution that has come to be known derisively as the Swinging Sixties, could be labelled sick or perverted and thought of as at best a great handicap.[12] (vi)

In the novel Paddy has a close and affectionate relationship with her mother and her aunts but no positive relationships with male figures. In an interview Maureen Duffy explicitly links homosexuality with the absence of father figures: "There are . . . certain patterns which appear too often in the childhoods of homosexuals to be chance—statistically there are too many important mothers and unimportant fathers."[13] In the novel Paddy is born illegitimate. Her biological father deserts her mother when Paddy is two months old, and Paddy sees her stepfather as a rival:

> I no longer cared what I said to him and delighted in goading him . . . picking on his ignorance, his mispronunciation of even the simplest words.
> She charged me with jealousy and I gloried in it. I sang songs of envy and desire, made us private jokes and a language of our own that shut him out. (171)

The "psychological result" of adult lesbianism, however, is not really explored in the novel since it ends with her mother's death when Paddy is fifteen. The focus on the novel is primarily on Paddy's love, admiration, and concern for her mother, and on her mother's determination that her own illness and their poverty will not keep Paddy from an education and a better chance in life.

The Microcosm

The idea of the archeological dig first occurs in Duffy's work in her third novel, her one specifically lesbian novel, *The Microcosm* (1966). This novel juxtaposes the stories of several lesbian couples and several individual lesbians who often meet together at a lesbian club.[14] The first reference to an archeological site is an isolated line; Steve, the gym teacher, thinks of two of her colleagues and wonders about their relationship:

> Mrs. Masters is potty about her even though she's got a husband and two children. Wonder if she realizes. . . . They went on holiday together on an archeological dig. One of those great emotional relationships with queer overtones.[15]

The archeological dig comes into the plot unexpectedly at the end of the novel. Matt, the major character, has been worrying about "his" relationship with Rae (Duffy uses masculine pronouns for the "butch" characters). Though educated in archeology, Matt is currently working in a garage. Suddenly, a former professor drives up and invites Matt to come on a dig to Italy. When the professor finds out that Rae is currently working for a museum, drawing artifacts, he invites her to come along as well. As a plot device, the offer is pure coincidence, *deus ex machina* (the literal *machina* is a big Wolsey); as Matt comments to Rae, "eight million people in London and you happen to bump into just the one, way outside the laws of averages and statistics" (307). This trip will take Matt and Rae away from the tiny microcosm of the club and towards a study of the larger society.

Another recurrent image in Duffy's work that is associated both with the mother figure and with the archeological dig is that of the rockpool, the small tidepool, filled up and then washed out again by the ocean's tides. At the end of *The Microcosm*, Matt uses this image to define the world of the lesbian club:

> I conceived this idea of a rockpool, of the gay world as a universe in little where you could find all the human processes, life and death and love, rich and poor, successful and otherwise, moral and amoral, just as in a pool on the shore you can find crustaceans and fish, dozens of different forms of plant and animal life. . . . Then I found I wasn't studying them from a distance . . . but swimming about down there among them. (311)

Duffy acknowledges that the tidepool itself is an image that can be psychologically associated with the mother; the enclosed pool is like the womb filled with amniotic fluid. It is also, she says, a very personal image dating back to her early childhood, when she lived near the sea after being evacuated from London during the World War II bombing:

> My mother would sit on the beach, sometimes with one of her sisters or a friend, and I would go off along the beach. The beach was divided by a series of breakwaters . . . and I would go along climbing over these breakwaters, getting further and further away from them and then suddenly I would realize, stand up and look back to see where she was and she would have to reassure me by waving. . . . I was looking for rockpools and treasures as I went along and I was drawn on as if it were a sort of quest, which

is a . . . curiously fictional structure because it's allied to the saga, and the romance, the quest, the looking for treasures brought in by the tide. [I remember a series of photographs] of myself on the beach, taking away a rockpool from two small boys.[16]

The rockpool is thus associated with the mother not only on a Freudian level but also on a very personal experiential level. As a quest for treasures, it is also associated with an archeological dig. It is not surprising that the image of the ocean with its tides and rockpools often occurs in *Londoners*. In *Capital* it specifically combines with the archeological dig in the references to the drowned city of Atlantis. As Matt continues the image in *The Microcosm*, "he" uses it to explain to Rae why they must move out of the solely lesbian world into the larger world:

We're terrified of what's out there, of the competition, of being laughed at . . . and so we make this little world for ourselves. . . . But it's a fallacy. There's no such thing as a microcosm. You're walking along the shore and you come across the rockpool. You think it contains all you want, all varieties of human experience and just as you're becoming thoroughly absorbed in it a great wave washes over it and you realize it's not complete in itself, it's only part of the whole and all the little fishes . . . have to make a run for it out into open sea because that's the only place they'll ever grow up. . . . we have to learn to live in the world and the world has to live with us. . . . Society [is] . . . an infinitely complex living structure. (312–313)

Matt rejects the rockpool of the lesbian club as a fallacy and moves out with Rae into the world at large to analyze the infinitely complex structure that is society.

Male Characters in Duffy's Nonurban Novels

In her next novels Duffy herself turns away from the strictly lesbian novel to analyze society at large.[17] Six of her next eight novels have clearly identifiable male protagonists. (The narrator of her 1971 novel, *Love Child*, is a child.) *Paradox Players* (1967) and *Capital* (1975) have male "I" narrators, as does the novel that precedes *Microcosm, The Single Eye* (1964). *I Want To Go To Moscow* (1973; the American title is *All Heaven in a Rage*) and *Gor Saga* (1981) have male protagonists and focus on speciesism. *I Want To Go To Moscow* is a thriller whose hero, Jarvis Chuff, is hired to blow up experimental animal laboratories and slaughterhouses, and *Gor Saga* has a hero who, Duffy explains, is "a person of two worlds, animal and human, which translates into speciesism that class and cultural division I have always lived with." ("Preface," *That's How It Was*, x). *Change* (1987), which is about a number of different characters during World War II, shows Duffy's continuing interest in speciesism, for it includes a group of chimpanzees. Among the characters it also includes a young girl, Hilary, who discovers her love for another woman. Although Leah Fritz thought that Hilary would be the character with whom Maureen Duffy would most identify, Duffy, however, said that she most identifies with Lennie, "a working-class boy evacuee."[18]

Two of the later novels have minor characters who are lesbians, but the focus is on male heterosexual characters. *Wounds* (1969) juxtaposes a heterosexual love affair with numerous vignettes of painful love in which many forms of lovers, father, husband, mother, friend, can neither protect the loved one nor prevent the loved one's pain or loss. Although one of these vignettes is about an elderly lesbian, Kingy, who mourns for her lost lover and tries to stand up to the men in a bar who want to mock her, the novel as a whole reflects society at large. *Housespy* (1978) has a male protagonist, Scully, who is sent to be a bodyguard and detective to a Socialist Minister for Economic Planning. Scully discovers that the minister's wife is being blackmailed for lesbianism. Scully is sympathetic to the wife and gets fired for contradicting his superior in order to save her life.

Duffy explains that she uses male narrators for two reasons. The first is the "psychological aspect," that is, her lesbianism. The second relates to the position of women in contemporary literature. Like Iris Murdoch (see Ch. 4, p. 115), Duffy uses male narrators because "males in our society have done more than females (in the past and mercifully this is changing). If a story is about a woman spy, conductor, gorilla/human, it will be about that combination which, at present, will be the over-riding concern not the job or activity itself."[19] In *Housespy, I Want To Go To Moscow,* and *Gor Saga,* her focus would have been shifted away from the issues of spying or speciesism if she had used female protagonists.

Londoners

In *Londoners* this pattern shifts, because Al's sex is intention-ally "ambiguous."[20] In some ways the setting of the novel and many of Al's experiences as a writer parallel Maureen Duffy's own. Rachel Gould notes that "in many ways *Londoners* is a very exactly autobiographical novel. . . . Al is a writer who lives alone in a bedsit in Earls Court, where Maureen Duffy has been for fifteen years. . . . Al leads a life of Indian take-aways, fish and chips, public transport, sleazy pubs with tense atmospheres, transitory relationships, frequent solitariness and sometimes loneliness. Most of that is autobiographical too."[21] Not only the setting and atmosphere but many of the events in *Londoners* are autobiographical. A man with a bleeding hand did come in Duffy's basement window and sub-sequently fall to his death; his parents did come speak to her. The affectionate portrait of Hector Spalding is of her friend, Angus Wilson. The more satiric portraits, like Goetzle, are sometimes blends of individuals but are nonetheless based on experience. The two homosexual pubs in the novel are ones Duffy used to frequent when she lived in Earls Court; they were quite safe places for women, she explained.[22]

In spite of the autobiographical element, Duffy did not por-tray Al as specifically female for two reasons. Her main reason for making Al's sex ambiguous is similar to her choice of male protagonists for some of her novels: Duffy wants the reader of *Londoners* to focus on the problems of the writer, not of the woman writer. She explains that she did not make Al female because she did not want readers to think that Al is rejected as a scriptwriter or that Al's views are dismissed because Al is a woman.[23] At the same time, Al is not a typical male writer because Al's female qualities are important; they allow Al to celebrate the city and to notice parts of the city that might otherwise be missed. Gould mentions a second, more general reason for the ambiguity about Al's sex: Duffy's interest in the individual person. According to Gould, Duffy

> didn't want to mystify readers or to disguise the homosexual element, but to make the point that "a person is ultimately a person. You don't constantly look in the mirror and say: 'I am a woman' or 'I am a man' unless you see yourself in terms of a Mills & Boon romance. You see yourself as an 'I,' an ego, a personality."[24]

Furthermore, even when Duffy uses material from life, she consciously structures it. As she said to Gould, "there is always an element of sharpening when you put something in a novel."[25] In her interview with Dulan Barber, Duffy explained that "experience has to be worked on, wrought up and transformed, not simply regurgitated. . . . If you are trying to make an artefact you are wanting to achieve balance, colour, relevance and character. Life simply as it is lived, as a rule, is extremely untidy and things don't end. . . . I like to have a feeling of structure, a balanced skeleton underneath."[26] Even if many of the incidents in *Londoners* are from life, the structuring element, the skeleton of the novel, is *The Inferno*. Villon, Al's guide, functions like Dante,[27] and many of the sins and geography of *The Inferno* are intertwined with the contemporary events of the novel. *Londoners* is thus a blend of contemporary London life and literary allusion, and Al, its central character, is androgynous in his perceptions, sometimes presenting a male view, sometimes a female.[28]

Al sees the role of the artist and the nature of the city in both male and female terms. For Al, the artist has a dual role in society: a masculine role of being in conflict with society and a feminine one of nurturing society. While traveling beneath the city on the subway to various professional meetings and luncheons, Al thinks:

I seem to live half my life underground journeying. I travel about like a corpuscle in the veins of the city, red or white. Writers should be both, like oysters changing their sex every seven years. Sometimes we nourish the body, feed the imagination, and sometimes we fight off its enemies, the invaders that would destroy and pollute it. (115)

Part of the time the artist is in conflict with society, especially for Al in the struggle against censorship. In this role the artist has the masculine role, the role of the white corpuscle. It is this role that involves most of Al's public life in the city, the meetings with editors and committees. In testifying before a Parliamentary Select Committee on Censorship, Al says: "Artists and society have always been in conflict. . . . It may even be part of the artist's function to be so. Graham Greene certainly thinks it is" (92). This masculine role is also reflected in Al's perceptions of the city's landmarks and its crime. At other times Al sees the artist's role as more female, the red corpuscle feeding and nourishing the body politic. This conception of the artist's role as nurturing fits well with the compassionate side of Al's nature in private thoughts and interactions with people. Al is sympathetic to others' problems whether it be David's arrest for hugging a young man in the street, Léonie's pregnancy, an Indian storekeeper's worry over his nephew's immigration papers, Mary's sorrow over the rejection of her novel, a wounded drug addict's terror, or Paul's venereal disease. This side of Al's nature allows the observation of small details about city life and, like the female protagonists of Lessing and Drabble, the celebration of the districts and streets and parks of the city. In both cases Al sees the city in layers and as continuous with earlier time periods. In this sense Al is like Meepers in *Capital,* who is male and heterosexual, but not assertive. Meepers is old, shy, the victim of an old war wound and a recent mugging, but he too reaches out to the young students and the professor when they approach him and he too focuses on the little details that make up the city of London and its history. Maureen Duffy's urban observers are thus not typical women, nor egotistical men like those in many of Iris Murdoch's novels. They are instead

The Houses of Parliament, "The Mother of Parliaments."

either male loners who have feminine perceptions and concerns, like Meepers, or androgynous characters, like Al. Unlike some of Doris Lessing's and Margaret Drabble's characters, they do not plunge enthusiastically into the city; rather,
they observe it carefully from the sidelines, analyzing each
layer and pondering over it like archeologists.

Londoners is subtitled *an Elegy* and, like Al and the city of
London itself, the subtitle has a dual implication. Like the
contemporary definition of elegy, the novel is a meditation on
the death of the London of pre–World War II, the London Al's
father knew, as well as of the medieval London and Paris of
Villon's time. *Londoners* also, however, is an elegy in the Eliz-
abethan sense of the word, a love poem to the city of London
and its inhabitants, a "complaint" that both recognizes the
sorry state of the contemporary world and declares the speak-
er's love for the city even when it spurns him. The novel describes the sordid side of contemporary London in the homosexual clubs and crime and tawdriness of some of the old
landmarks, but it also celebrates the sensory appeal and variety of contemporary London that stimulates the imagination of the writer. On an intellectual level Al analyzes the historical layers beneath the contemporary city and identifies
the two aspects of the city, the sordid and the exciting. On a
more personal level, Al identifies with the city and sees it as
androgynous. Although Al usually refers to the city as female,
as mother, "great nurse, grand mother" (232), or as bride
(88), Al also conceives of London as androgynous, potentially
male or female:

> I join the tourists with their maps en route for the Mother of
> Parliaments, the Queen Ma'am and the mummies of the British
> Museum. It makes me suddenly wonder what sex London is.
> Other languages have to sex their capitals because of their own
> primitive genders but in any case there's no doubt. Paris is fe-
> male, so's Vienna; Berlin is masculine, Rome feminine. London
> is androgynous: all things to all men, and women too. We make
> our choice, make her in the image we need to love or hate. (88)

When Al observes the city, both sides of the city seem to appear. The landmarks and famous buildings, even when their

imposing qualities are deflated by Al's remarks, represent the masculine side of the city. The varied districts and the parks represent the female side. In both sides, however, Al sees the layering of time that ties the city to the image of the archeological dig.

As a writer, Al is an archeologist who continually sees layers of predecessors in the sights of London. One day while viewing London as female, as bridal, Al celebrates contemporary London as continuous with the London of Samuel Johnson and William Wordsworth:

> In that sense as well Johnson was right and he that is tired of London is tired of life. This morning because I have a purpose, belong . . . she is bridal, promising. When I get out at Westminster and come up beside the bridge with the great liner of County Hall moored on the opposite bank "earth hath not anything to show more fair." (88)

On a walk through a local park, Al sees this same continuum of writers in the various London trees:

> That's a plane [sycamore] I know by the patch-peeled bark, a Londoner. The spirit of Etherage [*sic*] could be locked in there. . . . And there are limes [lindens] by the gate that hang their sweet pea scent in the air above the traffic on warm evenings: Cavalier poets carved by Gibbons fine-grained. Those high climbers must be acacias, the feathers of Prince Henry James. (105)

Al's ability to mine the layers of the city and to unearth the tradition of London poets is a model for the reader who wants to unearth the "balanced skeleton" of the *Inferno* that forms the structure of *Londoners*. Villon, as Al's guide, parallels Virgil, and the descending spiral of sins is carefully recreated by allusion. Villon does not, however, like Virgil represent reason. Villon is for Duffy an urban anti-hero who, in his struggles with the literary and political establishment in the Paris of his day, can provide guidance and solace for Al. Duffy herself did write a play on Villon, and in the preface to that unpublished[29] play she describes the appeal of the anti-hero:

> One of the most potent contemporary figures is the anti-hero. . . . not someone who awes us with the weight of his decisions or actions but by his on-goingness, by his affirmation, he attains

heroism for us in situations and ways which we feel are within our grasp. He is frightened and weak yet at the same time curiously brave and strong. He may be caught, destroyed but not quite defeated. This makes him a hero though not heroic. Villon typifies the anti-hero. . . . He was a petty criminal because of his own wanton drive for self-destruction egged on by a society which educated him to a high standard and then gave him no acceptable outlet for his abilities. (i,ii).

Villon is thus an appropriate guide for Al, since Al also struggles to make a living by writing and is often rejected by the literary establishment. After experiencing rejection or fighting censorship, Al turns to Villon:

You, master, my guide are . . . a thief and a manslaughterer. . . . I understand all the twists and shifts . . . to go on writing without conforming. You could have given in, trimmed the tonsure you kept like a bald spot in the middle of your thinning hair. . . . You could have . . . taken a job with the establishment, written sermons instead of ballades in thieves cant. (*Londoners*, 15–16)

Even Al's financial problems are put into perspective by turning to Villon:

my master . . . you wrote *The Legacy* without enough even to buy a drink and warming your mittens at the candle flame you wrote by in your upstairs room alone while the Sorbonne rang its nine o'clock curfew knell on the day. Sometimes I'm more there with you than here; others you're here in this room with me. (16)

When Al's editors say that the language of the translation of Villon must be altered, Al wants "to shout: 'But it's true, it's true. I haven't made it up out of prurience. The words are there in the poems.'" Knowing that it's "Revise, trim or no production" (29), Al turns silently to Villon instead: "Did you have this trouble? Did church and state rail at you for your verses in thieves' cant, your cries of compassion for the blackened sinews of the hanged and the withered tits of the whores?" (29).

As Al leaves the editors, and the first literary battle, the journey down through the circles of Hell begins both in specific allusion and in Dantean parallels in the surface plot. Using the same image of the subway as a place of oblivion that

Hilary Burde does in Murdoch's *A Word Child*, Al thinks: "It isn't the swart boat to hell we most of us fear but the inner circle underground of oblivion. . . . Hell has become Hades again, the shadow kingdom of the heart, not of punishment but of non being, of sighs not howls" (32–33). The "swart boat" is Charon's ferry across the Acheron, and those of the "shadow kingdom" are like the opportunists who refused to make a choice in life and thus circle endlessly in a state of nonbeing. Limbo, the first circle of Dante's hell, inhabited by virtuous pagans, is alluded to in Al's visit to a library: "Topography is the lowest and dimmest circle of this limbo" (38). The second circle of carnal sin is represented by a pair of homosexual lovers, Paul and Frank (Paolo and Francesca), who are friends of Al. Al's editor, Goetzle, whom Al nicknames, "Guzzle," embodies gluttony. "Guzzle" was a Jewish refugee and although now "Johnsonian in his girth" (50), he "eats like a man who might starve. He eats for all those who didn't have enough, the walking skeletons of the camps" (54). As he eats, Guzzle lectures Al about best-selling authors and urges Al to make the biography of Villon longer and to get it done on time. As Al bargains for reading fees in order to make a little money while finishing the biography, Guzzle "stabs with his fork at a cockle shell of profiterole" (55). The fourth circle of the miserly and profligate is portrayed in more general terms, with references to "this great metropolis of lucre, Mammonchester" (13) and perhaps to the debates about the amount of money attached to the Sabine Baring-Gould award. Al sits at the committee meeting feeling frustrated with the politics of awarding literary prizes and the arguments over whether the award money is a profligate "waste of public money" or a "measly five hundred" (62). The allusions become specific again with Al's reference to the Styx, the river that separates the fourth circle from the fifth:

> The rush hour flows down from St Paul's in a muddy Styx of struggling bodies and cars. Paul's is a gaunt sepulchre for Donne's bones against a sky of smoking clouds. Clerks and typists and bookkeepers froth through the drizzle from Mammon's heart to

. . . London Bridge . . . homewards to their suburban teas, through Eliotesquerie to Betjemania. (62–63)

Here surface and substructure blend as the litany of London's writers merges with the Dantean allusions and contemporary details of rush hour.

Details of the plot of *Londoners* relate more closely to the Dantean substructure as the descent continues. Contemporary London is not only like Villon's Paris, but also like the great underground city of the *Inferno*. All the sins and all potential corruptions are present in a great city. In the fifth circle Dante observes the angry and then expresses righteous indignation himself; so, too, Al first comments on the general anger among the commuters and then expresses personal anger against the *Peterloo Review*. Al describes the London commuters as the sullen of the fifth circle, who wallow in the mud of the Styx:

> All the frustration of the day, and of the ordered lives of the city damped down, suddenly seethe and boil, at the getting up every morning to a task that seems dictated by society not nature until we grow sullen inside, carrying a scummed and festering pool that slops up in our throats, a heavy bile to be soothed with booze and pills. (64)

Al's anger occurs when Al goes to the *Peterloo Review* and a young female editor explains that they are turning down Al's article because they "couldn't see its relevance to the present phase of the conflict" (68). Al's despair has a further parallel from Dante as Al puts on the music from *Hercules*. The words from the opera refer to the same three furies who appear to Dante, and Medusa follows on cue: "The adagio opening . . . *Alecto with her snakes, / Megaera fell, / and black Tisiphone.* Why should they come to me, when I'm the one sinned against, to cry their murder. That's what rejection is: a little piece of murder. . . . And then they hold up that Medusa head that turns to stone: failure of nerve. What if I can't do it any more?" (72).

As the descent continues into the lower circles of hell,

crimes that are typical of the city appear. Rejection as murder leads into the seventh circle of the violent. On the level of the surface plot, murder is present not only in rejection but in the newspaper account of a gruesome homosexual murder that Al reads about. Then Eamon O'Halloran, a drug addict, comes in Al's window in terror that the mafia are after him, and is later found dead. Suicide appears in Al's memory of his college friend MacShane's suicide, and then in the explicit allusion to Dante's branches dripping blood that combines with a reference to the female poets Anne Sexton and Sylvia Plath:

> The far end is a hedge of laurel sealing off the streets beyond, suburban shrubbery not Apollo's bay, that last image of all those women writers who cut their wrists, themselves their own muse while he ran them down: Anne and Sylvia whose limbs set into rigidity, and became the leafy branchings of a Daphne. These are the deathly dusty laurels that never die, of the plastic foliage, stitched on not budded out. Break a twig and no white blood flows although their fingers are sinewy and resilient. (103–104)

Several examples of the urban crime of fraud, Dante's eighth circle, also occur in the novel. Prostitution is represented by Sally, a young black woman who comes into the Knickers trying to escape her pimp, and by Bumps Brunet, an effusive and ridiculous editor who wants Al to write a novel about prostitution. In a parallel to Dante's use of vivid names for devils in the bolgia of the grafters, Al thinks of how to write a report on a public meeting: "What devil's dance shall I make of it, what infernal saltarello for Tusker Edwards, Cur, Dogstooth, to ballet with Cupidity Wirral, Swindler, Rogue?" (172). Hypocrisy enters in the trial of Al's friend David for "public indecency" because he kissed a young carpenter on the street. Al comments: "We have been playing the subtle game of hypocrisy where all the pieces are yellow and everyone loses" (177). Neither man dares plead "not guilty" lest they attract the attention of the press and lose their jobs, so both are forced to accept a fine and a police record. Theft is present both in the burglary of Al's house and, even more vividly, when the movie director, Larry Lofts, steals Al's script about Villon. Lofts casually suggests setting Villon's story during the French Revolution and making Villon homosexual. Al tries to maintain artistic and historical integrity by tactfully suggesting the correct time period and a woman as "the love interest," but Lofts decides to keep Al's synopsis and hire another writer. Lofts is clearly branded a thief through an allusion to the *Inferno* in which all the thieves turn into snakes and lizards: "Lofts lounges green lizard in a deep armchair" (180). The tongues of flame that surround the evil counselors in the eighth bolgia are illustrated by the Cockettes, a grotesque transvestite act of dancing with flaming torches that Paul takes Al to see at The Wookey Hole Tavern after Al's disastrous afternoon with Larry Lofts. There Al meets Lisa, a former girlfriend, who taunts Al about writing a radio program on Villon. She too is encased in a tongue of flame: "The fires of the camp crematoria play round her still, as they do round Guzzle, I suppose, but with Lisa they have always danced and flickered like an impulse from that magnetic shield we carry about with us, the aura of the parapsychologists" (194). After leaving the tavern, Al has a vision of the whole city burning: "Roofs, gantries, hoardings are cut out in black on the red sky. The whole city seems to be burning, falling into the dark Thames soundlessly and yet still the sky glows with a cold heat while its reflection drowns" (197).

The ninth circle is ushered in by a reference to the cold and to the river Cocytus: "It's colder this morning. A few flakes, Cocytus feathers, drift down to leave damp fingerprints on the pavement" (204). The giants of circle nine are represented by huge papier-mâché heads from a carnival shop that decorate the Nevern: "Giant heads hang from the ceiling turning slowly in the updraught of hot air" (220). The worst crime in Dante's view, treachery, is for Duffy the mindless violence of an attempt to blow up a pub, which even turns out to be the wrong pub. Al thinks while pulling a "glittering blade of glass from a pub mirror . . . [from] my right hand. . . . 'They've made a mistake. It's not this pub they want. It's the one down the road where the soldiers'll be drinking, not here'" (240). Like Dante, Al emerges from the pub to see the stars, and Al laughs, knowing that survival is possible.

The stores identify "Pickpocket Avenue" as Oxford Street; this is a shopping street, a crowded path. Lessing too mentions it in *The Four-Gated City*.

Londoners contains not only a substratum of Dante, but a vivid portrayal of the surface of the city, its landmarks, its famous buildings, its districts, its houses and its parks. Al still plays the archeologist, this time not with literary allusions but with allusions to the architectural history and changing nature of city districts. Given Al's male role of constant conflict (with the literary establishment, the Parliamentary Select Committee, the *Peterloo Review,* Guzzle, Bumps Brunet and Larry Lofts), it is not surprising that Al mocks the city's landmarks, the monuments of the establishment. Coming out of the Parliamentary hearing, Al passes St. Margaret's and Trafalgar Square: "The flags in the square hang damp tea towels in an element not brisk enough to stiffen them. I cross over to St Margaret's under a sudden wheel of pigeons circuiting before touchdown in Trafalgar Square" (94). The landmarks are deflated as the flags become damp tea towels and the square an airport for pigeons. Similarly, the famous clock tower is reduced to "Big Ben, straight off the sauce bottle" (93). Buckingham Palace shrinks to a child's toy as Al thinks: "The last of the tourists are . . . snapping the façade of the toy box with its lead soldier" (96). When Al brings in the element of time to the observation of the landmarks and buildings, however, the tone becomes elegiac rather than satirical. Al thinks of the Houses of Parliament:

> "As always I find the building ridiculous rather than impressive. . . . Why do I find it so disturbing to think that this vaulting is a copy not an original fan flight of fancy? We all incorporate, make over, dally with the past. Is it because they didn't cannibalize; they tried to clone? Or is it the nature of gothic that it can't be reworked by another age while classical can, endlessly into palladian and barococo and Victorian town halls" (89–90).

The same tone mixing satire and elegy occurs as Al mocks famous streets as well as landmarks. Oxford Street is evoked in renaissance and eighteenth-century guise as Pickpocket Avenue, and then its present variety and tawdry appearance are compared with its past glories:

> I am blundering down Pickpocket Avenue where the cutpurses fleece the tourist and the tourist loots the shops, where the prin-

cesses of Araby, unused to carrying little tin counters or cheque
books about with them, lightfinger the goodies, believing that
husbands, fathers, brothers can always settle such things, and
find themselves up before the beak like any overnight drunk.
The street is strangely tawdry, even the famous names: D. H.
Evans and Selfridges, are staled by recession and touting cheek
by heavy jowl with gimcrack and gewgaw, trumpery and vanity,
gaud and trifle, unionjacked and bearskinned plastic made in
Hong Kong. We took beads and looking glasses to colonize the
natives in our Empire days and now they are sending them back
coloured red, white and blue" (30).

On Oxford Street the renaissance cutpurse stands near the
contemporary Arabian princess and the gaudy beads sent out
to colonize the British empire are now sent back to sell to
local tourists.

Times merge again as Al sees the image of wartime bomb-
ings beneath contemporary demolition. Al feels sorry for a
building that is being torn down and envisions it as an elderly
stripteaser:

> Someone has tried to cover up the ravage with a board skirting
> but it doesn't reach high enough, as if an elderly stripteaser had
> dropped her veils to thigh level letting us see the demolition of
> time above. No one, I notice, has put a name to it. Above the
> boarding there's a Victorian rococo shell dome that might have
> backed a Venus birthing from the waves, broken columns and
> moulded frieze. The mechanical jaws have munched and torn
> away the whole façade so that the interior is exposed like the
> pitiful slashed houses of wartime I remember. (164)

Although the image of an "elderly stripteaser" belongs to the
pattern of mockery, Al creates the tone of elegy in the description of the building's anonymous destruction in the jaws of a
mechanical monster.

The image of the "slashed houses" of wartime is related to
a pattern of archeological images, but this time Al's perception of a larger-than-life observer taking the lid off the bedsitters like the lid of a doll's house is female in its associations:

> If the giant came with his spade and sheared away one wall he
> would see us all; like opening the front of a doll's house. We each
> have a bed, a table, a chair, a radio. . . . we live vertically foot to

head. . . . I'm the eldest in this stack of lives. Right then that I should be the old mole in the cellerage with them all standing on my shoulders, and the only native, elder statesman, oldest resident of this little slice of Empire. (9–10, 11)

As the archeologist digger, "the old mole," Al looks at the layers of "this little slice of Empire." Al celebrates the variety of contemporary London represented in this house inhabited by a French girl, a German girl, an Indian girl, an Indian man, and a retired English Major who grew up in Bangalore, "a character from mid-Greeneland" (160). Later, more pessimistically, Al changes the doll's house inhabitants from the mole to rats. The variety of people is now represented by the variety of meals, but the loneliness of the inhabitants is caught in the image of the laboratory rats:

> Suppers are being cooked throughout the house: noodles dropped into boiling water, beans ladled onto toast, instant drumsticks drawn from beds of limp chips. Each animal in its box sits down to eat alone. A godseye view with the lid off the dollshouse would show us like laboratory rats in solitary. Some munch reading; others gobble. (106)

Al mitigates the image of the laboratory rat, however, just like the thoughts about landmarks, by placing it back in time and relating it to Villon: "You could have . . . set yourself to walk the beat of the cloister instead of scurrying like a sewer rat through the alleys of Paris" (16). Later Al corrects the history, "I don't even know if there were any sewers in Paris then. Probably not" (233), but the connection is still comforting. In this series of archeological images Al takes off the lid of the doll's house and examines a slice of contemporary London life, and then goes back and merges that slice with medieval Paris, seeing similar problems for artists and similar qualities in urban life.

Al's feminine side is represented not only by images of a doll's house, but also by sympathy for problems of friends, and even strangers. At one point Al thinks: "Do I believe in love at all any more or have I grown heretic in middle age or that middle-way agnosticism we're all supposed to fall into after our midlife crisis?" (20–21). In a minute Al answers the question: "love. I still believe in that divinity; I must" (22). When Hector Spalding says to Al, "What you need is the love of a good woman," Al jokes, a "bad one would do. . . . The little black prostitute from the Knickers crosses my mind momentarily but how could I make love without saying: 'I love you.' I've no practice at it" (123). Al is not interested in sex without love, and waiting for love, Al makes do with friendship, compassion, and one attempt at masturbation (which is interrupted by a phone call). Al thinks momentarily about Léonie, the French girl who is in love with the Indian, Jemal: "Perhaps Léonie and I should comfort each other. But then we'd lose our comforting friendship and we'd both know it was only second best" (20). Hearing that Léonie is pregnant by Jemal, Al rejoices with her as a woman would and then thinks as a man: "For a moment I wish it was my child she was carrying with such pleasure" (222). Al shows not only sympathy and support for friends but compassion for strangers. It is actually compassion that Al feels for the young black prostitute, Sally. Al, admiring the merging of cultures she represents, wishes it were possible to protect her: "Her accent is South Thames, Lewisham to Peckam. The face is fine carved in ebony like an Ethiope" (141). Listening to her discussing whether to give up prostitution, Al thinks about rescuing her but recognizes that it would not do: "I'm too old for her. Crabbed age and youth and all that" (142). Al is likewise sympathetic to the drug addict's father who comes to see where his son died, and to a boy in the pub whose pick-up buys him drinks but refuses to buy him food. Al gives him money, recognizing that it may be a con, but not caring whether it is or not. Although the structure of the novel presents the city as hell, Al also portrays another side of the city in which love and compassion for other people prevail. Al's concern for others illustrates what Duffy calls an "ethic of compassion." Duffy says of *Londoners*: "When people attempt—this horrible phrase—to 'do good' to react to each other with sympathy, compassion, and care, that's what makes it tolerable. That and love—various kinds of love."[30]

It is this compassion, and this admiration for the variety and diversity of people, that underlies Al's celebration of the districts, streets, and nodes of contemporary London. In these perceptions, which grow out of Al's more feminine qualities, the same merging of time occurs that mitigated Al's satiric views of landmarks and the vision of the lonely doll's house full of isolated cubicles. This time the layers of time reinforce the celebration of the city. In a passage similar to some of Margaret Drabble's in *The Middle Ground,* Al describes the ethnic variety of the district of Earls Court. Al notes how the district reflects the cosmopolitan nature of the eighties and at the same time recalls earlier time periods:

> Once this road [Earls Court Road] was full of old commonwealth Aussies and Kiwis, now it's new oil that greases its turning wheels. Three black-masked and chotied girls, with tempting glimpses of eyes and vizard frames of ivory skin, chatter on the corner by Smith's. A young man . . . in a long gown of white silk and a white lawn headcloth . . . leads a curly haired child by the hand . . . the grey gown . . . doesn't hide one good and one twisted foot. . . . They have come looking for a modern miracle from Western doctors, the inheritors of Averroes and Avenzoar. The shops are calligraphed with the arabic script. (34–35)

Al thinks of the ancestry of some friends in the area and identifies with them all:

> Somewhere a thousand or so years ago Frank's ancestors were Phoenician traders, migrants from the island city of Tyre, Paul's were Scots from Celtic Ireland, Jemal's North West Indian, Suli's Sinbad's sailors and mine were mongrel, polymorph; a nexus, in me the lines meet. I know their pasts, their legends, I can hear the songs they sing. (223)

The variety of ethnic groups in the area provides a pungent sensory variety in the evening as "takeaway" shops vie for clientele: "The air is aromatic with fish and chips, roast meat from the great turning drums of Kebabed flesh, curry in battered samosa triangles, glossy with grease, and from the stainless steel vats of hot chick peas, mutton, ladies' fingers, saffron rice" (39).

The districts of Soho and Chinatown, Mayfair, Kensington,

and Hampstead are evoked with precise detail. On the way to lunch with Guzzle, Al admires Chinatown and compares an earlier Soho with the present one. The trips on the underground link the districts and bring out each district's own unique qualities as Al comes up from their depths:

> I emerge at Leicester Square and walk up through the edge of Chinatown, past the drab books and delicately painted eggshells of the People's Republic shop. They don't need to tart up literature to vie with soap powder for the people's pence. . . .
> Shaftesbury Avenue that used to glitter as theatreland is now a stream of traffic between clothes shops, but I still catch a breath of Turkish smoke from a hubble-bubble long holder and hear the click of a bead fringe. . . . I . . . turn up into Soho proper, scene of my youth, Salad Days when there were still coffee bars and pavement pros instead of strip celluloid. . . . There was a year when the girls . . . stood around as if posing for a Lautrec. . . . They were perched along the pavements like a row of exotic birds. (49)

Behind the contemporary layer of clothes shops and Soho celluloid is the layer of Al's youth with its coffee bars and exotic girls. An even more elegiac, almost nostalgic tone envelops Al's description of Regent Street and Mayfair. Emerging from the underground on the way to the *Peterloo Review,* Al thinks of the elegant John Nash buildings in Regent Street which had been commissioned by Parliament in 1813 and of the Mayfair of the late 1930s and early 1940s with its luxurious movie houses. These memories contrast starkly with the current commercialism as the three layers of time are presented simultaneously:

> Spewed out again at Piccadilly I lament as always Nash's Regent Street vandalized by commerce and cross over among the classical façades of Mayfair, remembering my first foreign film in the plush seats of the Curzon, treated to a lush taste of Italian poverty on a day's outing from my own. (65)

Four days later Al walks through Kensington on the way to a city zoning meeting to earn some money by writing up the meeting for Rick's preservation journal. As they walk Al thinks back to the handsome but class-bound Kensington of the earlier twentieth century. This time Al admires the variety and colorfulness of the present-day shoppers on High Street:

> Now we're beyond the tube station . . . and waiting to cross the dusty veldt of the Cromwell Road, whose plane trees pattern the air with their still leafless tracery. Once over we're in an older trellis of handsome streets, relic of the Kensington of cabs and housemaids. We pass the miniature crystal palace of the gardening shop, plucked out of Kew by a giant hand and set down here, and turn right along the High Street. We have walked for ten minutes into a different world of leisurely shoppers. . . . Sometimes a whole gaggle of brightly coloured girls breaks through the stream. (163–4)

The same layering of time occurs when Al goes to Hampstead for the interview with Larry Lofts. While walking through Hampstead, Al contrasts the area as it is now with what it was on earlier visits there to a schoolmate and remembers that Freud died in Hampstead. Even the tube stations are not seen merely as ways of connecting the districts but rather as places in their own right with their own layers of history. Looking for the Bakerloo line, Al thinks not only of Sherlock Holmes but also of the nineteenth-century engineer Sir Marc Brunel:

> I fight my way out a stop later and am swirled along in search of the Bakerloo, most ancient of underground ways only just modernized out of its Brunellian high hat brick arches. I've always believed it's named after Sherlock Holmes or rather for him. (65)

Just as Al noted the layers of time beneath the landmarks, so too Al comments on and celebrates the layers of time behind districts, streets, and even transportation lines.

Al's ability to focus on the details of daily life allows Al to see nature within the city. Like P. D. James, Maureen Duffy does not see nature in contrast to the city but as part of it. On the chimney pots, in the cracks in the concrete, in small patches of dirt, nature manifests itself in the city. Opening a window to air out a room, Al listens: "Sometimes a blackbird sings high up and unseen, vesper or hesper from a cold chimney pot (106). Al also notices that "where earth has pushed aside the thin broken skin of tarmac the sparrows have a puddle bath. . . . Only one can use it at a time and there seems to be some queueing system. . . . Other birds may chirp, spadgers cheep. Have I discovered avian cockney?" (47). Although the book is set in very early spring with its chill winds and rains and even hail, some flowers have come out, inspiring Al to meditate on urban plants:

> Outside my lit room the Spring afternoon has draped itself in a soft grey teagown, a crêpe de Chine of unmoving cloud. A buddleia grows opposite the window from a cranny of dirt beside the cinder service road. . . . In summer buddleia grows with a spindly strength, a green persistence that ends in purple pokers for insects to browse on. The fireweed roots there too but I expect that, knowing how it crept across bombed London, lacing over scars and fractures with its green lances of leaves and flowering pink starfish. (101–2)

When going out to the country, Al thinks, "I'd forgotten how London's walls bring the Spring, blossoms and all, on quicker" (227).

Not all of Al's observations associate nature with rebirth like the fireweed, however. The plane trees, which sometimes harbor the consoling spirit of Etherege, can also evoke terror:

> Tonight coming back, for a moment I saw the still unleafed plane trees, my old friends, as Snow White's Disney wood of terror,[31] a mesh keeping out the sky, a web above the streets that we scurry under believing ourselves free, the kind of vision that comes to the middle-raged. (10)

Here nature creates a mesh or a web, not Drabble and Carol Gilligan's[32] comforting network, but something that keeps out the sky and might entrap the inhabitants. Nature is no more a benign force than the city itself. It is part of the city, and like the city can be associated with lyricism or terror.

The city is also connected with nature in the ocean images that pervade *Londoners* and are associated in earlier novels with both the image of the mother and that of the archeological dig. In *Capital* the archeological image merges with that of the ocean:

A plane tree (sycamore) with its peeling bark. It is known as the London Tree. Duffy also describes it elsewhere in *Londoners*. It is referred to in Murdoch's *Nuns and Soldiers* and P. D. James' *Innocent Blood*.

> The city this morning was a drowned Atlantis under deep waves
> of mugginess and fumes as if the dew had been drawn up from
> the pavements . . . [to] hang in a damp ocean shroud over the
> streets.[33]

London is a drowned Atlantis, the underwater city that archeologists yearn to explore. In *Londoners* the image is often hu-
morous as Al uses it to classify the variety of the city:

> The pub is a wide estuary with different species taking up their
> territory to feed and squabble and mate but the tide-lines that
> mark out their boundaries, cliffs, high flotsam, shore or shallows
> are temporal as well as spatial. (77)

The bar in the pub becomes "a reef where we each have our
own school with its territory to browse and snap on morsels
of comfort" (9). Unlike the pubs in Lessing's *If the Old Could
. . .* , which are true microcosms, miniature reflections of the
city, in Duffy's novel the pubs are estuaries, reefs, tidepools,
only temporary places of retreat. Al describes the young boys
and girls who come into the pub as "migrating birds [who] . . .
vanish from one scene for a time, sometimes to come back
but sometimes to drop into the ocean of the city" (46). The
traffic of the city is particularly associated with ocean images:
"Sometimes a bus pulls in from the endless surf of traffic"
(30). There is wry humor in Al's observations: "The home-
going rush slows the millrace traffic to a packed sardine crawl,
each little fish in its tin nose to tail" (105). Al's friend Rick is
"impervious to the noise of traffic. He booms above it: a Cap-
tain Ahab in a school of combusting whales" (163). Harrods
becomes the "*QE II* of commerce, a twenties liner dressed all
over with fairy lights at Christmas . . . now sailing through
late Spring towards where mosque and oratory confront each
other, clashing rocks in a Protestant sea, diagonally across the
strait where Brompton Road grows old" (32). The ocean imagery merges with the Dantean substructure when Al observes that the "rush hour flows down from St Paul's in a
muddy Styx of struggling bodies and cars" (62–63). A similar
image occurs in *Capital* when the narrator sees the traffic as
"a flowing Styx of black cars and cabs" (83). The ocean im-

agery functions like the rest of nature in the novels. It is associated with respite, humor, and variety.

At the end of the novel, Al finishes the radio program on Villon, accepts a job as the resident creative writer in "Ledwitch," and contemplates starting a relationship with an attractive woman writer on the interviewing panel who had looked up smilingly. Al tells the panel: "It will be good not to be a Londoner for a while at least, to stand back and look at it" (231). Al plans to leave London, but not forever, and to use that time to stand back and analyze the city. Not even the explosion in the pub at the end of the novel can discourage Al:

> I'm all right. I'm going to be all right. . . .
> The sky has cleared and there are stars. They seem to be laughing. And I'm laughing too. (240)

Al has meditated upon the city both in the role of attacking satirist and in that of nurturing celebrator. Al has analyzed the layers of the city beneath the cosmopolitan surface and has written an elegy for the city. Now Al is ready to leave the archeological site and go elsewhere, but both Al and London are assured of survival.

Capital

Duffy's earlier novel *Capital: a Fiction* is not as lyrical as *Londoners*. In *Capital* the city as an archeological dig is conveyed not primarily in the imagery and the observations of the city, but in the structure and plot of the novel. In structure the book alternates the story of Meepers with the letters of a professor of eighteenth-century history to his absent love. To these two layers of stories is added a third layer of vignettes from different time periods in London, from a Stone Age story of childbirth and death to a contemporary scene of children playing and roses growing in front of a small brick London house that still remains despite large blocks of redevelopment. Yet another layer occurs in a brief prologue and epilogue set sometime in the future. Commenting on the layered structure of the novel, Anatole Broyard identifies the city strongly with Meepers:

> *Capital* must be praised in layers. It is a wonderful idea that could not have come at a better time. . . . Miss Duffy has given Meepers the shabby majesty of the city he wishes to save, a city with false teeth, a vagrant city in the history books, one whose past is as ambiguous as any madman's childhood and adolescence. Meepers' musings are worthy of a saviour of cities.[34]

The plot of the novel, which is carried in both the Meepers sections, with their omniscient narrator, and in the professor's letters as he becomes increasingly interested in Meepers, picks up the idea of the city as an archeological dig in Meepers' attempts to prove that London remained inhabited even after the Romans left in the fifth century A.D. Meepers literally digs in excavation sites around London to find evidence for his theory. When Meepers explains the importance of his project to the professor, he emphasizes the issue of the survival of the city:

> The city, this city. This concept or medium of civilization. Did it survive? Or did it collapse and the rats and rabbits nibble among the ruins of an unburied Pompeii, along with a few impoverished squatters? Or did it hold out, make terms with the barbarians. . . . Was there in fact no break in continuity? . . . If the city survived then I think it will again. It's threatened . . . by lack of faith. We are out of love with it because we are out of love with ourselves. What might really destroy us is human self-disgust. (133)

One place Meepers looks for evidence is in a site being excavated for high-rise towers near where an old Roman road once was. In spite of falling into a pit and breaking his false teeth, Meepers finds a shard of pottery that is enough to convince the professor to request a colleague in computer science to run Meepers' data on the university computer. With these two narrative strands, the novel picks up a dual vision similar to Al's in *Londoners*. The professor, who comments so wittily and caustically on the city of London and the negative changes that have occurred since the eighteenth century, parallels the satiric, masculine Al in conflict with society.

Meepers, quiet and unobtrusive, parallels the nurturing, female side of Al as Meepers tries to prove that London's existence was continuous and can remain so if people can learn to love and have faith in themselves. Although Meepers does not survive to prove London's continuity, he does bring out in the professor a new quality of compassion that teaches the latter to value the city.

The image of the city as archeological dig, the layered city, is made explicit by Meepers. Not only is the novel structured with layers of stories from different times breaking through the narrative, but Meepers, as an amateur archeologist, thinks of the city that way. The opening passages about Meepers reveal his layered perception of the city:

> He couldn't help it if the bones poked through the pavements under his feet; plague victims, there was a pit hereabouts he was sure, jumbled together, massacred Danes weighted by their axes to the river-bed, the cinders of legionaries in porphyry and glass urns gritting beneath the soles of his thin shoes. . . . As he passed below, long buried noblemen looked down at him from the portrait gallery of street names. . . . They had found mammoth bones here, he remembered, when they were digging the first underground in the 1860s. (15)

For Meepers the city streets barely cover the bones of the victims of the plague in the 1600s and 1300s, and those bones are mingled with those of the Danes who invaded England in the late 800s. The remains of Roman legionnaires from the 400s also lie beneath the city streets. Prehistoric mammoth bones lie below the underground. When Meepers looks down at the Thames, he thinks:

> The dun-coloured mousse was full of treasures: flints, battle axes, shards, coins cast or fallen in, even whole ships. . . . The layers that lifted the city twenty feet above ground level were here compressed into the river bed. (87)

The same concept of the layered city appears again as Meepers wishes that the nineteenth-century excavations for the subway had been supervised by archeologists. He thinks of the layers of the city as those of a cake:

the train passed under St Paul's and the city. The deposits were stratified thick around and over him; his compartment nibbled its way through them like a mouse through a richly layered cake. He lamented the lost chances of nineteenth-century burrowing, the lack of knowledge and system, the brutality of the rape, the never-to-be repaired hymen of history. (105–106)

For Meepers each layer of the city's history is valuable, and he is interested in proving that the city and civilization belong together. A female image blends with that of the archeological dig as history becomes a woman whose hymen has been broken in a brutal rape, but Meepers plans to save her and cherish her.

Until he gets to know Meepers and value his project, the professor's view of the city is caustic, and he views the city much as Al does during Al's battles with the literary establishment. The professor criticizes the hasty renovation, the dampness, and the dowdiness of London. Like Meepers, he links the city to the past, although this past for him tends to be the eighteenth and nineteenth centuries rather than the earlier periods that interest Meepers. Like Al, the professor regrets the tearing down of John Nash's late eighteenth- and early nineteenth-century buildings, and the professor uses the same sort of ocean and fish imagery that Al often does:

> Then going up the Strand I noticed that they'd almost finished knocking down the North side, the last of the Nash, just the two pepperpots forlorn on the end and the middle of that beautiful building sliced out like a fillet from a dead fish; the windows whitely opaque too with the sky open behind them more dead cod, calcined eyeballs in the façade. (25)

Al's deflating "sauce bottle" image also appears as the professor scathingly mocks London's landmarks and buildings when he's driven through the city at night: "the Houses [of Parliament] looked more like illustrations for a sauce bottle than ever. County Hall exhibited a sort of foolish podgy dignity like a matron overblown in pastels with its green and pink floodlighting. Then it was a discreet flash of his elegancy Paul's once we were past the concrete droppings of a monstrous clay cow that's the National Theatre and next city cliffs, fascist classical of bank and brokers" (127). Also like Al, the professor thinks of the city as it has been presented by Wordsworth and other authors of the past:

> What he [Wordsworth] saw was the eighteenth-century London: "Ships, towers, domes, theatres and temples" . . . looking down towards St Paul's from the bridge. How is it that our air is so much cleaner than it used to be and yet I still get the drowned feeling? Perhaps it's because after that moment that he caught on the bridge, and Blake caught it too, the air got darker and thicker down through Dickens. (26)

Before he meets Meepers, however, the professor has no perception of the city's charm and variety such as that which balances Al's mocking vision. The professor admires a few Asian-Africans, but when he looks at the teenagers on the street, he sees nothing but dowdiness. He writes to his love:

> And now you're not here there's nothing to offset the sheer dowdiness of the city. Everywhere I look there's the same imitation of 'thirties, 'forties, 'fifties fashions that were hideous in their day and have gained nothing by regurgitation with a touch of green and mauve camp. (39)

The dowdiness turns to a vision of degeneration as he imagines London as an old eighteenth-century courtesan trying to attract the tourists:

> The pavements were choked with girl clerks in summer dresses and men in shirtsleeves with half moons of sweat under their armpits . . . interlaced with every nationality of tourist making for St Paul's. . . . They come to gape at the remains of this vast tel that's like a highdressed wig, powdered and bejeweled but where the mice have nested . . . and the lice run among its remaining hairs and drop from the thin ringlets on to the dirty tidemarked neck, the suburbs. (69–70)

The professor says he once had passion for London but now it's gone: "I feel it most in my lost passion for the city that's become an old wife I hardly speak to except to complain my dinner's cold and dry" (112). Though he is still wed to the city, he is repulsed by what it has become.

Meepers has many more problems than the professor, but

he sees London in a more positive light. Meepers was wounded in World War II and spent a long time as a prisoner of war. He still has shrapnel in his head, "fine metal fingers that had left his mind sharp but severed his emotions," except for an occasional "eruption of hot feelings" (35).[35] When he finally returns to London, he discovers that his parents have been killed in the war and that the house he grew up in was only rented. He has a small pension, but not enough for a London flat, so he becomes a squatter. He lives on the same square in which he grew up, but now only occupies the garden shed behind a fashionable new house where he works as a gardener. Most of his time, however, he spends on history, archeology, and his project to prove that London remained inhabited after the Romans left. He often gives lectures on archeology to local societies. It is on the way home from one of these lectures that Meepers is mugged in a suburban station, his wallet stolen, and his nose badly bruised. No sooner does he begin to recover than he returns one evening to find the garden shed padlocked. He realizes he must move on and finds an empty lodge in Kensington Gardens. When that starts to be renovated, he moves to the eleventh floor of an empty high-rise office building. Throughout all of this he gets discouraged but never becomes bitter, and he always retains his affection for the city. After he is mugged, Meepers longs to get back to the city: "He wanted to be sucked into the obliterating city where he would be supported and comforted by its very presence and continuity, by its millions of ant bodies busying around him" (35).

It is not just the millions of bodies who comfort him, however. Individuals also respond. The conductor on the train says he won't worry about the ticket and even offers Meepers some money. Meepers is almost afraid of such "dangerous kindness" (35) that could lead him to fall apart and lose his independence. He refuses the money, since he has enough change to take a taxi to the square with his garden hut. There he stops by a coffeestall bus where he usually gets a cup of hot tea every night. The woman who sells coffee brings him into the bus, gives him two aspirins, and laces his coffee with liquor: "The clichés of kindness as comforting as the fortified tea or old shoes slopped over him" (34). This individual act of kindness he accepts, and it does fortify him. The city can provide nurturance even in the unlikely figure of a woman selling coffee from a bus.

Later, when Meepers falls into a pit at the excavation site, he breaks his false teeth. The next day, when he goes out to have them fixed, he thinks: "Oh the convenience of a city: first that it should make false teeth at all and then that it should renew them in a twinkling when broken" (137). In spite of his problems as a squatter and in spite of his accidents, Meepers praises city life. When he stops to notice the people around him, he admires them even if he feels shy in their presence. In imagery like Al's in *Londoners,* Meepers views the cleaning women as exotic birds who possess the city during the early hours of the morning:

> A gaggle of cleaners broke from an office block, exotic and plump as bullfinches in their summer plumage, chivvying each other into loud laughter with tossed-off obscenities, their permed, dyed heads glittering like parakeet crests in the sun. . . . Meepers crossed the road afraid as a girl below a workmanned scaffolding to pass them by and run the gamut of their invitations and laughter, loud as their sons'. . . . At this time it was their city. Without them dust and trash would gradually silt it up. (85–86)

Although he appreciates their vividness and their contribution from a distance, Meepers has a young girl's sensitivity to their brashness. In an observation similar to Jane Somers' in Lessing's *The Diaries of Jane Somers,* Meepers recognizes that at this time of day, London is the women's city.

It is from Meepers that the professor learns both sensitivity and compassion as well as sympathy for Meepers' concern to prove the city's existence continuous. The professor first meets Meepers when he writes up his theory for the journal the professor edits and the professor rejects it because it is "too early and conjectural" (102). Meepers is angry and frustrated, but decides to take a job as a porter at the university in order to sit in on the professor's lectures and learn how to prove that he is right. The professor, recognizing him, is afraid of him at first: "suppose he's decided to blow the place up because of my recalcitrance in not accepting his wretched piece?" (19). Soon, however, the professor comes to respect Meepers' knowledge as Meepers relates the early history of coins to the professor's class discussion of the South Sea Bubble, and the professor learns of Meepers' lecturing to historical societies. Meepers' accident on the excavation site provides the professor with an opportunity for compassion. When Meepers, exhausted and unable to talk after breaking his teeth, is picked up by the police, he gives the professor's address as his own lest he be locked up as a vagrant. Meepers explains later to the professor that he had looked up the professor's address after the professor returned his article and remembered it because it was the house next to the one in which he was born. He didn't think the police would call the professor, but they did. The professor, who had been thinking about Meepers and writing of him in most of his letters, comes to Meepers' defense and takes him home. It is then that Meepers, lisping without his upper plate of false teeth, has an opportunity to explain his project and gives the professor the fragment of first-century Samian pottery that he found in the pit. After this experience, the professor becomes interested in Meepers' idea and suggests trying Meepers' data in the university computer.

Gradually the professor becomes less "out of love" with himself and less disgusted with the city around him, the two qualities that Meepers thinks most threaten the survival of the city. And because of Meepers, the professor gets to know some of his students. One evening the professor finds himself standing in line behind two students, Robin and Jenny, and he asks them, for something to say, if they know Meepers. The professor buys them a drink and they respond by inviting him to their flat in Hammersmith which they share with a young black girl, Martha, and her baby. The students ask about "the old guy who knows so much" (111) and later invite Meepers to dinner. When Meepers reciprocates that invitation and invites Robin, Jenny, and Martha to the eleventh floor of the office building in which he is a squatter, they all get in trouble because the police see them. Robin quickly pretends that they are occupying the buildings as a housing protest, and the professor and his colleagues go over to rescue the students. The students are easily rescued, but when the professor discovers that Meepers is homeless again, he takes him in. Living in the professor's house, Meepers is able to finish his data for the computer, and the professor, finishing his course, decides to go to America to find his lover, to whom he writes: "Without you my veneer of civilization breaks down. I become brutish and stupid. You are my city and I am coming to find you" (182). Now it is the professor's lover who has become the city, not an eighteenth-century courtesan or an old wife. The professor has learned in his contact with Meepers what Duffy calls an "ethic of compassion," that impulse to "'do good' to react to each other with sympathy, compassion and care" and it is that ethic, along with love, that makes life "tolerable."[36] The professor, in responding to Meepers' needs and interests, has learned to be compassionate and sympathetic. He has learned, like the androgynous Al, some feminine virtues.

Meepers never gets the computer's answer (nor does the reader) because he has a heart attack and dies after the professor has already left for America but before the program is run. Although Meepers dies, an image of compassion precedes his death, and a scene of continuity follows it. These qualities of compassion and interrelationship predict the city's survival better than the computer. After Meepers hands his data over to the computer specialists, he stops once again by the coffee-stall bus to visit with the woman who was kind to him after the mugging. She is delighted to see him again and still has his thermos sitting on her shelf. They chat briefly about the war and her vacation, and Meepers turns to go. As Meepers leaves the bus, he turns "to look up at her framed in the doorway as if like a Byzantine portrait she had been painted on a timeless golden backdrop. Her face was dark and featureless against the light which caught at her pepper-and-salt hair and turned it into a flaring halo. . . . He almost waved" (184). For Meepers, her earlier kindness and simple friendliness have given her an aura of the early saints. When Meepers sits down at the professor's desk that evening, the sharp pains of a heart attack strike him. He worries that he has failed. People from all layers of history seem to be calling out to him: "They were pushing up through the ground, standing on each other's shoulders and calling to him not to leave them out as if he was their last hope of immortality" (186). Meepers scrawls "Sorry so sorry" on the professor's pad as the pain abates for a minute, and then dies.

This time, however, the novel does not shift directly to the vignettes as it does elsewhere, but stays with the omniscient author to shift to the young black mother, Martha, who is taking her son, Ben, through Westminster Abbey to introduce him to his heritage. As Duffy emphasizes in the Preface to *That's How It Was,* "mother and child effectively open and close *Capital*" (xi). The opening vignette portrays a Stone Age woman dying in childbirth, but the closing maternal scene portrays survival and celebration. Martha is charmed by the "delightful gaudiness of it all . . . a riot of gilt and enamel on white stone and polished marble" (187). Ben is "very happy to be carried about and shown his inheritance" (187). Just as Meepers thought about the graves of the earlier London inhabitants, so Ben is being introduced to the tombs that represent London's history. Martha looks for the tomb of the Black Prince, "but his only appearance was . . . on his father's monument. It didn't matter. There were enough kings, queens and princes for Ben not to feel without antecedents" (188). The choir begins to sing "Kings shall be thy nursing fathers and their queens thy nursing mothers" (188). Ben, with his black face and cockney accent, represents cosmopolitan London, and it is he who will inherit the many-layered history of London and the "ethic of compassion," represented by his mother's nurturance, that will ensure its survival.

The historical vignettes that are interspersed between the episodes about Meepers and the professor's letters undergird Meepers' vision of the layered city. The novel is divided into a prologue and epilogue and five sections based on the vignettes. The prologue and epilogue are the most pessimistic. They present an aerial view of England set some time in the

future. In the Prologue the island is overcrowded and people
rush to the polluted sea shore like lemmings: "The cities
seemed half empty, plague stricken under the dust-veiled sun,
trussed by flat tapes of motorways. . . . Along the highways to
the capital itself the land was pocked by abandoned diggings
and scarred with decaying commercial buildings" (12). In the
epilogue two men in a helicopter hover over England to take
pictures and discuss its overpopulation. They already have
pictures of "the old Paris area. . . . Kilometers of weeds and
rusting iron between broken walls like a filmset. . . . the Eiffel
Tower . . . lies there like the spine in a skeleton leaf" (191–
192). Paris seems not to have survived. Will London? The answer is implied in the last line, which belongs not to the helicopter pilot but to a narrator: "Or Hierusalem . . . " (192).
The city can deteriorate, as the prologue and epilogue illustrate, but there is also the alternative of the new Jerusalem
that can be brought about by the ethic of compassion.

The history of London is represented in the vignettes that
alternate with the story of Meepers and the professor's letters.
The individual vignettes, which are arranged chronologically
from prehistoric times to the present, are artfully crafted and
sometimes refer obliquely to the text of the plot. Several small
notebooks of dates and historical facts and a newspaper clip-
ping of archeological discoveries in the Duffy manuscript collection at King's College attest to how carefully she researched
these sections of the novel. The details and even the styles of
the sections are historically accurate. The influence of Joyce,
who Duffy says led her back to the genre of the novel again
after she had turned away from it in adolescence,[37] is evident
in sections where the style is reminiscent of the "Oxen in the
Sun" chapter of *Ulysses*. The long vignette on the Saxon experience of the Norman Conquest is written with modern versions of words that would have been in the Old English vocabulary at the time.[38] A later vignette about a poet replicates
the alliteration of *Piers Plowman:* "The poet came to the pul-
pit and preached above them. . . . He was mild in his manner
and gave them sops to soothe them" (117). As James Brockway notes in a review, the description of eighteenth-century

courtesans is a take-off of Sacheverell Sitwell:[39] "Ah, Cre-
morne, what pleasurable anticipation dwells in your name
alone. Let us enter the gardens just as the evening is beginning when the daytime denizens have gone East in calico"
(149). Sometimes themes in the vignettes follow themes from
the main plots. The description of the courtesans follows a
letter of the professor that describes a postcard of a portrait
of Venus and Mars he receives from his love and the physical
longing it arouses in him. A section about a woman selling
watercress is similar to Mayhew's descriptions of Victorian
poverty and follows a segment of the plot in which Meepers
shows the professor and Robin and Jenny a third- or fourth-
century skeleton of a woman who died of malnutrition. Centuries may pass, but both lust and hunger endure. Sometimes
the vignette seems to comment ironically on the text. After
the professor tells Meepers that he would like to read Meepers'
article again, "not for *Studies* you understand . . . For my own
interest" (103), a vignette follows in which a French Jew who
comes to England soon after the Norman Conquest lends
money at forty percent interest. At other times the connections between vignettes and plot are more oblique. Duffy says
that she got the idea of Meepers' false teeth from Genet; in
tribute to Genet, she refers obliquely to his novel entitled
Lady of the Flowers in the name "Flower de Luce" that she
uses in a vignette about a fourteenth-century prostitute that
follows the section in which Meepers' teeth are broken.[40]

The first of the five sections of the novel, entitled "The City
of the Dead," contains four vignettes from prehistoric times.
The first describes the prehistoric mother who dies in childbirth, the "Swanscombe Man, who was probably a woman
aged about twenty-five, was dying beside the Thames" (18),
though an older son survives her. The second is more humor-
ous: the vignette brings contemporary and ancient time together by having Neanderthalensi shiver in Whitehall, pick
berries in Piccadilly, walk across Hyde Park, and fall asleep
listening to the hyenas on Hampstead Hill. The third vignette
recounts the story of the "seal people" as they fish for salmon
in the Thames. The fourth is a parody of the King Arthur

story. "Artor" travels with "Murddin" and sleeps with Murddin's sister. However, when at Murddin's command Artor throws the sword he pulled from a stone into a lake, it merely sinks down: "What did you expect? A white arm dressed in fine linen?" cackles Murddin (57). History is not romanticized, nor is its violence hidden, as the next section, "New Troy," illustrates in four vignettes from the time of the Roman occupation to the Battle of Hastings. Llyr visits Lludd and Lludd admires Llyr's two ferocious daughters, Gonerilla and Regan. The narrator describes Llyr's thoughts: "He was getting old but his girls would defend him" (65). The ironic reference to the situation in *King Lear* makes clear that the violence can come from within as well as from without. Next a young Roman soldier admires the public buildings and well-laid-out streets of Lundinium. Violence comes to the forefront in "Fragments from the Berkynge Chronicle, probably spurious" that tells of Danish invasions in the 800s and 900s and in the vivid account from a Saxon point of view of the Battle of Hastings.

In the third section, "Respublica Londiniensis," the relationship between plot and vignettes shifts, and the structure alters. At this point in the plot, the professor speaks to Meepers, and as their stories come closer together, the vignettes come more often: first Meepers' story, then a vignette, then the professor's, then another vignette. "Respublica Londiniensis" has nine vignettes and stretches from the reign of William the Conqueror with the vignette about the French Jew who comes to England to lend money at forty percent to the mid-seventeenth century with a vignette about Ranter Coppe, who defies the godliness of the Commonwealth. Violence is present in this section, too: one vignette personifies Death during the Black Plague of 1348 and another both grimly and humorously describes the success of the young prostitute, Flower de Luce, during the Peasant's revolt in Richard II's reign. Favorite historical legends are gently mocked. Richard Whittington, for example, explains that the real way to become rich is to marry well, run for office in the guild, and lend money. "King Elizabeth" appears, irritated by the sluggishness of his barge and the pain in "his womb" (133) and wondering how much money he'll get in the traditional cup full of coins at Guildhall. The eighteenth and nineteenth centuries are represented in a section entitled "Babylon" that includes four vignettes, among them a lush description of eighteenth-century courtesans and a Dickensian description of young pickpockets working a Chartist gathering. The success of these pickpockets is counterbalanced by another vignette describing the suffering of prison life. The fifth section, showing twentieth-century life, is entitled "Cockaigne" (after the legendary land of luxury and indolence), but the vignettes are of simple people: a working-class boy and girl visit their grandmother in the country, a young couple meet at "the Workes" and marry, a West Indian immigrant tries to find a job. The wars are represented by "old man Moloch" eating soldiers in World War I and a couple drinking gin in the London blitz during World War II.

The final vignette turns away from both violence and humor to become elegiac in tone as it portrays Londoners who

> still grow roses out of the thin top soil above the brick earth that the house is built from, pied yellow and black London brick. . . . Streets are torn down around then to be replaced by complexes of flats. . . . Container lorries park . . . like the carcasses of tin dinosaurs. Behind their front room curtains they watch the comings and goings of the street: the children playing out, the workmen renovating number 2, Mr. Goodenough taking his first steps . . . after an operation, a car drawing up, returning men and women from work. "We always say to them when they go away: Come back to civilization." (190)

In spite of the violence of wars, the loneliness of individuals left to die on prehistoric plains or locked up in the Tower of London, and the persecution or exploitation of some people by others, London has survived all these years and civilization has been continued by ordinary people who grow roses in the city, who live in their houses despite redevelopment, and who keep track of their neighbors. The epilogue that follows this vignette shows that it is possible still for the life of the city to be destroyed, but it is also possible that these very people can create the new Jerusalem by exercising an "ethic of compassion" and by having faith in the value of the city. For those like Meepers and Al and the professor and even Ben, who have learned to see the city as an archeological dig with layers of past that are worth preserving and a varied present that is worth celebrating, London can be the new Jerusalem.

CHAPTER 7

Conclusion

In the late twentieth century, the worldwide migration to cities continues, but so does a general disparagement of urban life and the future of cities. Many who work in cities are still afraid of them and retreat to the suburbs for housing and leisure activities. At such a time it is encouraging to find a whole tradition of writers who celebrate the city and portray its varied detail. The novels of Doris Lessing, Margaret Drabble, Iris Murdoch, P. D. James, and Maureen Duffy are "recording instruments" that have given us a "section map in depth"[1] of London. But even more than just the detailed portrayal of one specific city, they have given us a new attitude with which to approach cities, a new way of seeing cities, a woman's view. The dangers of the late twentieth-century city are still present in these novels, but the dangers are only part of a complex matrix that also includes a willingness to accept change and fragmentation in the city, the valuing of a variety of different people, and a nonhierarchical appreciation of all the elements that make up a city. The matrix images' celebration of the city counterbalances the negative images of the city in much modern literature, both British and American.[2] They also provide new, flexible images of the city that can replace the nonfunctional images of the city as an organism or machine[3] so often used in city planning.

In their flexibility and expandability, the matrix images convey an acceptance of change and a toleration of fragmentation in the city. A palimpsest or an archeological dig has no fixed number of layers; a network or a mosaic is expandable; a labyrinth can have an infinite number of turnings. Likewise, because there is no specific closure to these images, one can analyze in depth a part of any of them as well as look at each of them as a whole. The images of the city in these novels, unlike, for instance, those Dickens used, embrace change, both architectural and natural, and thereby allow the dimension of time to be part of the perception of the city. Martha Quest in Doris Lessing's *The Four-Gated City,* Cordelia Gray in P. D. James' *Skull Beneath the Skin,* and Al and Meepers in Maureen Duffy's novels view the city as having evolved over time. The city's earlier layers of time are preserved in Martha Quest's imagination as she remembers the older structures on a street when she looks at the new ones. In P. D. James' works the presence of time and change is signaled by buildings that have been renovated and thus incorporate both the old and the new simultaneously. It is only P. D. James' female characters, however, who fully appreciate the renovated structures; Cordelia Gray, for instance, is delighted by her new flat in an old Victorian warehouse that overlooks the Thames. The passage of time moves into the very structure of Duffy's works. In *Londoners* it appears in the literary allusions of Al, who sees present-day London coexisting with Villon's Paris and Dante's *Inferno;* in *Capital* it is found in the layering of vignettes of London's past with the narratives of Meepers and the professor.

An acceptance of change and passing time within the city implies an acceptance not only of architectural and historical change but also of the rhythmic changes of nature and the presence of nature within the city. Nature is no longer contrasted to the city but seen as a part of it. The old baulk of timber that sprouts a flower is an important symbol of the city in Doris Lessing's *The Four-Gated City.* In *The Diaries of Jane Somers* and in P. D. James' *Innocent Blood* the parks of the city are as vividly portrayed as the city streets. Margaret Drabble's characters in *The Radiant Way* create gardens in their backyards and notice the roaming cats and budding buddleias underneath the huge highway bridges. Iris Murdoch creates both atmosphere and the passage of time in her novels by her description of seasons and changing patterns of light. Maureen Duffy uses natural images to convey city life and describes the small natural details one often does not notice in urban scenes, for instance the "cockney" sparrows and the fireweed slowly covering and reclaiming old bomb sites.[4] In many of the novels, the "London Tree," the plane tree (or sycamore) with its peeling bark, plays a major role in expressing the presence of nature and the rhythms of the seasons. The "long-armed plane trees" slowly dropping autumnal leaves[5] preside over Tim's mystical experience in Hyde Park in Murdoch's *Nuns and Soldiers.* They grow in the back yards of Pimlico and Delaney Street in P. D. James' *Innocent Blood,* and the winter silhouettes of their bare branches create a "Disney Wood of terror"[6] for Al in *Londoners.* Like the city itself, nature in these novels is not always benign, but it is part of the city and illustrates the changes within the city. Although some of the novels, like Drabble's *The Radiant Way* and Murdoch's *Nuns and Soldiers,* have contrasting rural and urban scenes, nature is not the nostalgic refuge from the city that appears in much American and earlier British literature.

The flexibility that allows these female matrix images to accommodate change also allows fragmentation. A city cannot be encompassed all at once, but if one is not afraid of gathering fragments of lives, fragments of vistas, fragments of city life over different periods of time, a full image of the city can be assembled out of those fragments. The novels of Lessing and Duffy in particular illustrate this approach to seeing the city. Martha Quest in Lessing's *The Four-Gated City* carries with her a fragment of wallpaper that represents her way of seeing the layers of the city. Acceptance of fragmentation also allows one to analyze the boundary areas of the city. At the edges of a fragment of palimpsest, the layers of text are most visible. So also in the boundary areas of the city, on an invisible borderline where one district melds into the next, or on an edge that separates a park or river from the rest of the district, one can see aspects of the city that are often ignored or overlooked. Just as Martha Quest keeps her fragment of wallpaper, so in Duffy's *Capital* the amateur archeologist Meepers uses a fragment of pottery as proof of the continuity of London's civilization from the end of the Roman occupation to present times. The fragments of other stories, the vignettes of London's past which are built into the very structure of the novel emphasize that the proper way to read cities is to accept the fragments as a representation of the whole and to see the layers of the past embedded in the present. Archeologists, whether Duffy's Meepers or Margaret Drabble's Frances Wingate in *The Realms of Gold,* must create the story of a city from fragments. As Frances says to herself, "I imagine a city, and it exists."[7] A willingness to accept fragments and to preserve the ordinary details of "window sills, skins of paint, replaced curtains and salvaged baulks of timber" is what allows the city to be imagined and recorded in "women's brains."[8]

An equally important theme in all these novels is the valuing of the variety of people in cities and the emphasis on connection with and compassion for others. The matrix images all imply connection. It is the relationship between layers that creates a palimpsest or an archeological dig. It is the connection between nodes or tiles or turnings that creates a network, a mosaic or a labyrinth. Chodorow and Gilligan's emphasis on women's fluid ego boundaries and relational qualities and Jessica Benjamin's thesis that women's psychic structure is best represented by an image of "intersubjective space" provides a striking parallel to these images. Benjamin explains that "intersubjective space" includes "the space between the I and the you" and implies an involvement with others.[9] This concern for other people and the vision of the city as having space for others echoes through Lessing's descriptions of "women's time"[10] in cities in *The Diaries of Jane Somers,* in Drabble's description of connection in *The Middle Ground* and *The Radiant Way,* in Murdoch's morality of attachment,[11] in P. D. James' condoning of the involvement of her female detectives, and in Maureen Duffy's "ethic of compassion."[12] These women writers celebrate the city as a place for people.

The variety of the city and the connection between people of disparate classes, races, and backgrounds is strongest in the novels of Margaret Drabble. Since Drabble's female characters often have professions such as social work or journalism that take them all over the contemporary city, Drabble portrays the breadth of that connection and the variety of city structures and institutions. Her characters know recent immigrants from Pakistan and Jamaica, inmates from female detention centers, and working-class rock singers. Moreover, Drabble's protagonists see the connections between these varied groups of people. In Drabble's vision all of the city is connected together, by the network of sewer pipes below the city, by the streets and alleys that run through the surface of the city and by the human relationships that cross the lines of class, institution, and city district.

Although Drabble portrays the greatest variety of characters, all five of the novelists emphasize openness to relationships as an important part of the ability to see the city. In Lessing's *The Diaries of Jane Somers* it is not until Janna Somers gets to know Maudie that she can see and appreciate all the old women of the city and understand the dimension of women's time in the city. It is as Tim and Anne discover problems in human relationships in Murdoch's *Nuns and Soldiers* that they go out to walk the streets of the city and observe it. Philippa Palfrey in P. D. James' *Innocent Blood* has to go out into the city to get to know her mother. Meepers' vision of the survival of the city in Duffy's *Capital* will persist after his death because of his relationship with the professor and the group of students.

Paradoxically, in these novels the urban experience of anonymity does not lead to impersonality and alienation but instead establishes the freedom to seek out new relationships. Martha Quest in *The Four-Gated City* must experience the freedom of the city before she can shake off old confining roles and commit herself to new relationships. It is only in the anonymity of London that Janna Somers and Richard Curtis can have even a fleeting relationship in Lessing's *If the Old Could.* . . . Anonymity also allows Anne Cavidge in Murdoch's

Nuns and Soldiers to express her love for Peter by following him through the city and Philippa and her mother in P. D. James' *Innocent Blood* to live together and get to know one another. It is anonymity that permits Meepers in *Capital* to exist as a squatter in London, but it does not prevent his giving a party for the students or calling on the professor when in need.

In accordance with the emphasis on horizontal connections between people and the valuing of all the little ordinary details of city structure and city life, these novels offer a strong critique of hierarchy and the need to control. City landmarks are mocked when they represent domination and hierarchy, and male characters who see the city only in terms of landmarks are severely criticized. Martha Quest laughs at Trafalgar Square and Nelson's Column as she rejects the value system of Britain's colonial past. Al in Duffy's *Londoners* mocks "Big Ben, straight off the sauce bottle,"[13] implying that it cannot represent all that London is. In Margaret Drabble's *The Ice Age,* Anthony Keating reveals his preoccupation with domination and control through his idealization of phallic landmarks like his own gasometer and various monuments like the Eiffel Tower and the Post Office Tower. Margaret Drabble is equally critical of new towns developed by male architects and real estate developers with this mind set. In *The Ice Age* Allison sees the new town center in Northam as "monstrous, inhuman, ludicrous,"[14] and in *The Middle Ground* the new town, Romley Riverside, has "pleasure gardens of concrete"[15] with little spindly trees about to die. Iris Murdoch is the most critical of egocentric male characters who are obsessed both by landmarks and by the need to control. Hilary Burde in *A Word Child* is fixated on Big Ben, which represents his need to control time and the events of the past. Instead of making connections between all the districts or "villages" of London as Philippa Palfrey does in P. D. James' *Innocent Blood,* Hilary tries desperately to control his life by going ritualistically to a different district each night. Unlike Martha Quest in *The Four-Gated City,* Hilary fears the edges of the city and a meeting on Chelsea Embankment leads to a drowning, the engulfment Hilary so fears. In his fanatic attempts to control, Hilary circles endlessly in a moral labyrinth of his own making.

There is a hint, however, that male characters can learn to see the city in terms of a matrix if they are willing to give up this need to control it. If Hilary in *A Word Child* is willing to give up his attempt to control the past and accept his girl-friend Tommy's forgiveness by entering into a real relation-ship with her, he can perhaps escape his moral labyrinth. It is only as P. D. James' rational and detached male detective, Adam Dalgleish, becomes emotionally involved in a case and almost loses his self-control in *A Taste for Death* that he has a vision of the beauty of the city. In many of the novels it is a new kind of man with "female" qualities of empathy and con-cern for others who can value the city. One of Murdoch's few admirable male protagonists is Danby Odell in *Bruno's Dream,* who takes care of his dying father-in-law. Like other male characters in Murdoch, Danby sees landmarks, but for him the towers of Lots Road power station are symbols of di-vine protection, not of man's control over the city. Duffy's characters are clearly not traditional males. Al in *Londoners* has as many female qualities as male and is specifically not identified as either a man or a woman. Meepers in *Capital* is male but one of the dispossessed, homeless and disabled be-cause of the war. Although his meekness may contribute to his being mugged, it also gives him the sensitivity and humil-ity to be open to other people and to the past of the city. Clearly, men too can have this new vision of the city as a place of connection if they are capable of giving up the need to dom-inate and can forgo seeing the city only in terms of landmarks to their own egos. Only then can all humanity perceive what Drabble calls "the city, the kingdom. . . . where all connec-tions are made known,"[16] where people are related in "a vast web, a vast network . . . humanity itself."[17]

If we need to go beyond the modernist tradition in literature with its vision of the city as wasteland or, as Irving Howe de-scribes it, "pesthole and madhouse,"[18] we also need to go beyond modernism in architecture, which was characterized by extreme rationalism and an attempt to dominate nature and ordinary man (see Ch. 1, pp. 22–24). A recent movement in architecture called "postmodernism" and such formerly modernist architects as Philip Johnson at first seem to do this in their experimentation with breaking up the rectilinear geometry of modernism. This experimentation may seem analogous to literary modernism's breaking up the forms of nineteenth-century realism and going beyond rationalism in the stream-of-consciousness style. However, it is questionable whether the new architectural forms are not just as rationalistic; they merely use different geometries. Most of Philip Johnson's new office towers are still egocentric landmarks that call attention to themselves and boast of man's achievement. They would fit Anthony Keating's litany of monuments in Drabble's *The Ice Age*. Postmodernist buildings may seem to bring historical references into their architecture with such devices as Philip Johnson's "Chippendale clock" pediment on top of the AT&T building in New York or his use of gothic forms for the Pittsburgh Plate Glass (PPG) building, but, however beautifully detailed, these buildings[19] do not really bring time into the city in the sense that planner Kevin Lynch calls for in *What Time Is This Place* or in the way it is incorporated into all aspects of the city by many contemporary British women novelists. In many postmodernist buildings the historical references seem "appliquéd" or tacked on to the modern buildings. Sometimes, as for instance, in the PPG building, the gothic form wars with the glass of the material. The resulting empty concrete plaza and soaring glass structures of PPG seem as sterile as any building of more traditional modernism. Postmodernist buildings may be more "playful" than modernist buildings, but only to the small degree that play is permitted by a father who is firmly in control. The postmodernist movement remains paternalistic and elitist. For example, Philip Johnson's plan for Boston's Post Office–Customs House was called "parachute architecture" by the architectural critic Robert Campbell because it seemed to be dropped in from above without regard to its surroundings.[20]

A group of architects in Great Britain have called for a new movement in architecture to oppose the tradition of modernism and postmodernism. Their movement, which they call "community architecture," embraces the feminist (although they do not use the term) values of a nonhierarchical approach to architecture and the involvement of ordinary people in designing their own communities. Like philosophers Byrne and Keeley, architects Wates and Knevitt call for an end to the patriarchal tradition of modernism in architecture:

> The ghosts of the degenerate inheritors of the Modern Movement in architecture and planning—whose paternalistic, technocratic and dehumanizing influence for the last fifty years has made it the single most disastrous episode in the whole history of the built environment—can finally be laid to rest.[21]

In place of paternalism and "hierarchies" [which] cannot deal effectively with complexity,"[22] Wates and Knevitt call for a new role for architects and planners, that of an "enabler" who helps ordinary people to participate in the creation of their environment. What Wates and Knevitt do not acknowledge is the extent to which ordinary women play an important role in all the community architecture projects they describe. They quote Maureen Doyle, a member of the Prince Albert Gardens Co-operative, as saying, "It's learnt me an awful lot in the process of doing it. When I first came on to this scheme I couldn't open my mouth I was so timid. . . . I've achieved something in my life I never thought I would."[23] Dolly Pritchard, a tenant of Lea View House, which is a renovated public housing project, is quoted as saying, "I just walk around my place. I'm so chuffed with it. It's been worth every meeting, every protest."[24] A day-care center was built because "some young parents (mostly, but not all, women) in the Poplar area of London's East End" expressed a need and the Greater London Council's Women's Unit funded it.[25] When Wates and Knevitt describe how Rod Hackney, who in 1987 was elected president of the Royal Institute of British Architects, became a community architect, they quote from an interview with him in *Woman* magazine: "Black Road [a housing rehabilitation project] taught me the greatest lesson of my life. . . . Architects, councils and government planners all have to get closer to the wishes and needs of ordinary families."[26] Clearly, the ordinary woman's willingness to work for family and community makes this kind of approach to architecture possible and reinforces the images of the city in women's novels.

If we are to create new ways of living in cities and of valuing them, we need to look at women's perception of cities not only as they participate in individual architectural projects but also as they envision cities as a whole. The matrix images of Doris Lessing, Margaret Drabble, Iris Murdoch, P. D. James, and Maureen Duffy provide a female vision of the city, a vision that cherishes all the little details and variety of the city, one that celebrates urban life. It is a vision worth reading about and imagining. It is a vision worth planning for and designing.

Notes

CHAPTER 1
Introduction

1. Maureen Duffy, "Foreword," *20,000 Streets under the Sky: The London Novel 1896–1985,* catalogue of an Exhibition at The Bookspace, Royal Festival Hall, London, Feb. 17–Mar. 12, 1986 (London: The Bookspace, 1986), 7.

2. Kevin Lynch, *A Theory of Good City Form* (Cambridge, Mass.: MIT Press, 1981), 147, 150. Dickens' qualities as an urban novelist are discussed by Donald Fanger, *Dostoevsky and Romantic Realism: a Study of Dostoevsky in Relation to Balzac, Dickens and Gogol* (Cambridge, Mass.: Harvard Univ. Press, 1965); Alexander Welsh, *The City of Dickens* (Oxford: Clarendon Press, 1971); and Raymond Williams, *The Country and the City* (New York: Oxford Univ. Press, 1973).

3. Doris Lessing, *The Four-Gated City* (New York: Knopf, 1969), 10. All further citations will be to this edition.

4. Phyllis Rose, "Our Chronicler of Britain," *New York Times Book Review,* 7 Sept. 1980, 1.

5. Louis Martz, "Iris Murdoch: the London Novels," in *Twentieth Century Literature in Retrospect,* ed. Reuben Brower (Cambridge, Mass.: Harvard Univ. Press), 66.

6. Some works that have analyzed the tradition of urban literature are as follows. The emphasis, as the titles make clear, is on male writers. Marc Eli Blanchard, *In Search of the City: Engels, Baudelaire and Rimbaud,* Stanford French and Italian Studies 37 (Saratoga, Calif.: Anma Libri, 1985), focuses on his three subjects as investigator, flâneur, and spectator, respectively. Murray Baumgarten's *City Scriptures: Modern Jewish Writing* (Cambridge,

Mass.: Harvard Univ. Press, 1982) is on American Jewish writing; it treats primarily male authors but does include some discussion of Anzia Yezierska and Joanna Kaplan. Max Byrd, *London Transformed: Images of the City in the Eighteenth Century* (New Haven: Yale Univ. Press, 1978), discusses eighteenth-century urban literature up to Blake and Wordsworth. Diana Festa-McCormick, *The City as Catalyst: a Study of Ten Novels* (Rutherford, N.J.: Fairleigh Dickinson Univ. Press, 1979), uses primarily French novels from Balzac to Butor but includes Dos Passos and Durrell. Blanche H. Gelfant, *The American City Novel* (Normal: Univ. of Oklahoma Press, 1954), discusses three types of twentieth-century American urban novels. Irving Howe gives a summary of urban literature in "The City in Literature," *Commentary* 51, no. 5 (May 1971): 61–68. Michael C. Jaye and Anne Chalmers Watts, eds., *Literature and the Urban Experience: Essays on the City and Literature* (New Brunswick, N.J.: Rutgers Univ. Press, 1981), have essays by Joyce Carol Oates, Toni Morrison, and Marge Piercy, but focus mainly on modern male writers. John H. Johnston, *The Poet and the City: a Study in Urban Perspectives* (Athens: Univ. of Georgia Press, 1984), includes British and American poets from the eighteenth to the twentieth centuries. Amy Kaplan's article, " 'The Knowledge of the Line': Realism and the City in Howells's *A Hazard of New Fortunes*," *PMLA* 101, no. 1 (Jan. 1986): 69–81, shows how an attempt to learn about the city is thwarted by the characters' focus on the "line" that separates rich and poor. Gail K. Paster discusses the image of the city in Renaissance drama in *The Idea of the City in the Age of Shakespeare* (Athens: Univ. of Georgia Press, 1985). Burton Pike, *The Image of the City in Modern Literature* (Princeton: Princeton Univ. Press, 1981), uses nineteenth and twentieth-century British and European literature to look at certain urban themes: stasis and flux, the individual and the mass, and utopia. William Sharpe and Leonard Wallock, *Visions of the Modern City: Essays in History, Art and Literature*, 2nd. ed. (Baltimore: Johns Hopkins Univ. Press, 1987), have a good introduction and interesting chapters on Dickens and on Bellow. Monroe K. Spears, *Dionysus and the City: Modernism in Twentieth Century Poetry* (New York: Oxford Univ. Press, 1970), discusses modern American and British poetry. William B. Thesing, *The London Muse: Victorian Responses to the City* (Athens: Univ. of Georgia Press, 1982), looks at Victorian poets who write about the city. David R. Weimer, *The City as Metaphor* (New York: Random House, 1966), uses American novelists and poets. The most comprehensive work on British urban literature is Raymond Williams' *The Country and the City* (New York: Oxford Univ. Press, 1973). The one work that focuses on women's perception of the city is a collection of essays edited by Susan M. Squier, *Women Writers and the City: Essays in Feminist Literary Criticism* (Knoxville: Univ. of Tennessee Press, 1984). The standard work on the history of the city is Lewis Mumford's *The City in History* (New York: Harcourt Brace, 1961).

7. Nancy L. Paxton writes that on the subject of cities George Eliot's "silence seems to reflect her feelings that cities in general and London in particular were somehow threatening." "George Eliot and the City: The Imprisonment of Culture," in Squier, *Women Writers and the City*, 71. Paxton shows that even in Eliot's most urban novel, *Romula*, the city is often seen as confining. Elizabeth Gaskell is the primary exception to nineteenth-century women writers' avoidance of the city, but she writes mostly about an industrial city, Manchester, not London.

8. Elizabeth Abel, Marianne Hirsch, and Elizabeth Langland, eds., *The Voyage In: Fictions of Female Development* (Hanover, N.H.: Univ. Press of New England, 1983), 8.

9. Gelfant, *The American City Novel*, 11. Gelfant uses the novels of James Farrell to illustrate her concept of the ecological novel in American literature. This kind of novel is prevalent in American urban literature, which is more strongly influenced by naturalism and often portrays cities segregated by ethnic area. Black women writers of this type of novel include Ann Petry, *The Street* (1946), and Gloria Naylor, *Women of Brewster Place* (1982).

10. Peter Kemp, *Muriel Spark* (London: Paul Elek, 1974), 38.

11. Howe, 68.

12. Shari Benstock, *Women of the Left Bank: Paris 1900–1940* (Austin: Univ. of Texas Press, 1986), 449.

13. Sydney Janet Kaplan, " 'A Gigantic Mother': Katherine Mansfield's London," in Squier, *Women Writers*, 173.

14. Susan M. Squier, *Virginia Woolf and London: the Sexual Politics of the City* (Chapel Hill: Univ. of North Carolina Press, 1985), 186.

15. Deborah Johnson, *Iris Murdoch*, Key Women Writers Series, ed. Sue Roe (Bloomington: Indiana Univ. Press, 1987), 24–25.

16. Peter J. Conradi, *Iris Murdoch: the Saint and the Artist* (New York: St. Martin's, 1986), 264–65.

17. Quoted by Nancy Joyner, "The Underside of the Butterfly: Lessing's Debt to Woolf," *Journal of Narrative Technique* 4, no. 3 (Sept. 1974): 204–5.

18. Claire Sprague, *Rereading Doris Lessing: Narrative Patterns of Doubling and Repetition* (Chapel Hill: Univ. of North Carolina Press, 1987), 2.

19. Diana Cooper-Clark, "Margaret Drabble: Cautious Feminist," in *Critical Essays on Margaret Drabble,* ed. Ellen Cronan Rose (Boston: G. K. Hall, 1985), 30, 24.

20. Margaret Drabble, *Arnold Bennett* (New York: Knopf, 1974), 294.

21. Duffy says that after adolescence she turned away from reading novels because of the limited role for women in the classics of Austen, the Brontës, and George Eliot. She read only American novels of the 1930s and Russian novels. It was Joyce who brought her back to the genre of the novel. Interview with author, 30 June 1986.

22. Wendy Faris pointed out these distinctions in a general discussion at the International Association of Philosophy and Literature Conference on "City, Text, and Thought," New York, May 1985. She based some of her comments on William Henry Matthews, *Mazes and Labyrinths* (1922; rpt. New York: Dover, 1970), 184.

23. Sigmund Freud, *The Interpretation of Dreams,* vol. 4 of *The Standard Edition of the Complete Works of Sigmund Freud,* trans. James Strachey with Anna Freud, 8th. ed. (London: Hogarth Press, 1953), 135.

24. Sandra Gilbert and Susan Gubar, *The Madwoman in the Attic: The Woman Writer and the Nineteenth Century Literary Imagination* (New Haven: Yale Univ. Press, 1979), 73.

25. William Sharpe, "From 'Great Town' to 'Nonplace Urban Realm': Reading the Modern City," in Sharpe and Wallock, *Visions,* 9.

26. Kevin Lynch, *The Image of the City* (Cambridge, Mass.: MIT Press, 1960), 5.

27. Lynch, *Image,* 72.

28. Sharpe, 9.

29. Judith Kegan Gardiner, "Mind Mother: Psychoanalysis and Feminism," in *Making a Difference: Feminist Literary Criticism,* ed. Gayle Greene and Coppélia Kahn (New York: Methuen, 1985), 133.

30. Byrd, 31.
31. Williams, *Country and City,* 146, 145.
32. Lynch, *Theory,* 89.
33. Lynch, *Theory,* 95–96.
34. Lynch, *Theory,* 88.
35. Sharpe, 36.
36. Lynch, *Theory,* 335.
37. Lynch, *Image,* 47–48. Lynch lists these elements in a slightly different order. Since he gives no particular rationale for his order, I have rearranged them slightly to correspond to elements as they are often presented by urban novelists.
38. Nancy Chodorow, "Gender, Relation and Difference in Psychoanalytic Perspective," in *The Future of Difference,* ed. Hester Eisenstein and Alice Jardine (Boston: G. K. Hall, 1980), 14.
39. Nancy Chodorow, *The Reproduction of Mothering: Psychoanalysis and the Sociology of Gender* (Berkeley: Univ. of Calif. Press, 1978), 169.
40. Carol Gilligan, *In a Different Voice: Psychological Theory and Women's Development* (Cambridge, Mass.: Harvard Univ. Press, 1982), 29.
41. Gilligan, *In a Different Voice,* 48–49.
42. Some of the critics in Linda K. Kerber, Catherine G. Greeno and Eleanor E. Maccoby, Zella Luria, Carol B. Stack, and Carol Gilligan, "On *In a Different Voice:* an Interdisciplinary Forum," *Signs* 11, no. 2 (Winter 1986): 304–33, note that Gilligan allows her readers to come close to this interpretation. Chodorow is not as strongly criticized in this aspect. Criticism of her has instead focused on whether any of her theory is valid cross-culturally or historically. See Janice Haaken, "Freudian Theories Revised: a Critique of Rich, Chodorow and Dinnerstein," *Women's Studies Quarterly* 11 (Winter, 1983): 12–16; Marianne Hirsch, "Mothers and Daughters: a Review Essay," *Signs* 7, no. 1 (Autumn 1981): 200–22; Judith Lorber, Rose Lamb Coser, Alice S. Rossi, and Nancy Chodorow, "On *The Reproduction of Mothering:* a Methodological Debate," *Signs* 6, no. 3 (Spring 1981): 482–514.
43. Gilligan, *In a Different Voice,* 2.
44. Debra Nails, Mary Ann O'Loughlin, and James E. Walker, eds., "Women and Morality," spec. issue of *Social Research* 50, no. 3 (Autumn 1983). Several of the articles in this volume focus on the dangers of dualism.

45. Jonathan Culler, *On Deconstruction: Theory and Criticism after Structuralism* (Ithaca, N.Y.: Cornell Univ. Press, 1982), 172–73.

46. Joan Tronto, "Beyond Gender Difference to a Theory of Care," *Signs* 12, no. 4 (Summer 1987): 649.

47. N. Katherine Hayles, "Anger in Different Voices: Carol Gilligan and *The Mill on the Floss*," *Signs* 12, no. 1 (Autumn 1986): 23–39.

48. Jessica Benjamin, "A Desire of One's Own: Psychoanalytic Feminism and Intersubjective Space," in *Feminist Studies/Critical Studies*, ed. Teresa de Lauretis (Bloomington: Indiana Univ. Press, 1986), 93.

49. Benjamin, 94–95.

50. Benjamin, 95.

51. Murdoch's morality is made explicit in her philosophical work, *The Sovereignty of Good*, to which Gilligan refers in a 1984 article, "The Conquistador and the Dark Continent: Reflections on the Psychology of Love," *Daedalus* 113, no. 3 (Summer 1984): 75–95.

52. For the original essays see Richard Sennett, ed., *Classic Essays on the Culture of Cities* (Englewood Cliffs, N.J.: Prentice-Hall, 1969).

53. Sharpe, 3.

54. Richard Sennett, *The Uses of Disorder* (New York: Knopf, 1970), 38.

55. Sara Ruddick, "Maternal Thinking," *Feminist Studies* 6, no. 2 (Summer 1980): 342–67.

56. Dee Preussner, "Talking with Margaret Drabble," *Modern Fiction Studies* 25, no. 4 (Winter 1979–80): 575.

57. Gilligan, *In a Different Voice*, 154.

58. Sennett, *The Uses of Disorder*, 46.

59. Chodorow, *The Reproduction of Mothering*, 169.

60. Sennett, *The Uses of Disorder*, 135.

61. Blanche Gelfant, "Sister to Faust: The City's Hungry Woman" in Squier, *Women Writers and the City*, 279.

62. Sharpe, 7. Sharpe cites Leslie Fiedler's and Leo Marx's essays in *Literature and the Urban Experience*, ed. Michael C. Jaye and Ann Chalmers Watts, as expressing this view strongly. A classic work on antiurbanism in America is Morton and Lucia White's *The Intellectual Versus the City: From Thomas Jefferson to Frank Lloyd Wright* (Cambridge, Mass.: Harvard Univ. Press, 1962), which dis-

cusses the image of the city as wilderness. David R. Weimer in *The City as Metaphor* feels that the Whites are too pessimistic in their analysis of the role of the city in American writing, but he has to strain to find a sense of the miraculous in the city in the works of Crane and Dreiser.

63. Jean Paul Sartre, "American Cities," in *The City: American Experience*, ed. Alan Trachtenberg et al. (New York: Oxford Univ. Press, 1971), 202, 203–4.

64. Vincent Scully, *The Earth, the Temple and the Gods* (New Haven: Yale Univ. Press, 1962), 171.

65. Scully, 170.

66. Gail Kern Paster, *The Idea of the City in the Age of Shakespeare* (Athens: Univ. of Georgia Press, 1985), 3.

67. Carl Schorske, "The Idea of the City in European Thought from Voltaire to Spengler," in *The Historian and the City*, ed. Oscar Handlin and John Burchard (Cambridge, Mass.: MIT Press, 1963), 95–114.

68. Howe, 68.

69. Patrick Byrne and Richard Carroll Keeley, "Le Corbusier's Finger and Jacob's Thought: The Loss and Recovery of the Subject in the City," in *Communicating a Dangerous Memory: Soundings in Political Theology*, ed. Fred Lawrence (Atlanta: Scholar Press, 1987), 64.

70. Byrne and Keeley, 77.

71. Byrne and Keeley, 84.

72. Jane Jacobs, *The Death and Life of Great American Cities* (New York: Random House, 1961), 15.

73. Jacobs, 19.

74. Jacobs, 50.

75. Williams, pp. 9–45.

76. Squier, *Women Writers and the City*, 4.

77. Sidney H. Bremer, "Willa Cather's Lost Chicago Sisters," in *Women Writers and the City*, ed. Susan Squier, 212.

78. Jane Jacobs, *The Death and Life of Great American Cities* (New York: Random House, 1961), 443–44.

79. Lynch, *Theory*, 257. Although Lynch uses "man" here as a generic term, elsewhere in this book he uses female pronouns, cf. 142.

80. Maureen Duffy, *Londoners: an Elegy* (London: Methuen, 1983), 56.

81. Kevin Lynch, *What Time Is This Place* (Cambridge, Mass.: MIT Press, 1972), 173–174.

CHAPTER 2
The City as Palimpsest:
Doris Lessing

1. Kevin Lynch, *The Image of the City* (Cambridge, Mass.: MIT Press, 1960), 3. Recently the text image has become popular in several disciplines. The use of the text image among social scientists is discussed by Clifford Geertz in "Blurred Genres: The Refiguration of Social Thought," *American Scholar* 49 (Spring 1980): 175–77. Joyce Carol Oates refers to the city as a text in "Imaginary Cities: American," in *Literature and the Urban Experience: Essays on the City and Literature,* ed. Michael C. Jaye and Ann Chalmers Watts (New Brunswick, N.J.: Rutgers Univ. Press, 1981), 11.

2. Charles Abrams, *The City Is the Frontier* (New York: Harper and Row, 1965), 16.

3. Sandra Gilbert and Susan Gubar refer to women's writing as palimpsests in *The Madwoman in the Attic: The Woman Writer and the Nineteenth Century Literary Imagination* (New Haven: Yale Univ. Press, 1979), 73.

4. Mary Anne Singleton, *The City and the Veld: the Fiction of Doris Lessing* (Lewisburg, Pa.: Bucknell Univ. Press, 1977).

5. Ellen Cronan Rose, "Doris Lessing's *Citta Felice,*" *The Massachusetts Review* 24, no. 2 (Summer 1983): 369–86.

6. Claire Sprague, *Rereading Doris Lessing: Narrative Patterns of Doubling and Repetition* (Chapel Hill: Univ. of North Carolina Press, 1987), 9–10.

7. Doris Lessing, *The Four-Gated City* (New York: Knopf, 1969), 10. All further citations will be to this edition.

8. Lynch, *Image,* 2.

9. Nancy Chodorow, *The Reproduction of Mothering: Psychoanalysis and the Sociology of Gender* (Berkeley: Univ. of Calif. Press, 1978), 169.

10. Chodorow, *Reproduction of Mothering,* 166.

11. Chodorow, *Reproduction of Mothering,* 204.

12. Doris Lessing, *A Proper Marriage* (London: Michael Joseph, 1954), 37. All further citations will be to this edition.

13. Betsy Draine discusses the ferris wheel as both a negative and

a potentially positive symbol of repetition in *Substance Under Pressure: Artistic Coherence and Evolving Form in the Novels of Doris Lessing* (Madison: Univ. of Wisconsin Press, 1985), 52–53.

14. Claire Sprague focuses on the multilayered quality of Martha and her acceptance of a variety of roles for herself. She sees the piece of wallpaper as an image of Martha herself. "'Without Contraries Is No Progression': Lessing's *Four-Gated City,*" *Modern Fiction Studies* 26, no. 1 (Spring 1980): 102. A later version of this article is Chapter 5 of *Rereading Doris Lessing*.

15. Lynch, *Image,* 46–48.

16. Raymond Williams says that this movement of the city, the "random passing of men and women," is actually Dickens' "fictional method" and is one of his greatest strengths as an urban novelist. *The Country and the City* (New York: Oxford Univ. Press, 1973), 154–55.

17. Alexander Welsh, *The City of Dickens* (Oxford: Clarendon Press, 1971), 7.

18. John H. Raleigh, "The Novel and the City: England and America in the 19th Century," *Victorian Studies* 11, no. 3 (March 1968): 307.

19. Sara Ruddick, "Maternal Thinking," *Feminist Studies* 6, no. 2 (Summer 1980): 353. She bases the argument that maternal thinking will help better to study communities on Jean Baker Miller, *Towards a New Psychology of Women* (Boston: Beacon Press, 1976).

20. In response to a question as to whether her style is feminine and whether she should be grouped with other female British novelists, Lessing said that she does not believe "in this business of the feminine sensibility" and sees a lot of difference between the highly mannered style of Spark and Murdoch and the workaday style of Drabble. Bernd Dietz and Fernando Galván, "*Entrevista:* a Conversation with Doris Lessing," *Doris Lessing Newsletter* 9, no. 1 (Spring 1985): 6. Nonetheless, as her comments in *The Golden Notebook* and *The Four-Gated City* make clear, she does believe that "a woman's way of looking at life" may be different from a man's and that women may notice different things.

21. Doris Lessing, "Preface to *The Golden Notebook*" in *A Small Personal Voice,* ed. Paul Schlueter (New York: Knopf, 1973), 29.

22. Doris Lessing, *The Golden Notebook* (London: Michael Joseph, 1962), 229.

23. Chodorow argues that the "layering" in a woman's psychic configuration is established in the early preoedipal relationship with the mother and is related to the desire to have children: "As Deutsch makes clear, women's psyche consists in a layering of relational constellations. The preoedipal mother-child relation and the oedipal triangle have lasted until late in a woman's childhood, in fact throughout her development. . . . Given the triangular situation and emotional asymmetry of her own parenting, a woman's relation to a man *requires* on the level of psychic structure a third person, since it was originally established in a triangle" (*Reproduction of Mothering*, 200–1).

24. Doris Lessing, *The Marriages between Zones Three, Four and Five* (New York: Knopf, 1980), 54–55.

25. Yi-Fu Tuan picks up Lynch's terms and discusses people's tendency to define a city in terms of landmarks in *Topophilia: A Study of Environmental Perception, Attitudes and Values* (Englewood Cliffs, N.J.: Prentice-Hall, 1974): 204–6.

26. Lynch, *Image*, 46–48.

27. Ruddick mentions the dangers of "inauthenticity" in mothering: "Maternal thought embodies inauthenticity by taking on the values of the dominant culture. . . . Inauthenticity constructs and then assumes a world in which one's own values don't count" (354). Ruddick bases her ideas about inauthenticity on Adrienne Rich, *Of Women Born: Motherhood as Experience and Institution* (New York: Norton, 1976).

28. Hana Wirth-Nesher stresses that the city is best portrayed in its real heterogeneity, mysteriousness, and fragmentation in novels by outsiders who personally have experienced these aspects of the city. She focuses on male Jewish writers, but Doris Lessing as a woman and a colonist fits Wirth-Nesher's theory as well. "The Modern Jewish Novel and the City: Franz Kafka, Henry Roth and Amos Oz," *Modern Fiction Studies* 24, no. 1 (Spring 1978): 91–109.

Although Claire Sprague thinks that Woolf was not a strong influence on Lessing (see Ch. 1, p. 6), this sense of a woman's being an alien in the center of the city nonetheless echoes Woolf's comment that "if one is a woman one is often surprised by a sudden splitting off of consciousness, say in walking down Whitehall, when from being the natural inheritor of that civilization, she becomes, on the contrary, outside of it, alien and critical." *A Room of One's Own* (New York: Harcourt, Brace and World, 1929), 101.

29. Jessica Benjamin, "A Desire of One's Own: Psychoanalytic

Feminism and Intersubjective Space," in *Feminist Studies/Critical Studies,* ed. Teresa de Lauretis (Bloomington: Indiana Univ. Press, 1986), 95.

30. Roberta Rubenstein, in an interesting interpretation of *The Four-Gated City,* sees Erich Neumann's three dimensions of psychic and physical life, the domain of the outside world, the domain of the community, and the doman of the self, as being the three concentric circles in each section of the novel. The domain of the outside world would thus be London for Part I of the novel, but the "repressive political and social atmosphere" (138–139) in Part II, "the Alderston march" (149) in Part III, and the desensitization of the sixties in Part IV (151). Although Rubenstein concentrates more on the sphere of the community (the Coldridge household) and Martha's "self," her interpretation does show the connection between Lessing's vivid portrayal of London in Part I and later parts of the novel. *The Novelistic Vision of Doris Lessing: Breaking the Forms of Consciousness* (Champaign: Univ. of Illinois Press, 1979).

31. Dagmar Barnouw, "Disorderly Company: From *The Golden Notebook* to *The Four-Gated City,*" in *Doris Lessing: Critical Studies,* ed. Annis Pratt and L. S. Dembo (Madison: Univ. of Wisconsin Press, 1974), 87.

32. "Inner space fiction" is Mona Knapp's term in *Doris Lessing* (New York: Ungar, 1984); the term "apologue," a form that conveys a certain specific thesis, is used by Betsy Draine in *Substance Under Pressure* and Rachel Blau DuPlessis in "The Feminist Apologues of Lessing, Piercy and Russ," *Frontiers* 4, no. 1 (Spring 1979): 1–8. Katherine Fishburn also uses the term in *The Unexpected Universe of Doris Lessing* (Westport, Conn.: Greenwood, 1985) about Lessing's space fiction and attributes it to Sheldon Sacks, "Golden Birds and Dying Generations," *Comparative Literature Studies* 6, no. 3 (Sept. 1969): 274–291.

33. Mona Knapp, *Doris Lessing* (New York: Ungar, 1984), 138.

34. Doris Lessing, "Preface," *The Diaries of Jane Somers* (London: Michael Joseph, 1984), n.p.

35. Gayle Greene, *"The Diaries of Jane Somers,"* paper presented at the annual meeting of the Modern Language Association, New York, December 1985. Forthcoming in Greene's book, *Revisions: Contemporary Women Writers and the Tradition.*

36. Richard Sennett, discussing the concept of the city as theater, explains how valuable this concept of the city was to public

life in the eighteenth century and attributes the weak contemporary sense of a public life and the dead public spaces of some contemporary architecture to the loss of the idea of the city as theater. *The Fall of Public Man* (New York: Knopf, 1977).

37. Doris Lessing, *The Diaries of Jane Somers* (London: Michael Joseph, 1984), 322. All further citations will be to this edition.

38. Lessing says that Jane Somers is based on three friends of hers, one a rich woman to whom nothing bad had ever happened, another close friend "who's not only extremely beautiful, but very well dressed, and who, at the age of fifty, can still enter the room and stop a conversation. But she does it at the cost of unbelieveable hard work . . . an obsession," and a third friend who works for women's magazines. "Doris Lessing Talks About Jane Somers," *Doris Lessing Newsletter* 10, no. 1 (Spring 1986), 5.

39. Quoted by Mona Knapp in "Reports: Lessing in North America, March-April 1984: University of California, Los Angeles," *Doris Lessing Newsletter* 8, no. 2 (Fall 1984): 8. I am grateful to William Sharpe's article, "Urban Theory and Critical Blight: Accommodating the Unreal City," *New Orleans Review* 10, no. 1 (Spring 1983): 86, for directing me to this passage in Rushdie's novel.

40. Salman Rushdie, *Midnight's Children* (New York: Knopf, 1981), 81.

41. Greene, 9.

42. "Doris Lessing Talks About Jane Somers," *Doris Lessing Newsletter* 10, no. 1 (Spring 1986): 5.

43. Lessing, "Preface," *The Diaries of Jane Somers,*" n.p.

44. Pildar Hidalgo also compares *The Good Terrorist* to Conrad's *Secret Agent,* in "*The Good Terrorist*: Lessing's Tract for the Times," *Doris Lessing Newsletter* 11, no. 1 (Spring 1987): 7. For an analysis of the city in *The Secret Agent,* see Christine W. Sizemore, " 'The Small Cardboard Box': a Symbol of the City and of Winnie Verloc in Conrad's *Secret Agent,*" *Modern Fiction Studies* 24, no. 1 (Spring 1978): 23–39.

45. Doris Lessing, *The Good Terrorist* (London: Jonathan Cape, 1985), 90. All further citations will be to this edition.

46. Sprague, *Rereading Doris Lessing,* 112.

47. Virginia Tiger, "Lessing in New York City, April 1 and 2," *Doris Lessing Newsletter* 8, no. 2 (Fall 1984), 5.

48. On house imagery in Lessing's novels see Rubenstein (n. 30, above), and Sprague, *Rereading Doris Lessing,* 98–105 and 162–67.

CHAPTER 3
The City as Network:
Margaret Drabble

1. Carol Gilligan, *In a Different Voice: Psychological Theory and Women's Moral Development* (Cambridge, Mass.: Harvard Univ. Press, 1982), 33, 35.

2. Gilligan, 48.

3. Hans Blumenfeld's description is typical of urban planners' use of the term: "The city of industrial capitalism—in Europe as well as in America . . . was an assembly of real estate for various purposes, served by various networks. The networks multiplied as the cities grew larger and more complex. To the expanding networks of streets were added other networks for water, sewers, gas, electricity, rail traffic, and telephones." Hans Blumenfeld, "The Role of Design," in *The Growth of Cities,* ed. David Lewis (New York: John Wiley, 1971), 14.

4. Jane Jacobs, *The Death and Life of Great American Cities* (New York: Random House, 1961), 119.

5. The novel itself is like a collage or a network of texts since there are five narrative voices: the four protagonists and what Ellen Cronan Rose calls in *The Realms of Gold* "noisy declarations of authorial presence." *The Novels of Margaret Drabble: Equivocal Figures* (Totowa, N.J.: Barnes and Noble, 1980), 108. This narrative structure is discussed by Pamela S. Bromberg in "Narrative in Drabble's *The Middle Ground:* Relativity versus Teleology," *Contemporary Literature* 24, no. 4 (Winter 1983): 461–79, and by Lorna Irvine in "No Sense of an Ending: Drabble's Continuous Fictions," in *Critical Essays on Margaret Drabble,* ed. Ellen Cronan Rose (Boston, G. K. Hall, 1985), 73–86.

6. Margaret Drabble, *The Middle Ground* (New York: Knopf, 1980), 243–44. All further citations will be to this edition. Rose compares this passage to Mrs. Dalloway's "paean" to the city in the opening of Virginia Woolf's novel; see "Drabble's *The Middle Ground*: 'Mid-Life' Narrative Strategies," *Critique* 23, no. 3 (Spring 1982): 82. Drabble herself says that *The Middle Ground* was influenced by *Mrs. Dalloway:* "The book, in fact, ends up with a literary joke, a Mrs. Dalloway-type party"; quoted by Diana Cooper-Clark, "Margaret Drabble: Cautious Feminist" in Rose, *Critical Essays on Margaret Drabble,* 30. See Chapter 1, pp. 5–7, for further discussion of Woolf's influence on Drabble. In an interview with John Han-

nay, Drabble explains in more detail how she came to use the party to close the novel; see "Margaret Drabble: An Interview," *Twentieth Century Literature* 33, no. 2 (Summer 1987): 132.

7. This kind of view is possible from the twelfth floor of a city hospital in London because, like many European cities, London had until recently strict zoning laws that would not allow new buildings to be so high that they would block the view of the cathedral, St. Paul's in this case. Some exceptions like the Post Office Tower exist. Current buildings proposed for the area near St. Paul's are very controversial.

8. Margaret Drabble, *A Writer's Britain: Landscape in Literature* (New York: Knopf, 1979), 242.

9. Nancy Chodorow, "Gender, Relation and Difference in Psychoanalytic Perspective," in *The Future of Difference,* ed. Hester Eisenstein and Alice Jardine (Boston: G. K. Hall, 1980), 9.

10. Dee Preussner, "Talking with Margaret Drabble," *Modern Fiction Studies* 25, no. 4 (Winter 1979–80): 575.

11. Sara Ruddick, "Maternal Thinking," *Feminist Studies* 6, no. 2 (Summer 1980): 357–58.

12. Ruddick discusses attentiveness, which she develops from the theories of Simone Weil and Iris Murdoch (see Ch. 4, pp. 113–118, above, on Murdoch), as part of maternal thinking, pp. 357–358.

13. Mary Jane Elkins notes that one of the "threads" of the novel has to do with lost, dead and neglected babies. These references to babies "set . . . the backdrop of the primacy of family and specifically of maternity." "Alenoushka's Return: Motifs and Movement in Margaret Drabble's *The Middle Ground,*" in Rose, *Critical Essays on Margaret Drabble,* 176–77. In spite of her guilt, Kate's decisions about the baby and the abortion match the ethic of responsibility that Gilligan finds in her analysis of women's abortion decisions (*In a Different Voice,* 132–50).

14. Lynn Veach Sadler in "The Society We Have: The Search for Meaning in Drabble's *The Middle Ground,*" *Critique* 23, no. 3 (Spring 1982): 83–93, and Roberta Rubenstein in "From Detritus to Discovery: Margaret Drabble's *The Middle Ground,*" *Journal of Narrative Technique* 14, no. 1 (Winter 1984): 1–16, both briefly discuss the sewage imagery and Kate's need to come to terms with her past. Helen Druxes discusses the sewer as a "liminoid city space" in "Female Birth and Rebirth in the City: Moving from Margaret Drabble's *Jerusalem the Golden* (1962) to *The Middle Ground*

(1980)," a paper presented at the annual meeting of the Modern Language Association, San Francisco, December 1987.

15. The sewer, especially in Victor Hugo's *Les Misérables*, is described by Richard Lehan as an image of urban hell and a symbol of what the city discards. "Urban Signs and Urban Literature: Literary Form and Historical Process," *New Literary History* 18 (1986–87): 106.

16. Michael F. Harper shows how Douglas' ideas about marginality are developed in Drabble's novel. Marginality, according to Douglas, is perceived as dangerous, whether it be the marginality of bodily orifices and their products or social marginality as represented by people who do not fit the patriarchally imposed order. "Margaret Drabble and the Sense of Closure in *The Middle Ground*," paper presented at the annual meeting of the Modern Language Association, Washington, D.C., December 1984.

17. Mary Douglas, *Purity and Danger: an Analysis of Concepts of Pollution and Taboo* (New York: Praeger, 1966), 2, 4.

18. Class differences might also account for Kate Armstrong's positive view of the sewers; Kate's family were working-class. Leonore Davidoff discusses the class differences in Victorian society and the responses to dirt and bodily functions. Middle-class Victorians were obsessed with cleanliness and sanitary reform. Servants performed all the "dirty work" of caring for young children and cleaning the house. Working-class people had no such separation from nature or natural functions. Davidoff cites Munby's embarrassment in asking a female servant for the "water-closet" and his amazement at her comfortable response. "Class and Gender in Victorian England: The Diaries of Arthur J. Munby and Hannah Cullwick," *Feminist Studies* 5, no. 1 (Spring 1979): 99–100.

19. Nora Stovel, "Margaret Drabble's Golden Vision," in *Margaret Drabble: Golden Realms*, ed. Dorey Schmidt (Edinburg, Tex.: Pan American Univ. Press, 1982): 13.

20. Gilligan contrasts the female image of safety at the center of the net with the male image of safety at the top of the hierarchy: "As the top of the hierarchy becomes the edge of the web and as the center of a network of connection becomes the middle of a hierarchical progression, each image marks as dangerous the place which the other [sex] defines as safe" (*In a Different Voice*, 62).

21. Chodorow, "Gender, Relation and Difference," 11. Jane Flax disagrees with Chodorow on this point, maintaining that differentiation is still a major problem for women, but Flax, as she herself

points out, works primarily with very disturbed women. Chodorow admits that differentiation can be a problem, but not necessarily, and connectedness can be very comfortable. Jane Flax, "Mother-Daughter Relationships: Psychodynamics, Politics and Philosophy," in Eisenstein, *The Future of Difference,* 22–23.

22. Mary Hurley Moran stresses that Drabble dislikes the angry rhetoric of French's novel. *Margaret Drabble: Existing within Structures* (Carbondale: Univ. of Illinois Press, 1983), 11–12.

23. Ruddick, pp. 351, 357.

24. Robert Venturi et al., *Learning from Las Vegas* (Cambridge, Mass.: MIT Press, 1972).

25. In the interview with Diana Cooper-Clark, Drabble says: "Well, the older generation are [paralyzing], but my mothers usually get on well with their babies. The younger women do. . . . Being a daughter is not much fun. But being a mother is wonderful" (Rose, *Critical Essays on Margaret Drabble,* 28). This echoes Drabble's comments to Preussner on mothers of the older generation versus their daughters: they "tend not to be terribly good mothers, but they're all right. Their daughters get along with them all right" (569).

26. Dorothy Dinnerstein explores the rage children feel against the mothers who first set limits upon them, in *The Mermaid and the Minotaur: Sexual Arrangements and Human Malaise* (New York: Harper and Row, 1976).

27. Although Sebastian isn't developed enough as a character here to analyze in detail, it does seem as if he is finally managing to "accord" his mother "her own selfhood," rather than just seeing her as "object" or as a "narcissistic extension" of himself (Chodorow's terms in "Gender, Relation, and Difference in Psychoanalytic Perspective," 7–8). In extending his mother her selfhood, he too is growing up.

There are several other mainly positive portraits of "connected" mothers and sons in *The Middle Ground:* Hugo Mainwaring and his sophisticated mother who runs an art gallery have "a rapport . . . quick . . . sharp . . . intense" (122). Sam Goldman, the playwright, and his mother are intimate and affectionate despite a large culture gap (125); even Gabriel Denham from *Jerusalem the Golden* says how fond he is of his mother (221). Kate worried that she would be "one of those women designed to ruin their sons through excessive devotions, through emotional dependence," but realizes that "Mark had been saved from her attentions by her need to earn her own living, by the other two and their needs, by Hugh [sic], by the tatty diversities of tatty distracting modern life." She regards the grown Mark with "tenderness, delight, wonder [and] gratitude" (269).

28. Rubenstein comments on this symbol, saying the drainage of the can "form[s] the final flushing away of the old Kate that has been brought to the surface" ("From Detritus to Discovery," 13).

29. Margaret Drabble, "No Idle Rentier: Angus Wilson and the Nourished Literary Imagination," *Studies in the Literary Imagination* 13, no. 1 (Spring 1980): 128.

30. Preussner, 571.

31. Joanne V. Creighton, *Margaret Drabble* (London: Methuen, 1985), 65.

32. Margaret Drabble, *The Realms of Gold* (New York: Knopf, 1975), 28–29. All further citations will be to this edition.

33. Creighton, 88.

34. Joyce Carol Oates, *"The Needle's Eye," New York Times Book Review*, 11 June 1972, 23.

35. Margaret Drabble, *The Needle's Eye* (London: Weidenfeld and Nicolson, 1972), 53.

36. Ellen Cronan Rose, "Introduction," in *Critical Essays on Margaret Drabble*, 6.

37. Margaret Drabble, "The Author Comments," *Dutch Quarterly Review of Anglo-American Letters* 5, no. 1 (1975): 38.

38. Erik Erikson, *Childhood and Society*, 2nd. ed. (New York: Norton, 1963), 266–68.

39. Elaine Tuttle Hansen, "The Uses of Imagination: Margaret Drabble's *The Ice Age*," in Rose, *Critical Essays on Margaret Drabble*, 154–55.

40. Margaret Drabble, *The Ice Age* (New York: Knopf, 1977), 27–28. All further citations will be to this edition.

41. Drabble analyzes present-day Sheffield's economic problems in "A Novelist in a Derelict City," *New York Times Magazine*, 14 April 1985, 76–81. In this article she presents a different picture of Sheffield, in which no redevelopment is taking place: "There is an eerie silence, a sense of emptiness, a deathly calm. The scale of decay is daunting: the buildings look hopelessly dilapidated and, indeed, many are over a century old—historic, with touches of architectural beauty mingled in the rubble. This is no modern industrial quarter of gleaming factories with automated carparks: it is ancient, unplanned, accumulated, a maze of accidental growths. In its time it worked, but that time is over" (77).

42. Rose, *The Novels of Margaret Drabble,* 115.

43. Margaret Drabble, *The Radiant Way* (London: Weidenfeld and Nicolson, 1987), 14. All further citations will be to this edition.

44. John Updike, "Seeking Connections in an Insecure Country," *The New Yorker,* 16 Nov. 1987, 153.

45. I am grateful to John Hannay for pointing out this parallel with *The Realms of Gold.*

46. References to squatters occur briefly in two of Drabble's earlier novels. Drabble mentions that "vagrants" have been living in Jane Gray's house in *The Waterfall* (London: Weidenfeld and Nicolson, 1969), 239, and in *The Ice Age* Anthony Keating's house is described as "empty, squatted in, unsaleable." (9).

47. Eliot's "Metropole" was in Brighton. Gayle Greene says that Drabble's London in *The Radiant Way* has an "apocalyptic cast" like Eliot's "The Waste Land." "The End of a Dream," *Women's Review of Books* 5, no. 4 (Jan. 1988): 4. Drabble spent the years from 1980 to 1986 as the editor of the fifth edition of *The Oxford Companion to English Literature.*

48. "Lykewake Gardens," the street where Jilly Fox's murder took place, is not listed in *London A-Z* as a real street, but most of the streets Drabble uses are actual London streets. Drabble mixes her fictional street with actual ones to give a sense of reality to the novel. For instance, when Esther sits musing by the canal, she thinks of real streets, all close by Ladbroke Grove and Harrow Road, before mentioning Lykewake Gardens: "North Pole Road. Little Wormwood Scrubs. Droop Street. Warlock Street. Fifth Avenue, Sixth Avenue. She discovered a new cafe on the corner of Lykewake Gardens and Mortuary Road [also not in *London A-Z*]" (244).

49. Lynch criticizes the image of the city as organism because it can lead planners to try to "cut out" slums to prevent "infectious spread." See Ch. 1, p. 10.

50. Patrick Parrinder, "Speaking for England," *London Review of Books* 9 (21 May 1987), 21.

51. Le Corbusier, *The Radiant City, elements of a doctrine of urbanism to be used as the basis of our machine-age civilization,* trans. Pamela Knight, Eleanor Levieux, and Derek Coltman (1931; rpt. New York: Orion Press, 1967).

52. Jacobs, p. 22. See also Patrick Byrne and Richard Carroll Keeley, "Le Corbusier's Finger and Jacob's Thought: The Loss and Recovery of the Subject in the City," in *Communicating a Dangerous Memory: Soundings in Political Theology,* ed. Fred Lawrence

(Atlanta: Scholar Press, 1987), for criticism of Le Corbusier's Radiant City.

53. E. M. Forster, *Howards End* (New York: Knopf, 1921), 108.

CHAPTER 4
The City as Labyrinth:
Iris Murdoch

1. Margaret Drabble, *The Writer's Britain: Landscape in Literature* (New York: Knopf, 1979), 243, 244.

2. Donald Fanger, *Dostoevsky and Romantic Realism: a Study of Dostoevsky in Relation to Balzac, Dickens and Gogol* (Cambridge, Mass.: Harvard Univ. Press, 1965), and Alexander Welsh, *The City of Dickens* (Oxford: Clarendon Press, 1971), both discuss the variety of urban setting in Dickens.

3. Louis Martz, "Iris Murdoch: the London Novels," in *Twentieth Century Literature in Retrospect,* ed. Reuben Brower (Cambridge, Mass.: Harvard Univ. Press, 1971), 66.

4. Peter J. Conradi, *Iris Murdoch: the Saint and the Artist* (New York: St. Martin's, 1986), 4.

5. Martz, 69.

6. Michael Slater discusses Dickens' allegiance to the nineteenth-century "womanly ideal." He emphasizes "Dickens's extreme difficulty in reconciling the sexual with the domestic ideal. . . . Dickens is only able to present a woman as convincingly noble as wife and mother when she is, in fact, a childless single woman who adopts, sustains and protects a quasi-husband and also a child." *Dickens and Women* (London: J. M. Dent, 1983), 311–12. Even Bella Wilfer (in *Our Mutual Friend*), Slater describes as one of those "good wives . . . [portrayed] as though they actually were children" (312).

7. The adjectives describing Diana are based on the words of Elizabeth Dipple. Dipple notes Diana's development with surprise: "she begins as one of Murdoch's narrow types—the attractive, middle-aged woman, trapped by complacency and emotional greed—and the choice of her as a vehicle of knowledge shows Murdoch's perpetual capacity to mould her materials freely and unexpectedly." *Iris Murdoch: Work for the Spirit* (Chicago: Univ. of Chicago Press, 1982), 171.

8. Iris Murdoch, *Bruno's Dream* (London: Chatto and Windus, 1969), 291–92. All further citations will be to this edition.

9. Murdoch often uses water symbolism to express this release

from absorption with self that leads to beatific feeling. For instance, in *The Unicorn* as Effingham Cooper sinks slowly into a slimy wet bog, he realizes "with a clarity which was one with the increasing light, that with the death of the self the world becomes quite automatically the object of a perfect love." *The Unicorn* (London: Chatto and Windus, 1963), 189. Usually, however, this experience occurs far away from the city. There are similar near-drowning episodes in *The Unicorn, The Nice and the Good, The Sea, The Sea, Nuns and Soldiers,* and if not a near-drowning, then an ordeal associated with water, in the steamy, suffocating depths of Ennistone Institute Baths in *The Philosopher's Pupil.* Ordeal by water is not always redemptive, however. There are actual drownings in *The Unicorn, Bruno's Dream, A Fairly Honourable Defeat, A Word Child, The Sea, The Sea,* and *The Good Apprentice.* Conradi notes that Murdoch herself once almost drowned in the sea (109).

10. There are actually only two towers. Martz suggests that the trinity must be "symbolic" (68) but he doesn't say whether he considers them "protective" or "menacing."

11. Dipple, 166, 196. Conradi thinks Dipple correctly accounts for Murdoch's moral passion in this statement but does not include Murdoch's moral scepticism (62–64). Conradi may be more accurate in terms of the complex morality in Murdoch's novels, but Dipple's statement does give an accurate assessment of the tone of the novels of the 1970s.

12. Deborah Johnson, in a deconstructive reading of some of these novels, shows, for instance, how the complex relationship between author and narrator in *The Black Prince* illustrates Irigaray's "mimetism" in which the woman writer exposes "what it is she mimics." *Iris Murdoch,* Key Women Writers Series, ed. Sue Roe (Bloomington: Indiana Univ. Press, 1987), 35.

13. Jack I. Biles, "Interview with Iris Murdoch," *Studies in the Literary Imagination* 11, no. 2 (Fall 1978): 119. Murdoch made a similar response to Michael Bellamy's same question in 1976. "Interview with Iris Murdoch," *Contemporary Literature* 18, no. 2 (Spring 1977): 133.

14. Sara Ruddick, "Maternal Thinking, *Feminist Studies* 6, no. 2 (Summer 1980): 357–58. Murdoch also emphasizes the importance of Weil's concept of attention. In "Against Dryness," first published in 1961, Murdoch notes that "Simone Weil said that morality was a matter of attention, not of will. We need a new vocabulary of atten-

tion." "Against Dryness: a Polemical Sketch," in *The Novel Today: Contemporary Writers on Modern Fiction*, ed. Malcolm Bradbury (Totowa, N.J.: Rowman and Littlefield, 1978), 30.

15. Iris Murdoch, "The Sublime and the Good," *Chicago Review* 13, no. 3 (Autumn 1959): 52.

16. Carol Gilligan, "The Conquistador and the Dark Continent: Reflections on the Psychology of Love," *Daedalus* 113, no. 3 (Summer 1984): 77.

17. Carol Gilligan, *In a Different Voice: Psychological Theory and Women's Moral Development* (Cambridge, Mass.: Harvard Univ. Press, 1982), 151–54.

18. Gilligan, *In a Different Voice*, 42.

19. Iris Murdoch, *The Sovereignty of Good* (London: Routledge and Kegan Paul, 1970), 52. All further citations will be to this edition.

20. Peter Hawkins, *The Language of Grace: Flannery O'Connor, Walker Percy and Iris Murdoch* (Cambridge, Mass.: Cowley Publications, 1983), 95.

21. Dipple, 15.

22. Quoted by Conradi, 143.

23. Jessica Benjamin, "A Desire of One's Own: Psychoanalytic Feminism and Intersubjective Space," *Feminist Studies/Critical Studies*, ed. Teresa de Lauretis (Bloomington: Indiana Univ. Press, 1986), 81.

24. Peter Wolfe, "'Malformed Treatise' and Prizewinner: Iris Murdoch's *The Black Prince*," *Studies in the Literary Imagination* 11, no. 2 (Fall 1978): 98. He notes the phallic Post Office Tower and the corresponding womb-like apartment and Covent Garden Opera House, 102–3.

25. The image of the labyrinth in *Oliver Twist, Martin Chuzzlewit,* and *Little Dorrit* is discussed by J. Hillis Miller in *Charles Dickens: The World of His Novels* (Cambridge, Mass.: Harvard Univ. Press, 1958), 50–60, 110–115, 232–235; in *Oliver Twist* and *Nicholas Nickleby* by F. S. Schwarzbach in *Dickens and the City* (London: The Athlone Press, 1979), 41–68. For Samuel Beckett's use of the image, see Debra Castillo, "Beckett's Metaphorical Towns," *Modern Fiction Studies* 28, no. 2 (Summer 1982): 190–92.

26. A. S. Byatt ties the net imagery to Wittgenstein's net in *Tractatus Logico-Philosophicus* "in which he likens our descriptive languages to a mesh put over reality." *Iris Murdoch* (London: Longman

Group, 1976), 36. Murdoch confirmed this association in an interview done in 1983. William Slaymaker asked her if the title of *Under the Net* referred to Wittgensteinian language nets. Murdoch replied, "It's an obvious image for the understanding of particulars. . . . one constantly desires to get 'under the net' of language toward the thing itself." "An Interview with Iris Murdoch," *Papers in Language and Literature* 21, no. 4 (Fall 1985): 432. Conradi discusses the net's relationship to Wittgenstein and Plato (32).

27. Gilligan, *In a Different Voice*, 62.

28. There are unicursal church floor labyrinths that have safe centers; see William Henry Matthews, *Mazes and Labyrinths* (1922; rpt. New York: Dover 1970). However, the opening reference to the Minotaur in *Flight from the Enchanter* shows Murdoch's interest in the Greek myth.

29. Susan Squier, *Virginia Woolf and London: the Sexual Politics of the City* (Chapel Hill: Univ. of North Carolina Press, 1985), 84.

30. Gilligan, *In a Different Voice*, 31.

31. Iris Murdoch, *Under the Net* (London: Chatto and Windus, 1975), 38. All further citations will be to this edition.

32. Dipple, p. 139.

33. Iris Murdoch, *Henry and Cato* (London: Chatto and Windus, 1976), 22. All further citations will be to this edition.

34. Iris Murdoch, *The Nice and the Good* (London: Chatto and Windus, 1968), 131. All further citations will be to this edition.

35. Bellamy, 139. In the same interview Murdoch says, "Julius King is, of course, Satan, and Tallis is a Christ figure, and Tallis' father (Leonard Browne) is God the Father, who finds that it's all gone wrong. . . . Morgan . . . is the human soul, for which the two protagonists are battling" (135–36).

36. Iris Murdoch, *A Fairly Honourable Defeat* (London: Chatto and Windus, 1970), 139. All further citations will be to this edition.

37. Iris Murdoch, *A Word Child* (London: Chatto and Windus, 1975), 51. All further citations will be to this edition.

38. Dipple, 219.

39. Kevin Lynch, *The Image of the City* (Cambridge, Mass.: MIT Press, 1960), 47–48.

40. T. S. Eliot, "Burnt Norton," *The Complete Poems and Plays of T. S. Eliot* (London: Faber and Faber, 1969), 173, 174.

41. Bellamy, 135. Murdoch is discussing here the danger in art of imposing form arbitrarily, but since she includes in the artist figure both Julius King of *A Fairly Honourable Defeat* and Jake Donaghue

of *Under the Net,* who try to impose form on other people, Hilary Burde fits as well.

42. Lynch, *Image,* 62.

43. Conradi, 81.

44. Crystal is uneducated, but she does know the Bible. She quotes to Gunnar Jopling a passage from Philippians: "Whatsoever things are just . . . think on these things" (325). Murdoch uses the same passage in *The Sovereignty of Good* in discussing the right kind of attachment (56).

45. Both Conradi and Johnson say that *A Word Child* is about redemption: "fall and redemption" (Conradi, 230), "forgiveness, and redemption of the past" (Johnson, 99).

46. Murdoch says "Ann [Peronett] in *An Unofficial Rose* is a good character without being demonic, but . . . it may be that she's not interesting enough" (Bellamy, 136). Dipple, qualifying Ann's goodness, comments: "Although consistently handled as one of Murdoch's characters of the good, her renunciations and negatives mix curiously with her frequent muddy attempts at comprehension and her defeated struggles to assert a will she does not fully possess" (57).

47. Johnson, 72.

48. Iris Murdoch, *Nuns and Soldiers* (London: Chatto and Windus, 1980), 353. All further citations will be to this edition.

49. In *The Sovereignty of Good* Murdoch criticizes the romantic notion of suffering (82). Brendan Craddock, the good priest in *Henry and Cato,* also criticizes suffering as "breeding beautiful images" (336).

50. Dipple, 318.

51. Benjamin, 80.

52. Wendy Faris described the two kinds of labyrinths at the International Association of Philosophy and Literature Conference on "City, Text, and Thought," May, 1985. She mentioned the labyrinth in the floor of Chartres as a typical church labyrinth. They are also discussed in Matthews.

53. In "T. S. Eliot as a Moralist," *T. S. Eliot: a Symposium for his Seventieth Birthday,* ed. Neville Braybrooke (New York: Books for Libraries, Inc. 1958), 152–60, Murdoch illustrates how Eliot in the role of a literary critic is "one of our more important moralists," (152) and although she ultimately defends the liberalism which Eliot attacks, she returns at the end of the article to defend Eliot the poet: "Mr. Eliot has seen, and it is a great part of our 'health'

that we have a poet who can penetrate our anxious trivial world with such profound compassion. In his poetry Mr. Eliot is no Jansenist" (160).

54. T. S. Eliot, *The Cocktail Party* (New York: Harcourt Brace, 1950), 139–41.

55. Eliot, *The Cocktail Party,* 184.

CHAPTER 5
The City as Mosaic:
P. D. James

1. V. S. Pritchett explains the origins of the village structure of London in *London Perceived* (New York: Harcourt, Brace and World, 1962), 7–8.

2. P. D. James, *Unnatural Causes* (1967; rpt. London: Hamish Hamilton, 1976), 154. All further citations will be to this edition.

3. P. D. James, *Skull Beneath the Skin* (New York: Scribner's, 1982), 165. All further citations will be to this edition.

4. P. D. James, *Innocent Blood* (New York: Scribner's, 1980), 134. All further citations will be to this edition.

5. P. D. James, *A Taste for Death* (London: Faber and Faber, 1972), 157. All further citations will be to this edition.

6. Raymond Williams, *The Country and the City* (New York: Oxford Univ. Press, 1962), 221.

7. Williams, 227.

8. Carolyn G. Heilbrun, "A Feminist Looks at Women in Detective Novels," *Graduate Woman,* July/August 1980, 16, 19.

9. Heilbrun, "A Feminist," 20.

10. Lillian de la Torre says that Cordelia Gray is based on P. D. James' daughter: "Hers is the pixie face, the sturdy sense, the valiant heart." "Cordelia Gray: The Thinking Man's Heroine," in *Murdress Ink: The Better Half,* ed. Dilys Winn (New York: Workman, 1979), 113.

11. Carolyn G. Heilbrun, "James, P. D.," *Twentieth-Century Crime and Mystery Writers,* ed. John M. Reilly (New York: St. Martin's, 1980), 857.

12. Carol Gilligan, *In a Different Voice: Psychological Theory and Women's Moral Development* (Cambridge, Mass.: Harvard Univ. Press, 1982). Jessica Benjamin, "A Desire of One's Own: Psychoanalytic Feminism and Intersubjective Space," *Feminist Studies/Crit-*

ical Studies, ed. Teresa de Lauretis (Bloomington: Indiana Univ. Press, 1986): 78–101.

13. Jane S. Bakerman, "From the Time I Could Read, I Always Wanted to be a Writer: Interview with P. D. James," *The Armchair Detective* 10 (Jan. 1977), 92.

14. SueEllen Campbell, "The Detective Heroine and the Death of her Hero: Dorothy Sayers to P. D. James," *Modern Fiction Studies* 29, no. 3 (Autumn 1983): 498. Erlene Hubly also describes James' detective novels as "something other than the classical detective novel . . . a blend of several forms—the romantic and the realistic, the classical and the hard-boiled." "The Formula Challenged: the Novels of P. D. James," *Modern Fiction Studies* 29, no. 3 (Autumn 1983): 521.

15. P. D. James, *A Mind to Murder* in *Crime Times Three* (New York: Scribner's, 1963), 197. All further citations will be to this edition.

16. Dale Salwak, "An Interview with P. D. James," in *Mystery Voices: Interviews with British Mystery Writers* (San Bernadino, Ca.: Borgo Press, forthcoming).

17. P. D. James, *An Unsuitable Job for a Woman* (London: Faber and Faber, 1972), 214. In his article on *An Unsuitable Job for a Woman,* James F. Maxfield argues that Cordelia Gray is not an "exemplary feminist heroine" because she allows herself to become emotionally involved in Mark's death and even covers up for Miss Leaming. I argue that these qualities are precisely what make Cordelia a "feminist heroine;" she has the traditional male qualities of bravery and toughness, but she does not give up her female qualities of sympathy and involvement. "The Unfinished Detective: The Work of P. D. James," *Critique* 28, no. 4 (Summer 1987), 211–23.

18. Bernard Benstock, "The Clinical World of P. D. James," in *Twentieth-Century Women Novelists,* ed. Thomas F. Staley (New York: Barnes and Noble, 1982), 107.

19. Charles Dickens, *Little Dorrit,* (1857; rpt. New York: Penguin, 1967), 150.

20. Bakerman, 92.

21. Nancy Carol Joyner, "P. D. James," *10 Women of Mystery,* ed. Earl R. Bargainnier (Bowling Green, Ohio: Bowling Green State Univ. Press, 1981), 115.

22. Kevin Lynch, *The Image of the City* (Cambridge, Mass.: MIT Press, 1960), 103, 104.

23. *A–Z London Street Atlas,* edition 1A (London: Geographer's A–Z Map Co., n.d.), 188.

24. Joyner, 115.

25. Jane Jacobs, *The Death and Life of Great American Cities* (New York: Random House, 1961), 59.

26. Lynch, *Image,* 77.

27. Lynch, 104.

28. Lynch, 48.

29. Lynch, 104.

30. The context of this quotation is interesting in light of Philippa's later relationship with Maurice. In *The Jew of Malta* the monks are about to accuse Barabas of murder, but he cuts them off:

Friar Barnadine: Thou hast committed—
Barabas: Fornication? But that
Was in another country, and besides
The wench is dead. (IV i 40–44)

The Complete Plays of Christopher Marlowe, ed. Irving Ribner (New York: Odyssey Press, 1963), 217. It is not Maurice who commits a murder; Philippa feels that she is responsible for her mother's suicide. The "fornication" becomes a reestablishment of contact between Maurice and Philippa.

31. Richard B. Gidez, *P. D. James* (Boston: Twayne, 1986), 97. Norma Siebenheller also lists the references to rose and floral imagery in *Innocent Blood* but only mentions that this use of imagery goes beyond the genre of mystery. She does not suggest a meaning for the imagery. *P. D. James* (New York: Ungar, 1981), 70–71.

32. Bruce Harkness points out that the title of this work was originally intended to have been *Blood Tie*. "P. D. James," in *Art in Crime Writing: Essays in Detective Fiction,* ed. Bernard Benstock (New York: St. Martin's, 1983), 124. In the interview with Dale Salwak, P. D. James explains that that title was already in use by someone else (see note 16 above).

33. Harkness notes that incest is a "persistent topic" in James, occurring in *Death of an Expert Witness* and *Cover Her Face* as well as here (128). Siebenheller first describes it as a way of "repaying" Maurice: "Phillippa [sic] owes a great deal of herself to Maurice Palfrey, and somehow, in that bed in Ravenna, she repays it" (70). Later, however, Siebenheller "wonders why James was so eager to include" the incest since "it is not really crucial to the plot" (119). Gildez says the whole episode "strains credulity" (95). The incest

is sudden and Philippa's casual attitude towards it is almost unbelievable, but it does illustrate her renewal of a relationship with Maurice.

CHAPTER 6
The City as Archeological Dig:
Maureen Duffy

1. Maureen Duffy, "Foreword," *20,000 Streets Under the Sky: The London Novel 1896–1985,* catalogue of an Exhibition at The Bookspace, Royal Festival Hall, London, Feb. 17-March 12, 1986, 8.
2. Maureen Duffy, *Londoners: an Elegy* (London: Methuen, 1983), 23. All further citations will be to this edition.
3. Margaret Mead, "The Kind of City We Want," *Ekistics* 209 (April 1973): 206.
4. Kevin Lynch, *What Time Is This Place* (Cambridge, Mass.: MIT Press, 1972), 171.
5. Maureen Duffy, "Preface," *That's How It Was* (1962; rpt. London: Dial Press, 1984), x. All further citations will be to this edition.
6. Duffy actually grew up in Trowbridge.
7. Maureen Duffy, "Foreword," *20,000 Streets under the Sky: London Fiction 1896–1985,* 7.
8. In an interview with Christine Sizemore on June 30, 1986, Duffy said that she heard John Fowles make this statement on a TV show, and he did not elaborate on the idea. Fowles has commented in more detail elsewhere. In an interview with Raman K. Singh, Fowles refers to an article by an American professor of psychiatry, Gilbert J. Rose, on *The French Lieutenant's Woman.* Rose emphasizes that "the drive to re-establish unity with the lost mother of infancy is an important factor in the creative impulse." Rose explains further that "the unconscious roots of an author's giving birth to a novel lie deeper than latent homosexuality [Rose is discussing a male author here] or identification with the female reproductive ability. Author and novel together are mother and child, rejoined in bodily completeness, perfection and immortality." Gilbert J. Rose, *"The French Lieutenant's Woman*: the Unconscious Significance of a Novel to its Author," *American Imago* 29 (1979): 173. Fowles says of Rose's article: "I don't go all the way with his analysis, but I go totally with his theory that novelists are genetically made; and then by circumstances over which you have no control in the first few

years of your life." Raman K. Singh, "An Encounter with John Fowles," *Journal of Modern Literature* 8, no. 2 (1980): 184–85. Fowles' word "genetically" is odd because Rose discusses psychic development, not genetic influence. Psychoanalytic explanations are sometimes seen to be almost as deterministic as genetic explanations, but they are different. Fowles' point seems to be that authors are "made," have a natural inclination to be writers because of their early experiences, but he confuses genetic and psychic. Later in the same interview Fowles says that "it's pointless to teach people [to write] who haven't got the right genetic make-up; and who haven't had the right infancy experiences—I'm a Freudian— the right kind of separation trauma . . . [Singh's ellipses] because I think this really is the heart of all art; you must have had the right experience of separation of your own identity from other ones" (194). It would be interesting to know how much emphasis Fowles is putting on "separation" here. Of course, everyone must separate from the mother, but Nancy Chodorow argues in *The Reproduction of Mothering: Psychoanalysis and the Sociology of Gender* (Berkeley: Univ. of California Press, 1978) that girls maintain a connectedness that boys cut off. If Fowles is emphasizing separation as that typical of boys' experience rather than the "differentiation" that girls go through, then he is describing a new version of the old nineteenth-century phallic theory of writing that Gilbert and Gubar discuss in *The Madwoman in the Attic: The Woman Writer and the Nineteenth Century Literary Imagination* (New Haven: Yale Univ. Press, 1979).

9. I think Duffy means "Jarvis Chuff" here rather than "Scully." Scully is the hero of *Housespy* in which there is no recurring mother figure. Jarvis Chuff is the hero of *I Want to Go to Moscow* (American title *All Heaven in a Rage*), and his mother plays a very significant role in his memory throughout the novel.

10. Chodorow, *Reproduction*, 204.

11. Chodorow, *Reproduction*, 169.

12. Although *That's How It Was* deals with Paddy as a child rather than as a mature sexual adult, Catherine Stimpson notes that the search for the mother is "at the heart of the labyrinth of some lesbian texts. There she unites past, present, and future. . . . Of course lesbianism is far more than a matter of mother/daughter affairs, but the new texts suggest that one of its satisfactions is a return to primal origins, to primal loves, where female/female, not male/female relationships structured the world." Catherine R.

Stimpson, "Zero Degree Deviancy: The Lesbian Novel in English," in *Writing and Sexual Difference,* ed. Elizabeth Abel (Chicago: Univ. of Chicago Press, 1981), 256–57. Adrienne Rich criticizes Chodorow, Dinnerstein, and Jean Baker Miller for not including lesbians in their analysis of mother-daughter bonds but suggests that Chodorow comes closest to "an acknowledgement of lesbian existence," especially in Chodorow's argument that "in having a child a woman seeks to recreate her own intense relationship with her mother." "Compulsory Heterosexuality and Lesbian Existence," *Signs* 5, no. 4 (Summer 1980): 635, 636.

13. Rachel Gould, "Maybe It's Because I'm a Londoner," rev. of *Londoners," Manchester Guardian* 5 Oct. 1983: 18.

14. In a 1973 interview with Dulan Barber, Duffy says, "*The Microcosm* was conceived as a non-fiction book, and I built it up from there, incorporating lots of characters I had interviewed, and others I knew personally. I fitted bits of characters together so that I could get as full a range as possible. . . . I only discovered my homosexuality because I fell in love with somebody, so I was never alone. Also, I very quickly discovered the club scene and met a great number of people. . . . I never had any feeling of guilt, which is a great help. It never seemed to me in the least unnatural or immoral or even, once I'd made the intellectual discovery, particularly unusual. You see, one of the great virtues of a club is that if you go there and it's packed with about two hundred people on a Saturday night, it is a bit difficult to think of yourself as unique. . . . my writing certainly antedates my knowing I was a homosexual. There doesn't seem to be any break between what I was doing before I knew and what I've done since." "Maureen Duffy: Talking to Dulan Barber," *Transatlantic Review* 45 (Spring 1973): 7–8.

15. Maureen Duffy, *The Microcosm* (New York: Simon and Schuster, 1966), 40. All further citations will be to this edition.

16. Maureen Duffy, interview with author, "Interview with Maureen Duffy," London, 30 June 1986.

17. Since after *The Microcosm* none of Duffy's novels focuses exclusively on lesbian characters, I asked her if Matt's speech was a statement she was making as a novelist as well. She replied: "It wasn't consciously so, but I think it was probably sort of preconsciously so. . . . I don't want to keep repeating a novel" (Interview, 30 June 1986).

18. Leah Fritz, "Maureen Duffy: In a Class by Herself," *Women's Review of Books* 5, no. 2 (Nov. 1987): 25.

19. Maureen Duffy, letter to author, 21 March 1986.

20. Duffy, letter to author.

21. Gould, 18.

22. Duffy, interview, 30 June 1986.

23. Duffy, interview.

24. Gould, 18.

25. Gould, 18.

26. Barber, 5–6.

27. Duffy, interview.

28. The majority of reviewers presume Al is male, although several realize the possibility of ambiguity. One reviewer, Angela Robbie, in *The New Statesman,* who identifies Al as female, creates just the problem that Duffy seeks to avoid. Robbie says that *Londoners* is "depressing in the same way as *The Well of Loneliness. . . .* It, too, marks out the different sexual choice as a burden." "Underworlds," rev. of *Londoners, The New Statesman* 106 (21 Oct. 1983): 24. This distorts the novel because Al's burden is not sexuality but rather difficulties with the literary establishment. It is probably coincidence that the satiric portrait of the *Peterloo Review* in the novel is based on *The New Statesman;* Galen Strawson points out the connection in "Modestly Villonesque," rev. of *Londoners, Times Literary Supplement,* 7 Oct. 1983: 1095. Leah Fritz thinks Al is a woman because of "the condescension and pseudo-gallantry" publishers extend to Al (Fritz, 24). When I first read *Londoners,* I read Al as male, but I agree with Strawson's assessment that Al "is an indefinite sort of man—there is something shiftingly feminine in the quality of his perceptions, in the particular pattern of detail that he discerns as he moves among people and about the city. He is heterosexual certainly, but hardly sexual at all."

It is hard to know how to write about a character whose sex is ambiguous. Because constructions like "he/she" are awkward and call too much attention to gender, I have tried to avoid the third person singular pronoun when writing about Al. Since Duffy uses "he" in *The Microcosm* to refer to some lesbian characters, the use of "he" might be a possible choice, but since "he" usually carries only a masculine connotation, it might obscure Al's feminine qualities.

29. The manuscript is in the Duffy collection at the library of King's College, London.

30. Gould, 18.

31. Walt Disney is also mentioned several times in *I Want to Go*

to Moscow (American title: *All Heaven in a Rage*). Jarvis Chuff describes the exterior of the prison as "the bizarre fairy towers of a sadistic Walt Disney" in *I Want To Go to Moscow: a Lay* (London: Hodder and Stoughton, 1973), 43. In the prison cell the only light is "the artificial Disney moonlight of the pale bulb at the dead middle of the ceiling" (10). Later Chuff describes a suburban bedroom as "a glorified dwarf's house from Snow White, all chintz curtains and Windsor chairs" (53). In *The Single Eye* the image of the dwarf's house also appears in Mike Fannon's description of entering his brother's house: "The stairs were very high and twisting, and the odd shape of the flat, the sloping ceiling . . . made me feel as if I'd come into the dwarf's house in *Snow White*." *The Single Eye* (London: Hutchinson and Co., 1964), 152. Duffy said that this movie specifically, and cinema in general, has had a strong influence on her fiction." Duffy, interview.

32. Carol Gilligan, *In a Different Voice: Psychological Theory and Women's Development* (Cambridge, Mass.: Harvard Univ. Press, 1982).

33. Maureen Duffy, *Capital: a Fiction* (1975; rpt. London: Methuen, 1984), 26. All further citations will be to this edition.

34. Anatole Broyard, "Light for our Dark Ages," *The New York Times* 19 March 1976: 31.

35. Duffy describes Meepers as being "damaged." Interview with author, 30 June 1986.

36. Gould, 18.

37. Duffy, interview.

38. Duffy, interview.

39. James Brockway, "Homage to London," rev. of *Capital, Books and Bookman* 21 (May 1976): 43.

40. Duffy, interview.

CHAPTER 7
Conclusion

1. Doris Lessing, *The Four-Gated City* (New York: Knopf, 1969), 10.

2. See Irving Howe, "The City in Literature," *Commentary* 51, no. 5 (May 1971): 66–68.

3. These are criticized by Kevin Lynch in *A Theory of Good City Form* (Cambridge, Mass.: MIT Press, 1981), 81–98.

4. Maureen Duffy, *Londoners: an Elegy* (London: Methuen, 1983), 47, 101–2.

5. Iris Murdoch, *Nuns and Soldiers* (London: Chatto and Windus, 1980), 385.

6. Duffy, *Londoners,* 10.

7. Margaret Drabble, *The Realms of Gold* (New York: Knopf, 1975), 29.

8. Lessing, *The Four-Gated City,* 10.

9. Jessica Benjamin, "A Desire of One's Own: Psychoanalytic Feminism and Intersubjective Space," *Feminist Studies/Critical Studies,* ed. Teresa de Lauretis (Bloomington: Indiana Univ. Press, 1986), 95.

10. Doris Lessing, *The Diaries of Jane Somers* (London: Michael Joseph, 1984), 208.

11. Iris Murdoch, *The Sovereignty of Good* (London: Routledge and Kegan Paul, 1970). See Ch. 4, pp. 115–118, above, for a discussion of this theme in *The Sovereignty of Good.*

12. Rachel Gould, "Maybe It's Because I'm a Londoner," rev. of *Londoners, Manchester Guardian* 5 Oct. 1983, 18.

13. Duffy, *Londoners,* 93.

14. Margaret Drabble, *The Ice Age* (New York: Knopf, 1977), 172.

15. Margaret Drabble, *The Middle Ground* (New York: Knopf, 1980), 112.

16. Drabble, *The Middle Ground,* 243–44.

17. Margaret Drabble, *The Radiant Way* (London: Weidenfeld and Nicolson, 1986), 73.

18. Howe, 68.

19. Philip Johnson's beautiful IBM building in Atlanta is an exception to these other postmodernist buildings. As Allen Freeman writes, "The new IBM Tower in Atlanta isn't *like* a 1920's skyscraper, it *is* a 1920's skyscraper." "A Trip Back to the 20's in Atlanta." *Architecture,* Jan. 1988, 56–59. Like Johnson's other office buildings, however, it is still a landmark that calls attention to itself.

20. Patrick Byrne and Richard Carroll Keeley, "Le Corbusier's Finger and Jacob's Thought: the Loss and Recovery of the Subject in the City" in *Communicating a Dangerous Memory: Soundings in Political Theology,* ed. Fred Lawrence (Atlanta: Scholar Press, 1987), 77.

21. Nick Wates and Charles Knevitt, *Community Architecture: How People are Creating Their Own Environment* (London: Penguin, 1987), 157.

22. Wates and Knevitt, 118.
23. Wates and Knevitt, 79.
24. Wates and Knevitt, 74.
25. Wates and Knevitt, 86–87.
26. Wates and Knevitt, 73.

Bibliography

Margaret Drabble

Bromberg, Pamela S. "The Development of Narrative Technique in Margaret Drabble's Novels." *Journal of Narrative Technique* 16, no. 3 (Fall 1986): 179–91.

———. "Narrative in Drabble's *The Middle Ground:* Relativity versus Teleology." *Contemporary Literature* 24, no. 4 (Winter 1983): 461–79.

Campbell, Jane. "Reaching Outwards: Versions of Reality in *The Middle Ground.*" *Journal of Narrative Technique* 14, no. 1 (Winter 1984): 17–32.

Creighton, Joanne V. *Margaret Drabble.* London: Methuen, 1985.

Davidoff, Leonore. "Class and Gender in Victorian England: The Diaries of Arthur J. Munby and Hannah Cullwick." *Feminist Studies* 5, no. 1 (Spring 1979): 87–141.

Douglas, Mary. *Purity and Danger: an Analysis of Concepts of Pollution and Taboo.* New York: Praeger, 1966.

Drabble, Margaret. *Arnold Bennett.* New York: Knopf, 1974.

Drabble, Margaret. "The Author Comments." *Dutch Quarterly Review of Anglo-American Letters* 5, no. 1 (1975): 35–38. [A response to the Mannheimer article.]

———. *The Garrick Year.* London: Weidenfeld and Nicolson, 1964.

———. *The Ice Age.* New York: Knopf, 1977.

———. *Jerusalem the Golden.* London: Weidenfeld and Nicolson, 1967.

——— and B. S. Johnson, eds. *London Consequences.* London: Greater London Arts Association, 1972.

———. *The Middle Ground.* New York: Knopf, 1980.

————. *The Needle's Eye.* London: Weidenfeld and Nicolson, 1972.

————. "No Idle Rentier: Angus Wilson and the Nourished Literary Imagination." *Studies in the Literary Imagination* 13, no. 1 (Spring 1980): 119–29.

————. "A Novelist in a Derelict City." *New York Times Magazine,* 14 April 1985: 76–81.

————. *The Radiant Way.* London: Weidenfeld and Nicolson, 1987.

————. *The Realms of Gold.* New York: Knopf, 1975.

————. *The Waterfall.* London: Weidenfeld and Nicolson, 1969.

————. *A Writer's Britain: Landscape in Literature.* New York: Knopf, 1979.

Duxes, Helen. "Female Birth and Rebirth in the City: Moving from Margaret Drabble's *Jerusalem the Golden* (1967) to *The Middle Ground* (1980)." Paper presented at the annual meeting of the Modern Language Association, San Francisco, December 1987.

Greene, Gayle. "The End of a Dream." Rev. of *The Radiant Way. Women's Review of Books* 5, no. 4 (Jan. 1988): 4–5.

Hannay, John. *The Intertextuality of Fate: a Study of Margaret Drabble.* Columbia: Univ. of Missouri Press, 1986.

————. "Margaret Drabble: an Interview." *Twentieth Century Literature* 33, no. 2 (Summer 1987): 129–49.

Harper, Michael F. "Margaret Drabble and the Sense of Closure in *The Middle Ground.*" Paper presented at the annual meeting of the Modern Language Association, Washington, D.C., December 1984.

Mannheimer, Monica L. "The Search for Identity in Margaret Drabble's *The Needle's Eye.*" *Dutch Review of Anglo-American Letters* 5, no. 1 (1975): 24–35.

Moran, Mary Hurley. *Margaret Drabble: Existing within Structures.* Carbondale: Univ. of Southern Illinois Press, 1983.

Myer, Valerie G. *Margaret Drabble: Puritanism and Permissiveness.* London: Vision Press, 1974.

Oates, Joyce Carol. "*The Needle's Eye.*" *New York Times Book Review,* 11 June 1972: 23.

Parrinder, Patrick. "Speaking for England." *London Review of Books,* 21 May 1987: 21–22.

Preussner, Dee. "Talking with Margaret Drabble." *Modern Fiction Studies* 25, no. 4 (Winter 1979–80): 563–77.

Rose, Ellen Cronan, ed. *Critical Essays on Margaret Drabble.* Boston: G. K. Hall, 1985.

——. "Drabble's *The Middle Ground:* 'Mid-Life' Narrative Strategies." *Critique* 23, no. 3 (Spring 1982): 69–82.

——. *The Novels of Margaret Drabble: Equivocal Figures.* Totowa, N.J.: Barnes and Noble, 1980.

Rose, Phyllis. "Our Chronicler of Britain." *New York Times Book Review,* 7 Sept. 1980: 1+.

Rubenstein, Roberta. "From Detritus to Discovery: Margaret Drabble's *The Middle Ground.*" *Journal of Narrative Technique* 14, no. 1 (Winter 1984): 1–16.

Sadler, Lynn Veach. "The Society We Have: The Search for Meaning in Drabble's *The Middle Ground.*" *Critique* 23, no. 3 (Spring 1982): 83–93.

Schmidt, Dorey, ed. *Margaret Drabble: Golden Realms.* Edinburg, Texas: Pan American Univ. Press, 1982.

Updike, John. "Seeking Connections in an Insecure Country." Rev. of *The Radiant Way. New Yorker* 16 Nov. 1987: 157–59.

Maureen Duffy

Barber, Dulan. "Maureen Duffy: Talking to Dulan Barber." *Transatlantic Review* 45 (Spring 1973): 5–16.

Brockway, James. "Homage to London." rev. of *Capital. Books and Bookman* 21 (May 1976): 43–44.

Broyard, Anatole. "Light for Our Dark Ages." rev. of *Capital. New York Times,* 19 March 1976: 31.

Duffy, Maureen. *All Heaven in a Rage.* New York: Knopf, 1973.

——. *Capital.* 1975. Reprint. London: Methuen, 1984.

——. *Change.* London: Methuen, 1987.

——. "Foreword." *20,000 Streets Under the Sky: The London Novel 1896–1985.* Catalogue of an Exhibition at The Bookspace, Royal Festival Hall, London, Feb. 17–March 12, 1986. London: The Bookspace, 1986: 7–8.

——. *Gor Saga.* New York: Viking, 1982.

——. *Housespy.* London: Hamish Hamilton, 1978.

——. *I Want to Go to Moscow: A Lay.* London: Hodder and Stoughton, 1973. [American edition entitled *All Heaven in a Rage.*]

——. Interview with author. London, 30 June 1986.

——. Letter to author, 21 March 1986.

——. *Londoners: an Elegy.* London: Methuen, 1983.

———. *Love Child.* New York: Knopf, 1971.

———. *The Microcosm.* New York: Simon and Schuster, 1966.

———. "A Nightingale in Bloomsbury Square." In *Factions,* ed. Giles Gordon and Alex Hamilton. London: Michael Joseph, 1974.

———. *The Paradox Players.* New York: Simon and Schuster, 1967.

———. *The Single Eye.* London: Hutchinson and Co., 1964.

———. *That's How It Was.* 1962. Reprint. London: The Dial Press, 1984.

———. *Villon.* Unpublished play. Duffy Manuscript Collection. Library of King's College, London.

———. *Wounds.* London: Hutchinson and Co., 1969.

Fritz, Leah. "Maureen Duffy: In a Class by Herself." *Women's Review of Books* 5, no. 2 (Nov. 1987): 24–25.

Gould, Rachel. "Maybe It's Because I'm a Londoner." Rev. of *Londoners. Manchester Guardian,* 5 Oct. 1983, 18.

King, Francis. "Ambivalent." Rev. of *Londoners. Spectator* 251 (29 Oct. 1983): 28.

Marcus, Frank. "Maureen Duffy." In *Contemporary Dramatists,* 3rd. ed., 207–9. New York: St. Martin's, 1982.

Robbie, Angela. "Underworlds." Rev. of *Londoners. New Statesman* 106 (21 Oct. 1983), 24.

Strawson, Galen. "Modestly Villonesque." rev. of *Londoners. Times Literary Supplement,* 7 Oct. 1983: 1095.

P. D. James

Bakerman, Jane S. "From the Time I Could Read, I Always Wanted To Be a Writer: Interview with P. D. James." *The Armchair Detective* 10 (Jan. 1977): 55–57, 92.

Benstock, Bernard. "The Clinical World of P. D. James." In *Twentieth-Century Women Novelists,* ed. Thomas F. Staley, 104–29. New York: Barnes and Noble, 1982.

Campbell, SueEllen. "The Detective Heroine and the Death of Her Hero: Dorothy Sayers to P. D. James." *Modern Fiction Studies* 29, no. 3 (Autumn 1983): 497–510.

Cooper-Clark, Diana. *Designs of Darkness: Interviews With Detective Novelists.* Bowling Green, Ohio: Bowling Green State Univ. Popular Press, 1983.

de la Torre, Lillian. "Cordelia Gray: The Thinking Man's Heroine." In *Murdress Ink: The Better Half,* ed. Dilys Winn, 111–13. New York: Workman, 1979.

Gildez, Richard B. *P. D. James*. Boston: Twayne, 1986.

Harkness, Bruce. "P. D. James." In *Art in Crime Writing: Essays in Detective Fiction*, ed. Bernard Benstock, 119–41. New York: St. Martin's, 1983.

Heilbrun, Carolyn G. "A Feminist Looks at Women in Detective Novels." *Graduate Woman*. July/Aug. 1980: 15–21.

———. "James, P. D." In *Twentieth Century Crime and Mystery Writers*, ed. John M. Reilly, 856–57. New York: St. Martin's, 1980.

Hubly, Erlene. "The Formula Challenged: The Novels of P. D. James." *Modern Fiction Studies* 29, no. 3 (Autumn 1983): 511–21.

James, P. D. *Innocent Blood*. New York: Scribner's, 1980.

———. *A Mind to Murder*. In *Crime Times Three*. New York: Scribner's, 1963.

———. *Shroud for a Nightingale*. In *Crime Times Three*. New York: Scribner's, 1971.

———. *The Skull Beneath the Skin*. New York: Scribner's, 1982.

———. *A Taste for Death*. London: Faber and Faber, 1986.

———. *Unnatural Causes*. 1967; rpt. London: Hamish Hamilton, 1976.

———. *An Unsuitable Job for a Woman*. London: Faber and Faber, 1972.

Joyner, Nancy Carol. "P. D. James." In *10 Women of Mystery*, ed. Earl R. Bargainnier, 108–23. Bowling Green, Ohio: Bowling Green State Univ. Popular Press, 1981.

Maxfield, James F. "The Unfinished Detective: The Work of P. D. James." *Critique* 28, no. 4 (Summer 1987), 211–23.

Salwak, Dale. "An Interview with P. D. James." *Mystery Voices: Interviews with British Mystery Writers*. San Bernadino, Ca.: Borgo Press, forthcoming.

Siebenheller, Norma. *P. D. James*. New York: Ungar, 1981.

Doris Lessing

Barnouw, Dagmar. "Disorderly Company: From *The Golden Note-Book* to *The Four-Gated City*." In *Doris Lessing: Critical Studies*, ed. Annis Pratt and L. S. Dembo, 74–97. Madison: Univ. of Wisconsin Press, 1974. [All the articles originally appeared in *Contemporary Literature* 14, no. 3 (Fall 1973).]

Dietz, Bernd, and Fernando Galván. "*Entrevista:* A Conversation with Doris Lessing." *Doris Lessing Newsletter* 9, no. 1 (Spring 1985): 5–6, 13.

Draine, Betsy. *Substance Under Pressure: Artistic Coherence and Evolving Form in the Novels of Doris Lessing*. Madison: Univ. of Wisconsin Press, 1985.

DuPlessis, Rachel Blau. "Feminist Apologues of Lessing, Piercy and Russ." *Frontiers* 4, no. 1 (Spring 1979): 1–8.

Fishburn, Katherine. *The Unexpected Universe of Doris Lessing*. Westport, Conn.: Greenwood, 1985.

Gardiner, Judith Kegan. "Evil, Apocalypse, and Feminist Fiction." *Frontiers* 7, no. 2 (Summer 1983), 74–80.

Greene, Gayle. *"The Diaries of Jane Somers."* Paper presented at the annual meeting of the Modern Language Association, New York, December 1985.

Hidalgo, Pilar. *"The Good Terrorist:* Lessing's Tract for the Times." *Doris Lessing Newsletter* 11, no. 1 (Spring 1987): 7–8.

Joyner, Nancy Carol. "The Underside of the Butterfly: Lessing's Debt to Woolf." *Journal of Narrative Technique* 4, no. 3 (Sept. 1974): 204–11.

Knapp, Mona. *Doris Lessing*. New York: Ungar, 1984.

———. "Reports: Doris Lessing in North America, March–April, 1984: University of California, Los Angeles." *Doris Lessing Newsletter* 8, no. 2 (Fall 1984): 8, 14.

Lessing, Doris. *Briefing for a Descent into Hell*. New York: Knopf, 1971.

———. *The Children of Violence*. 5 vols. London: MacGibbon and Kee, 1965–1969.

———. *The Diaries of Jane Somers*. London: Michael Joseph, 1984.

———. "Doris Lessing Talks About Jane Somers." *Doris Lessing Newsletter* 10, no. 1 (Spring 1986): 3–5, 14.

———. *The Four-Gated City*. New York: Knopf, 1969.

———. *The Golden Notebook*. London: Michael Joseph, 1962.

———. *The Good Terrorist*. London: Jonathan Cape, 1985.

———. *The Marriages between Zones Three, Four and Five*. New York: Knopf, 1980.

———. *Martha Quest*. London: Michael Joseph, 1952.

———. *The Memoirs of a Survivor*. London: Octagon Press, 1974.

———. *A Proper Marriage*. London: Michael Joseph, 1954.

———. *Shikasta*. New York: Knopf, 1979.

———. *A Small Personal Voice*. Ed. Paul Schlueter. New York: Knopf, 1974.

———. *The Summer Before the Dark*. New York: Knopf, 1973.

Rose, Ellen Cronan. "Doris Lessing's *Citta Felice*." *Massachusetts Review* 24, no. 2 (Summer 1983): 369–86.

———. *The Tree Outside the Window: Doris Lessing's Children of Violence*. Hanover, N.H.: Univ. Press of New England, 1976.

Rubenstein, Roberta. *The Novelistic Vision of Doris Lessing: Breaking the Forms of Consciousness*. Champaign, Ill.: Univ. of Illinois Press, 1979.

Singleton, Mary Anne. *The City and the Veld: The Fiction of Doris Lessing*. Lewisburg, Pa.: Bucknell Univ. Press, 1977.

Sprague, Claire, ed. *Critical Essays on Doris Lessing*. Boston: G. K. Hall, 1986.

———. *Rereading Doris Lessing: Narrative Patterns of Doubling and Repetition*. Chapel Hill: Univ. of North Carolina Press, 1987.

———. " 'Without Contraries Is No Progression': Lessing's *The Four-Gated City*." *Modern Fiction Studies* 26, no. 1 (Summer 1980): 99–116.

Taylor, Jenny. *Notebooks/Memoirs/Archives: Reading and Rereading Doris Lessing*. Boston: Routledge and Kegan Paul, 1982.

Tiger, Virginia. "Lessing in New York City, April 1 and 2." *Doris Lessing Newsletter* 8, no. 2 (Fall 1984): 5–6.

Walker, Melissa. "Doris Lessing's *The Four-Gated City*: Consciousness and Community—A Different History." *The Southern Review*, n.s. 17 (1981): 97–120.

Iris Murdoch

Bellamy, Michael O. "An Interview with Iris Murdoch," *Contemporary Literature* 18, no. 2 (Spring 1977): 129–40.

Biles, Jack I. "Interview with Iris Murdoch." *Studies in the Literary Imagination* 11, no. 2 (Fall 1978): 115–25.

Byatt, Antonia S. *Iris Murdoch*. London: Longman Group Ltd., 1976.

Cohen, Steven. "From Subtext to Dreamtext: The Brutal Egotism of Iris Murdoch's Male Narrators." *Women and Literature* 2 (1982): 222–42.

Conradi, Peter. *Iris Murdoch: the Saint and the Artist*. New York: St. Martin's, 1986.

Dipple, Elizabeth. *Iris Murdoch, Work for the Spirit*. Chicago: Univ. of Chicago Press, 1982.

Hawkins, Peter. *The Language of Grace: Flannery O'Connor, Walker Percy and Iris Murdoch.* Cambridge, Mass.: Cowley Publications, 1983.

Johnson, Deborah. *Iris Murdoch.* Key Women Writers Series, ed. Sue Roe. Bloomington: Indiana Univ. Press, 1987.

Martz, Louis. "Iris Murdoch: the London Novels." In *Twentieth Century Literature in Retrospect,* ed. Reuben Brower, 65–86. Cambridge, Mass.: Harvard Univ. Press, 1971.

Murdoch, Iris. "Against Dryness: a Polemical Sketch." In *The Novel Today: Contemporary Writers on Modern Fiction,* ed. Malcolm Bradbury, 23–31. Totowa, N.J.: Rowman and Littlefield, 1978.

———. *The Black Prince.* London: Chatto and Windus 1973.

———. *The Book and the Brotherhood.* New York: Viking, 1987.

———. *Bruno's Dream.* London: Chatto and Windus, 1969.

———. *A Fairly Honourable Defeat.* London: Chatto and Windus, 1970.

———. *The Flight from the Enchanter.* London: Chatto and Windus, 1956.

———. *The Good Apprentice.* London: Chatto and Windus, 1985.

———. *Henry and Cato.* London: Chatto and Windus, 1976.

———. *The Nice and the Good.* London: Chatto and Windus, 1968.

———. *Nuns and Soldiers.* London: Chatto and Windus, 1980.

———. *The Philosopher's Pupil.* London: Chatto and Windus, 1983.

———. *The Sandcastle.* London: Chatto and Windus, 1957.

———. *The Sea, the Sea.* London: Chatto and Windus, 1978.

———. *The Sovereignty of Good.* London: Routledge and Kegan Paul, 1970.

———. "The Sublime and the Good." *Chicago Review* 13, no. 3 (Autumn 1959): 42–55.

———. "T. S. Eliot as a Moralist." In *T. S. Eliot: a Symposium for his Seventieth Birthday,* ed. Neville Braybrooke, 152–60. New York: Books for Libraries, Inc., 1958.

———. *Under the Net.* London: Chatto and Windus, 1954.

———. *The Unicorn.* London: Chatto and Windus, 1963.

———. *An Unofficial Rose.* London: Chatto and Windus, 1962.

———. *A Word Child.* London: Chatto and Windus, 1975.

Roxmann, Susana. "Contingency and the Image of the Net in Iris Murdoch, Novelist and Philosopher." *Edda: Nordisk Tidsskrift for Litteraturforskning/Scandinavian Journal of Literary Research* 2 (1983): 65–70.

Slaymaker, William. "An Interview with Iris Murdoch." *Papers in Language and Literature* 21, no. 4 (Fall 1985): 425–32.

Wolfe, Peter. "'Malformed Treatise' and Prizewinner: Iris Murdoch's *The Black Prince*." *Studies in the Literary Imagination* 11, no. 2 (Fall 1978): 97–114.

Literary Criticism and General Literature

Abel, Elizabeth, Marianne Hirsch, and Elizabeth Langland, eds. *The Voyage In: Fictions of Female Development*. Hanover, N. H.: Univ. Press of New England, 1983.

Abel, Elizabeth, ed. *Writing and Sexual Difference*. Chicago: Univ. of Chicago Press, 1980–82.

Bainbridge, Beryl. *The Bottle Factory Outing*. London: Duckworth, 1975.

———. *The Dressmaker*. London: Duckworth, 1973.

Bennett, Arnold. *Riceyman Steps*. New York: G. H. Doran Co., 1923.

Brookner, Anita. *Look At Me*. New York: Pantheon, 1983.

Culler, Jonathan. *On Deconstruction: Theory and Criticism after Structuralism*. Ithaca, N.Y.: Cornell Univ. Press, 1982.

Dickens, Charles. *Little Dorrit*. 1857; rpt. New York: Penguin, 1967.

Dunn, Nell. *Up the Junction*. Philadelphia: Lippincott, 1966.

DuPlessis, Rachel Blau. *Writing Beyond the Ending: Narrative Strategies of Twentieth-Century Writers*. Bloomington: Indiana Univ. Press, 1985.

Eliot, T. S. *The Cocktail Party*. New York: Harcourt Brace, 1950.

———. *The Complete Poems and Plays of T. S. Eliot*. London: Faber and Faber, 1969.

Forster, E. M. *Howards End*. New York: Knopf, 1921.

Flynn, Elizabeth and P. Schweikart. *Gender and Reading: Essays on Readers, Texts and Contexts*. Baltimore, Md.: Johns Hopkins Univ. Press, 1985.

Geertz, Clifford. "Blurred Genres: the Refiguration of Social Thought." *The American Scholar* 49 (Spring 1980): 165–79.

Gelfant, Blanche. *Women Writing in America: Voices in Collage*. Hanover, N. H.: Univ. Press of New England, 1984.

Gilbert, Sandra, and Susan Gubar. *The Madwoman in the Attic: The Woman Writer and the Nineteenth Century Literary Imagination*. New Haven: Yale Univ. Press, 1979.

Greene, Gayle and Coppélia Kahn, eds. *Making a Difference: Feminist Literary Criticism*. London: Methuen, 1985.

Kemp, Peter. *Muriel Spark*. London: Elek, 1974.

Manning, Olivia. *The Doves of Venus*. 1955; rpt. London: Virago, 1984.

Marlowe, Christopher. *The Complete Plays of Christopher Marlowe*. Ed. Irving Ribner. New York: Odyssey, 1963.

Matthews, William Henry. *Mazes and Labyrinths*. 1922. New York: Dover, 1970.

Miller, J. Hillis. *Charles Dickens: The World of His Novels*. Cambridge, Mass.: Harvard Univ. Press, 1958.

Naylor, Gloria. *The Women of Brewster Place*. New York: Viking Press, 1982.

Oates, Joyce Carol. *Them*. New York: Vanguard Press, 1969.

Petry, Ann. *The Street*. New York: Houghton Mifflin, 1946.

Piercy, Marge. *Fly Away Home*. New York: Random House, 1984.

Piercy, Marge. *Going Down Fast*. New York: Trident Press, 1969.

Pym, Barbara. *Excellent Women*. London: Jonathan Cape, 1952.

Pym, Barbara. *A Glass of Blessings*. London: Jonathan Cape, 1958.

Rosaldo, Michelle Z., and Louise Lamphere. *Woman, Culture and Society*. Stanford, Calif.: Stanford Univ. Press, 1974.

Rushdie, Salman. *Midnight's Children*. New York: Knopf, 1981.

Sacks, Sheldon. "Golden Birds and Dying Generations." *Comparative Literature Studies* 6, no. 3 (Sept. 1969): 274–91.

Showalter, Elaine. *A Literature of Their Own: British Women Novelists from Brontë to Lessing*. Princeton: Princeton Univ. Press, 1977.

———. *The New Feminist Criticism: Essays on Women, Literature and Theory*. New York: Pantheon, 1985.

Singh, Raman K. "An Encounter with John Fowles." *Journal of Modern Literature* 8, no. 2 (1980): 181–202.

Slater, Michael. *Dickens and Women*. London: J. M. Dent and Sons, Ltd., 1983.

Spark, Muriel. *The Bachelors*. Philadelphia: Lippincott, 1960.

———. *The Ballad of Peckham Rye*. London: Macmillan, 1961.

———. *Girls of Slender Means*. New York: Knopf, 1963.

———. *Loitering with Intent*. New York: Coward, McCann & Geoghegan, 1981.

———. *Memento Mori*. Philadelphia, Lippincott, 1959.

Stimpson, Catherine R. "Zero Degree Deviancy: the Lesbian Novel in English." In *Writing and Sexual Difference,* ed. Elizabeth Abel, 243–59. Chicago: Univ. of Chicago Press, 1981.

Weldon, Fay. *Down Among the Women*. London: Heinemann, 1971.

Weldon, Fay. *The President's Child.* London: Hodder & Stoughton, 1982.

Williams, Raymond. *The English Novel: from Dickens to Lawrence.* New York: Oxford Univ. Press, 1970.

Woolf, Virginia. *Mrs. Dalloway.* New York: Harcourt Brace, 1925.

———. *Night and Day.* New York: Harcourt Brace, 1920.

———. *A Room of One's Own.* New York: Harcourt Brace, 1929.

———. *The Years.* New York: Harcourt Brace, 1937.

Zimmermann, Bonnie. "What Has Never Been: an Overview of Lesbian Feminist Literary Criticism." *Feminist Studies* 7 (1981): 451–75.

Psychological Theory

Bem, Sandra. "Gender Schema Theory and Its Implications for Child Development: Raising Gender-aschematic Children in a Gender-schematic Society." *Signs* 8, no. 4 (Summer 1983): 598–616.

Benjamin, Jessica. "A Desire of One's Own: Psychoanalytic Feminism and Intersubjective Space." In *Feminist Studies/Critical Studies,* ed. Teresa de Lauretis, 78–101. Bloomington: Indiana Univ. Press, 1986.

Chodorow, Nancy. "Gender, Relation and Difference in Psychoanalytic Perspective." In *The Future of Difference,* ed. Hester Eisenstein and Alice Jardine, 3–19. Boston: G. K. Hall, 1980.

———. *The Reproduction of Mothering: Psychoanalysis and the Sociology of Gender.* Berkeley: Univ. of Calif. Press, 1978.

Dinnerstein, Dorothy. *The Mermaid and the Minotaur: Sexual Arrangements and Human Malaise.* New York: Harper and Row, 1976.

Eisenstein, Hester and Alice Jardine. *The Future of Difference.* Boston: G. K. Hall, 1980.

Erikson, Erik. *Childhood and Society.* 2nd. ed. New York: Norton, 1963.

———. "Womanhood and the Inner Space." In *Identity Youth and Crisis,* 261–94. New York: Norton, 1968.

Freud, Sigmund. "Female Sexuality (1931)." In vol. 21 of *The Standard Edition of the Complete Psychological Works of Sigmund Freud.* Trans. James Strachey, with Anna Freud. 8th. ed. London: Hogarth Press, 1953.

———. *The Interpretation of Dreams.* Vol. 4 of *The Standard Edi-*

tion of the Complete Psychological Works of Sigmund Freud. Trans. James Strachey, with Anna Freud. 8th. ed. London: Hogarth Press, 1953.

Gardiner, Judith Kegan. "Mind Mother: Psychoanalysis and Feminism." In *Making a Difference: Feminist Literary Criticism,* ed. Gayle Greene and Coppélia Kahn, 113–45. New York: Methuen, 1985.

Garner, Shirley H., and Claire Kehane, eds. *The (M)Other Tongue: Essays in Feminist Psychoanalytic Interpretations.* Ithaca, N.Y.: Cornell Univ. Press, 1985.

Gilligan, Carol. "The Conquistador and the Dark Continent: Reflections on the Psychology of Love." *Daedalus* 113, no. 3 (Summer 1984): 75–95.

——. *In a Different Voice: Psychological Theory and Women's Moral Development.* Cambridge, Mass.: Harvard Univ. Press, 1982.

Haaken, Janice. "Freudian Theories Revised: a Critique of Rich, Chodorow, and Dinnerstein." *Women's Studies Quarterly* 11 (Winter 1983): 12–16.

Hayles, N. Katherine. "Anger in Different Voices: Carol Gilligan and *Mill on the Floss. Signs* 12, no. 1 (Autumn 1986): 23–39.

Henley, Nancy M. "Psychology and Gender: Review Essay." *Signs* 11, no. 1 (Autumn 1985): 101–19.

Hirsch, Marianne. "Mothers and Daughters: a Review Essay." *Signs* 7, no. 1 (Autumn 1981): 200–22.

Kerber, Linda, et al. "On *In a Different Voice:* an Interdisciplinary Forum." *Signs* 11, no. 2 (Winter 1986): 304–33.

Lorber, Judith, et al. "On *The Reproduction of Mothering:* a Methodological Debate." *Signs* 6, no. 3 (Spring 1981): 482–514.

Miller, Jean Baker. *Toward a New Psychology of Women.* Boston: Beacon Press, 1976.

Nails, Debra, Mary Ann O'Laughlin, and James E. Walker, guest eds. "Women and Morality." rev. of *In a Different Voice. Social Research* 50, no. 3 (Autumn 1983).

Rich, Adrienne. "Compulsory Heterosexuality and Lesbian Existence." *Signs* 5, no. 4 (Summer 1980): 631–60.

——. *Of Woman Born: Motherhood as Experience and Institution.* New York: Norton, 1976.

Rose, Gilbert. "*The French Lieutenant's Woman:* the Unconscious Significance of a Novel to its Author." *American Imago* 29 (1979): 165–75.

Rossi, Alice S. "Gender and Parenthood: American Sociological Assoc. 1983 Presidential Address." *American Sociological Review* 49 (Feb. 1984): 1–19.

Ruddick, Sara. "Maternal Thinking." *Feminist Studies* 6, no. 2 (Summer 1980): 342–67.

Tronto, Joan. "Beyond Gender Difference to a Theory of Care." *Signs.* 12, no. 4 (Summer 1987): 644–63.

Winnicott, D. W. *Playing and Reality.* New York: Basic Books, 1980.

Urban Theory and Urban Literary Criticism

A–Z London Street Atlas. Ed. 1A. London: Geographer's A–Z Map Co. Ltd., n.d.

Abrams, Charles. *The City Is the Frontier.* New York: Harper and Row, 1965.

Baumgarten, Murray. *City Scriptures: Modern Jewish Writing.* Cambridge, Mass.: Harvard Univ. Press, 1982.

Benstock, Shari. *Women of the Left Bank: Paris 1900–1940.* Austin: Univ. of Texas Press, 1986.

Blanchard, Marc Eli. *In Search of the City: Engels, Baudelaire and Rimbaud.* Stanford French and Italian Studies, vol. 37. Saratoga, Calif.: Anma Libri, 1985.

Blumenfeld, Hans. "The Role of Design." In *The Growth of Cities,* ed. David Lewis, 14–18. New York: Wiley, 1971.

Bradbury, Malcolm. "The Cities of Modernism." In *Modernism 1890–1930,* ed. Malcolm Bradbury and James McFarlane, 96–104. Harmondsworth, Eng.: Penguin, 1976.

Byrd, Max. *London Transformed: Images of the City in the Eighteenth Century.* New Haven: Yale Univ. Press, 1978.

Byrne, Patrick and Richard Carroll Keeley. "Le Corbusier's Finger and Jacob's Thought: The Loss and Recovery of the Subject in the City." In *Communicating a Dangerous Memory: Soundings in Political Theology,* ed. Fred Lawrence, 63–108. Atlanta: Scholar Press, 1987.

Castillo, Debra A. "Beckett's Metaphorical Towns." *Modern Fiction Studies* 28, no. 2 (Summer 1982): 189–200.

Fanger, Donald. *Dostoevsky and Romantic Realism: a Study of Dostoevsky in Relation to Balzac, Dickens and Gogol.* Oxford: Clarendon Press, 1971.

Faris, Wendy. "The Labyrinth: Sign of City, Text and Thought." Paper presented at the International Association of Philosophy and

Literature Conference on "City, Text and Thought." New York, May 1985.

Festa-McCormick, Diana. *The City as Catalyst: a Study of Ten Novels.* Rutherford, N.J.: Fairleigh Dickinson Univ. Press, 1979.

Freeman, Allen. "A Trip Back to the 20's in Atlanta." *Architecture,* Jan. 1988, 56–59.

Gelfant, Blanche. *The American City Novel.* Norman: Univ. of Oklahoma Press, 1954.

Howe, Irving. "The City in Literature." *Commentary* 51, no. 5 (May 1971): 61–68.

Jacobs, Jane. *The Death and Life of Great American Cities.* New York: Random House, 1961.

Jaye, Michael C. and Ann Chalmers Watts, eds. *Literature and the Urban Experience: Essays on the City and Literature.* New Brunswick, N.J.: Rutgers Univ. Press, 1981.

Johnston, John H. *The Poet and the City: a Study in Urban Perspectives.* Athens: Univ. of Georgia Press, 1984.

Kaplan, Amy. "'The Knowledge of the Line': Realism and the City in Howell's *A Hazard of New Fortunes. PMLA* 101 (Jan. 1986): 69–81.

Le Corbusier, *The Radiant City, elements of a doctrine of urbanism to be used as the basis of our machine-age culture.* Trans. Pamela Knight, Eleanor Levieux, Derek Coltman. 1933; rpt. New York: Orion Press, 1967.

Lehan, Richard. "Urban Signs and Urban Literature: Literary Form and Historical Process." *New Literary History* 18 (1986–87): 99–113.

Lynch, Kevin. *The Image of the City.* Cambridge, Mass.: MIT Press, 1960.

———. *A Theory of Good City Form.* Cambridge, Mass.: MIT Press, 1981.

———. *What Time Is This Place.* Cambridge, Mass.: MIT Press, 1972.

Matrix (Jos Boys, Frances Bradshaw, et al.) *Making Space: Women and the Man Made Environment.* London: Pluto Press, 1984.

Mead, Margaret. "The Kind of City We Want." *Ekistics* 209 (April 1973): 204–7.

Mumford, Lewis. *The City in History.* New York: Harcourt Brace, 1961.

Paster, Gail Kern. *The Idea of the City in the Age of Shakespeare.* Athens: Univ. of Georgia Press, 1985.

Pike, Burton. *The Image of the City in Modern Literature,* Princeton: Princeton Univ. Press, 1981.

Pritchett, V. S. *London Perceived.* New York: Harcourt Brace, 1962.

Raleigh, John H. "The Novel and the City: England and America in the 19th Century." *Victorian Studies* 11, no. 3 (March 1968): 291–328.

Sartre, Jean Paul. "American Cities." In *The City: American Experience,* ed. Alan Trachtenberg et al., 197–205. New York: Oxford Univ. Press, 1971.

Schorske, Carl. "The Idea of the City in European Thought: Voltaire to Spengler." In *The Historian and the City,* ed. Oscar Handlin and John Burchard, 95–114. Cambridge, Mass.: MIT Press, 1963.

Schwarzbach, F. S. *Dickens and the City.* London: Athlone Press, 1979.

Scully, Vincent. *The Earth, the Temple and the Gods.* New Haven, Conn.: Yale Univ. Press, 1962.

Sennett, Richard ed. *Classic Essays on the Culture of Cities.* New York: Appleton-Century Crofts, 1969.

———. *The Fall of Public Man.* New York: Knopf, 1977.

———. *The Uses of Disorder.* New York: Knopf, 1970.

Sharpe, William. "Urban Theory and Critical Blight: Accommodating the Unreal City." *New Orleans Review* 10 (Spring 1983): 79–88.

———, and Leonard Wallock, eds. *Visions of the Modern City: Essays in History, Art and Literature.* 2nd. ed. Baltimore: Johns Hopkins Univ. Press, 1987.

Sizemore, Christine W. " 'The Small Cardboard Box': A Symbol of the City and of Winnie Verloc in Conrad's *Secret Agent." Modern Fiction Studies* 24, no. 1 (Spring 1978): 23–39.

Spears, Monroe. *Dionysus and the City: Modernism in Twentieth Century Poetry.* New York: Oxford Univ. Press, 1970.

Squier, Susan Merrill. *Virginia Woolf and London: The Sexual Politics of the City.* Chapel Hill: Univ. of North Carolina Press, 1985.

———. *Women Writers and the City: Essays in Feminist Literary Criticism.* Knoxville: Univ. of Tennessee Press, 1984.

Thesing, William B. *The London Muse: Victorian Responses to the City.* Athens: Univ. of Georgia Press, 1982.

Tuan, Yi-Fu. *Topophilia: a Study of Environmental Perceptions, Attitudes, and Values.* Englewood Cliffs, N.J.: Prentice-Hall, 1974.

Venturi, Robert, et al. *Learning from Las Vegas.* Cambridge, Mass.: MIT Press, 1972.

Wates, Nick, and Charles Knevitt. *Community Architecture: How People Are Creating Their Own Environment.* London: Penguin, 1987.

Weimer, David. *The City as Metaphor.* New York: Random House, 1966.

Welsh, Alexander. *The City of Dickens.* Oxford: Clarendon Press, 1971.

White, Morton, and Lucia White. *The Intellectual Versus the City: From Thomas Jefferson to Frank Lloyd Wright.* Cambridge, Mass.: Harvard Univ. Press, 1962.

Williams, Raymond. *The Country and the City.* New York: Oxford Univ. Press, 1973.

Wirth-Nesher, Hana. "The Modern Jewish Novel and the City: Franz Kafka, Henry Roth and Amos Oz." *Modern Fiction Studies* 24, no. 1 (Spring 1978): 91–109.

Index

A Female Vision of the City was designed by Dariel Mayer, composed by Graphic Composition, Inc., printed by Cushing-Malloy, Inc., and bound by John H. Dekker & Sons, Inc. The book is set in Caslon No. 224. Text stock is 60-lb. Glatfelter Natural Antique.